Nightmare in Laos

The True Story of a Woman Imprisoned in a Communist Gulag

NIGHTMARE IN LAOS

THE TRUE STORY OF A WOMAN IMPRISONED IN A COMMUNIST GULAG

KAY DANES

Published by Maverick House Publishers.

Maverick House, Main Street, Dunshaughlin, Co. Meath, Ireland.
Maverick House SE Asia, 440 Sukhumvit Road, Klongton, Klongtoey,
Bangkok 10110, Thailand.

info@maverickhouse.com
http://www.maverickhouse.com

ISBN: 1-905379-08-0
978-1-905379-08-8

5 4 3 2 1

The paper used in this book comes from wood pulp of managed forests.
For every tree felled, at least one tree is planted, thereby renewing
natural resources.

A CIP catalogue record for this book is available from the British Library
and from the National Library of Australia.

DEDICATION

I dedicate this book to all who have survived life's challenges and hope that this story will give courage to those who are continuing to endure their own personal struggles. This particular journey has shown me that the human spirit is capable of enduring the seemingly impossible and that we should never give up our hope!

ACKNOWLEDGEMENTS

Heartfelt appreciation goes to my husband Kerry Danes, who insisted we would regain our freedom without having to sell our integrity, and continues to inspire courage in me. The same applies to our children, Jessica, Sahra and Nathan, who bravely never gave up hope and made us so very proud. And to my parents Noela and Ernest Stewart and sister Karen who took such good care of our children and managed to stay sane under the pressure.

I would like to thank the Australian Government, Prime Minister Mr John Howard for believing in us and promising our children he was doing everything possible to bring us both home safely, and the Australian Foreign Affairs Minister, the Honorable Alexander Downer, who kept calling for our release and made his staff, the often unsung heroes, available to provide 24 hour support to our families, in particular, our children.

Huge thanks to the former Australian Ambassador to Laos, His Excellency Jonathan Thwaites, who will always be my real life hero and to whom we owe our freedom. He held us both together when the way forward seemed impossible, and became a friend for life. Thanks too to his wife Eve who opened her home and her heart.

Thanks too to the former Director of Consular Operations, Ian Kemish, who negotiated the 'form of words' that finally secured our release from prison.

My sincere thanks go to the tremendous Australian Foreign Affairs staff who do so much for Australians detained overseas and rarely get any credit for their tireless efforts. Special thanks to John McCarthy who went to Laos as a special envoy to engage Lao Officials on behalf of the Australian Government, Louise Waugh who provided personal care and professional Consular support far beyond expectations, Robin Hamilton-Coates who gave us encouragement and honest advice prior to us being returned to the prison following Consular access, Dr Ben Burford, John Judge, Keith Gardner, and all the staff of the Australian Embassy for their support.

My added thanks to: Greg Walsh, Tony Fox, Martin Hodgson, Geoff Spiller, Lowell Tarling, Norma and Bill Jamieson, Colonel Paul Noonan and the Australian Department of Defence (Army), Con Sciacca MP, Michael Choi MP, Andrew Hellewell, Dr Sin Vilay, Kat Ditthavong and the Assembly of Lao Representatives Abroad, Noel Scott, Geoff Thompson, Kimina Lyall, Nelson Rand, Stuart Bromley, Mark Brockhurst, Dr Pao Saykao, Australian SAS Association, Robert Allen Jr, David Corretore, and Harold Christensen.

Special appreciation to: John Mooney and all the team at Maverick House Publishing for making this publication possible.

INTRODUCTION

The memories of the time I spent in Phonthong Prison will never go away. When I close my eyes, I can recall even the minutest details of the prison. I can see the faces of the guards and those prisoners I left behind who helped me to survive; their faces remain etched in my mind.

The prison was hell on earth. Sometimes I wonder how I endured its squalid conditions. I can think of nothing positive to say about it except perhaps that now I am more aware of the plight of political prisoners in Laos; and their untold suffering.

Serving time in Laos for a crime I didn't commit was a nightmarish experience. It began as a dispute between a foreign investor and the Lao Government, but turned into an ordeal of catastrophic proportions, for me, my husband and for my family.

There are many rights we sometimes take for granted, but few of us ever ask what would happen if those rights were taken away? I've always believed in democracy and free speech but I never fought for these privileges. I only realised how valuable they were once they were taken away.

As you read about the degrading experience that I lived through, I hope firstly that you'll be encouraged and strengthened by my story. But more than anything else, I hope this book will highlight the perpetual suffering of the people of Laos and the unfolding tragedy that has befallen their country.

CHAPTER ONE

The Abduction

My nightmare began when the Secret Police came and took my husband Kerry away. It was the afternoon of 23 December 2000 in the city of Vientiane in Laos, and the day had started out like any other. There was no dramatic prelude to his abduction; there were no telltale signs that anything was wrong. We had no idea that we were in danger. You could say our lives were absolutely normal. The only indicator that something was seriously wrong came just as we were preparing to leave our office. We were on our way to Thailand for our Christmas holidays when we were suddenly faced with an interruption, in the form of a visit from a colonel of the Lao Secret Police. His name was Bounmaly Vilayvong.

Laos was full of corrupt officials like Bounmaly and they extorted money and gifts from foreigners whenever they got the chance. Bounmaly was different; he was dangerous as well as being sleazy. He was also known to intimidate foreign businesses in order to gain control of their investments.

Our company provided security to many local and foreign companies in Laos on a contract basis, and I was wary of his reputation. Both Kerry and I knew what he was capable of. With my business acumen and Kerry's experience with the Australian

SAS and the contacts that gave him, we had established ourselves as *the* reputable security company, and we had heard many rumours about Bounmaly muscling in on foreign investors. He had left us more or less alone up until now, but on that day he was insistent that he talk to Kerry about one of our 75 clients, a company called Gem Mining Laos. Neither of us realised that Bounmaly was deadly serious when he said he wanted to talk. Our minds were on other things. We were looking forward to Bangkok.

Kerry assured him that he'd meet him the following week after our holiday. Bounmaly agreed and we thought nothing more of it.

Two hours later, Bounmaly returned. This time he was accompanied by several police who arrived in six black cars, which pulled up one after another outside our security headquarters.

I was the first one to sense that something was wrong. I'd seen them coming from my office window. When I told Kerry what I saw, he told me to leave immediately. Obviously he agreed that trouble was on the way.

'Take the kids and go. I'll catch up with you later,' Kerry said.

Within minutes, Bounmaly had forced his way past our staff to storm into our office just as Kerry picked up the telephone to alert his superiors.

'I think we can talk now!' he said as he signalled Kerry to put the phone down.

Neither Bounmaly nor his police team seemed to have any interest in me. Kerry just looked me in the eye, urging me to go. I made for the door at my husband's instructions and ignored the apprehension that swelled inside me. I would collect my children and make our way to Bangkok.

Our driver was waiting downstairs. When I stepped into the car, I instructed him to get me home fast. I prayed that whatever was going on with Bounmaly would not delay Kerry too long.

As our car headed home, I stared at the phone and waited for Kerry to call. I tried to remain calm but inside I began to fall apart.

I just continued to stare at my mobile, wishing for it to ring. It took me a few minutes to realise that I'd actually picked up Kerry's mobile phone. Then it rang.

'Madam ... they take Kerry!'

It was Kerry's assistant, Ting. I could barely make out her words.

'They take him to Hatsady, to Immigration. Don't worry Madam, I follow Vilayvong on motorbike.'

This was not the news that I wanted to hear as I felt my heart race. I begged Ting to keep following them while I rang our company lawyer.

Robert 'Bobby' Allen (Jnr) answered in his usual Boston drawl. I quickly explained what had just happened. He assured me that he would go straight to the Immigration Centre and sort things out. I ended the call and tried to ring the Australian Embassy but I couldn't remember the number. My mind had gone blank. I was now shaking. After taking a few slow breaths, I managed to call my company's Contract Manager and asked her to call Louise Waugh, a diplomat at the Embassy. I knew she would help.

I was brought back to reality by two of my children when I arrived home. With our eldest, Jess, back in Australia, Sahra who was eleven and Nathan who was seven, were still at the excitable age coming up to Christmas and were eager to get going on our trip to Thailand. They had heard the car approach and had run outside to meet me, but they were expecting the two of us.

'Where's Dad?' Nathan asked.

'I don't know. Bounmaly took him away,' was all I could say, and shoved the children and our bags into the car.

In those few moments I received a string of calls. The most important came from Louise Waugh, who called to say she was working on the case. In fact, she said she was at the Immigration Centre demanding access to Kerry. This was news I desperately wanted to hear but it gave me a false sense of security. I convinced myself that Kerry would be freed at once. In my own mind, I convinced myself that once free, Kerry would make his way to Thailand and we'd be well beyond the reaches of Bounmaly. I convinced myself to stay strong.

I bundled the children into the car and ordered the driver to head for the Friendship Bridge on the Laos-Thai border—just as Kerry had told me to. As we sped off, Louise called again and promised to meet me at the border crossing. The drive took less than an hour and we got there before she arrived. By this time I'd become frantic. No matter what I did, I couldn't stop thinking about Kerry. I stared into oblivion thinking only that I had to get my children to safety. That's why I didn't notice the policeman approach our car and take our passports from our driver.

Before Kerry was taken, we'd often crossed the bridge but we had never been stopped or questioned. Moments later the police surrounded the car. It was Bounmaly and his men.

'Hello Madam,' he said, as I spun around to see him standing just behind me.

He blew smoke into my face as he spoke. The next few minutes passed in a blur. My mind went completely blank as he started ranting about missing sapphires and Gem Mining Laos, a company we had provided security for in the past. I insisted he search my bags. I had nothing to hide. Seconds later, he ordered his men to take our bags from the car. They scattered their contents all over the side of the road.

I couldn't believe what was happening. I controlled my emotions for the sake of my children but Bounmaly sensed my fear and took advantage of the situation. He stared at me, never once breaking eye contact. He then mouthed a few orders to his police and one by one, they produced knives and began to cut open Nathan's soft toys. This was sick; he was only seven years old, and they were slicing open his favourite toys, traumatising him with their unnecessary cruelty. When they'd finished, they threw the toys away and I grabbed at them to stuff them back into a suitcase. Bounmaly never said a word. He just looked in my direction.

Nathan was in tears, but there was nothing I could do to stop what they had done. Louise arrived minutes later but she too was powerless to stop them. The rest happened in slow motion, or at least that's how I remember it.

At this point, I began to lose grip of my emotions. I was overcome by a sinking feeling. I was carrying US$50,000 in my rucksack to pay subcontractors I was due to meet in Thailand. This was for my own business, completely separate from Lao Securicor. I was terrified that Bounmaly would find the cash and condemn me, or simply steal it.

Looking back on that day, I think Bounmaly sensed I was hiding something. Rather than let me go, he insisted on searching my rucksack. His men had searched everything else and found nothing. Rather than allow him to find the cash, I told Waugh to tell Bounmaly about it. On hearing this, he marched me into the border's Immigration Building. I just had enough time to tell the kids to stay close to the car and wait for me to return; hopefully when everything was sorted out and explained.

Once inside the room I emptied my rucksack onto a small rattan table. By his startled reaction, you'd have thought I'd placed a kilo of heroin in front of him. Bounmaly insisted I'd broken some law but couldn't think which one. I argued that I hadn't because the Government had relaxed its law to accommodate foreign investors. The money was the payroll for my Thai subcontractors. Bounmaly was having none of it. He next insisted on a strip search and moved menacingly towards me. The thought of his filthy hands touching my body made my stomach churn. I backed away in fear, which caused him to laugh. When he saw my reaction, he laughed and ordered a female officer to search me in another room.

With nothing incriminating found, he then made his move. He instructed his officers to seize the money. There was nothing I could do. He had got what he wanted.

When he took the cash I thought I would be freed. For a moment, I actually managed to convince myself that I was heading for Thailand. But I was wrong. Hours had passed and it was now dark outside. The border crossing was completely deserted. Eventually they agreed to allow me to check on my children, who were still waiting downstairs by the car.

I reassured them that things would be okay. Suddenly, I remembered Kerry's cell phone tucked under my shirt. I told the policeman escorting me that I needed to use the toilet. Once inside, I switched on the phone and scrolled through its electronic phonebook, looking for Kerry's Special Forces contacts, but I stopped when I heard someone approach.

'Mum?' Sahra spoke through the doorway. 'Where's Dad? When can we go?'

I put the phone back under my shirt and left the confines of the toilet to hug my daughter. 'I don't know.'

'I'm scared,' she whispered.

'It's gonna be alright. Don't worry, okay?' my voice broke and I held back my own fears. 'I have to go back upstairs, take care of your brother.'

'I will.'

I hoped and prayed that this would all be over soon. I couldn't leave my children standing around the car much longer. They were hungry, tired, and confused, not to mention scared. I wanted to get them out of this situation as fast as I could, and only hoped I could, and soon.

I didn't need anyone to tell me I was in serious trouble though. In my heart I knew I wasn't going to be freed. This suspicion was confirmed when I was taken back into the building's custody suite. One of the officers produced some paperwork, which looked like a statement. I was told to sign it. I refused, arguing that it was improper for me, as a foreigner, to sign something I couldn't read. I pointed out that I didn't have a lawyer present but this meant nothing to my interrogators. They seemed content to let the hours pass by. As time went on, I couldn't help but fear for my children. I needed to see them. Eventually I agreed to sign my name at the bottom, with the words that my money had been unlawfully detained pending investigation.

The police couldn't read what I'd written but took it as a confession and marched me out the door. They escorted me downstairs and tried to force me into their car. I resisted. I demanded to be transported by the Australian Embassy. I wanted Louise to know where they were taking me. We spent the next hour arguing until finally they agreed to allow my driver to take me in our car on the strict condition that I was accompanied by a police officer.

Once we'd sat into the car, the policeman said we were going to the Immigration Centre at Hatsady. I prayed it was true as I sat in the back seat with my two frightened children.

We arrived at the centre, with Louise in tow. She arranged for Sahra and Nathan to be taken to my sister-in-law's house. I kept calm as I didn't want to frighten them. Although I was terrified, I felt slightly better once I knew they were going to be safe.

The officer who travelled with me in the car then ordered me inside. I told my driver to stay with our children and reassured them everything would be okay.

Louise attempted to follow me inside the building but they wouldn't allow her entry. Instead she handed me her phone and I vaguely recall talking to an Australian government official who was reassuring me that everything would be fine.

When the police took me inside the building, they marched me up a dark stairwell to a small room on the third floor. The door slammed shut moments later. When my eyes adjusted to my surroundings I saw two women asleep in the corner on a bunch of wooden school desks. They were Thai.

The police had allowed me to take a bag with me into the holding cell. This contained Nathan's army sleeping bag and a jacket. I wrapped myself up in the sleeping bag and used the jacket as a pillow. With my back to the Thai girls, I curled into the foetal position and stared blankly towards the dirty windows a few feet away. I kept wishing that Kerry was somewhere in the building but eventually gave up trying to figure out where he was as exhaustion set in. I tried to will my mind into blankness but it didn't work, and with frightened thoughts swirling around my head, eventually, I cried myself to sleep. I was frightened, worried, and had no idea of what lay ahead.

***

Over the next two days, our lawyer and the Embassy tried to make sense of what was going on. But it was increasingly clear to them, if not to me, that our lives were in grave danger. I just didn't understand the gravity of the situation. We had dealt with difficult situations before, but this was something that could really put my life at risk. I still didn't know where Kerry was and just assumed there had been some terrible mistake that prevented us from leaving Laos. I'd been looking forward to a new stage in my family's life, but this was far from what I had expected. I'd signed a lease on a new four bedroom penthouse apartment in the heart of Sukhumvit, Bangkok, where I planned to expand my bodyguard business. My two youngest children, Sahra and Nathan, had no idea that I'd enrolled them in an international school that boasted the latest computer technology, air-conditioned classrooms and playing fields that stretched for miles like oceans of green. It was a huge contrast to Laos where facilities were not always very good, if they were to be found at all.

It was to be a great surprise but instead, I found myself pacing the floor inside a room at the Lao Immigration building. After some frantic planning and upon my agreement, the Australian Embassy staff managed to evacuate our children from the country. It was a hell of a thing to expect from an eleven year old girl—to take her seven year old brother across two countries. But the Embassy had insisted that it was for the best. I hugged my children goodbye, kissed them gently on each cheek and prayed they would remain safe under the watchful eye of Embassy staff, until they arrived back in Australia.

They hadn't taken Kerry's phone from me so I rang his military commander in Australia and told him what had happened. I then rang my father and he promised me that he would find a way to bring me home. That same afternoon, the police came and took me from the Immigration holding cell. I had seen my husband taken from me, seen my children forced to flee the country, and had been taken into custody for some unknown reason. It had been a traumatic couple of days, but things were only going to get worse. My nightmare was only just beginning.

CHAPTER TWO

Behind the Razor Wire

As the pickup truck drove south, away from the city of Vientiane, four armed police sat either side of me. The dust swirled around, obscuring the landmarks. It seemed important to me to plot our route but the vehicle bounced left and right so many times that I quickly became disorientated in the catacomb of narrow streets. My fingers gripped the red vinyl bench seat as dry wind whipped my hair across my face, blinding me. People regularly vanished without a trace in Laos. My husband was snatched from his office two days ago and now, after I had been in custody for two days, I was on my way to God-knows-where. I attempted to talk with the skinny officer beside me, but he just told me to be patient.

Half an hour later, the pickup skidded to a halt. I grimaced with pain when my head collided with the metal roll bar that separated us from the driver's cabin.

'Get out!' the officer yelled.

'Quickly!' he shouted.

'Where am I?' I asked, looking around bewildered.

'Go!' yelled the officer. He had tobacco stained teeth and looked like a hard bastard. He directed me towards a dilapidated building in a forbidding complex. An intimidating hammer and sickle flag flew overhead and before me loomed Phonthong Prison. I didn't know what was going on. Why was I being taken to prison? The guards marched me to a large black gate that was at least twelve feet high and twice that distance across. When I craned my neck to the guard tower high above, I saw a guard pointing an AK rifle at my chest. His face was expressionless. Nervously, I waited for the pedestrian gate to open. Within minutes I was on the other side. My eyes followed the light green hedges bordering a murky coloured pond, until I stood in a dilapidated room with brown shuttered windows.

'Sit!' the officer commanded.

A rusty ceiling fan hung precariously overhead. I sat down on a rickety wooden bench, hoping it would hold my weight. The officer looked about my age, thirty-three. His light brown hair parted to one side and fell carelessly over his face. He looked expressionless. I was just another prisoner. I quickly realised that he couldn't speak a word of English. Hence he just sat there with his forearms resting heavily on the desk. The door creaked open a few minutes later and a skinny, dark-haired man dressed in grey summer pyjamas and faded blue flip-flops walked in. He knelt before the officer in charge.

He said: '*Jao, jao,*' while nodding his head, and then turned and addressed me in English. 'Hello, Madam. I am Anouhack from Canada but I was born in Laos,' he explained.

'Where's Kerry?' I demanded.

The officer shouted something unintelligible.

'Listen,' said Anouhack. 'I will explain everything later but now just co-operate.'

'Who are you?' I began curiously.

'I'm a prisoner just like you!' he responded quietly, before turning back to the officer.

Anouhack acted as a type of translator. He asked me a few basic questions and everything I told them was written down in a red book—my name, my age and the village where we lived. I learned nothing from them except that the officer's name was Tan Sombut. A second man, dressed in black, came in and sat beside me. Anouhack laughed when I asked if he was a priest.

'No. He is a policeman. His name is Tan See-Sye!' replied Anouhack.

Tan See-Sye just sat there, his thin lips curled into a smile. Then seemingly embarrassed by my close scrutiny, he laughed and looked away. The interview took an hour and still I had no idea where my husband was. Again the door creaked open to a Laotian woman wearing a Lao skirt, a *Pha sin*. Her hair was neatly coiled into a bun.

'Don't worry,' Anouhack explained. 'Her name is Pon-Phit. She must search you.'

I was humiliated as their eyes roved every inch of my body but relieved when her search ended.

Moments later I followed her outside with Anouhack walking beside me, telling me to be patient. The adrenaline pumped through my veins until I could hear my pulse thumping. We crossed the patch of dirt that took us to a grey-white building with a rusted tin roof. Four concrete stairs led us to a narrow veranda that ran parallel to five dingy, dark cells.

'What's happening?' I cried. 'Where's Kerry?' A guard's strong hands pushed me towards one of the cells.

'It's okay,' Anouhack whispered. 'I'll see you in the morning.'

I clung to the door to prevent them from pushing me inside but they were too strong. I literally fell into the room. When I picked myself up from the floor, I turned and grabbed at the heavy steel door but the bolt slid firmly into the lock. Through the bars I pleaded to be set free.

'Don't worry Kay, I'll explain in the morning,' said Anouhack, before disappearing along the veranda.

I was in shock as an old woman clutched my arm to gently pull me towards the centre of the room. I barely felt the hard wooden floorboards beneath my feet, or noticed the other women in the room. Where was Kerry? Why had they lied? Whose nightmare had I entered? Where was I?

The old woman gave me a morsel of sticky rice and dipped hers into a bowl of watery soup. Instinctively I ate but tasted nothing as the tears ran down my cheeks.

My body became numb. It was my mother's birthday, Christmas Day, and the worst day of my life. Hours later, as I sat in the corner of the 3 X 4 metre cell, a Thai woman, John-korn Jar-ear-atikorn, otherwise known as Mon, tried to reassure me that everything would be okay.

'*Pai norn*,' she said, motioning towards the blankets spread across the floor next to the rear wall. She meant I should go to sleep.

***

It took me forever to get to sleep. I tossed and turned all night. The floorboards dug into my back but I supposed it was better than sleeping on the dirty concrete floor with God-knows-what. Tormented, I dreamed my first dream in Phonthong Prison. Inevitably, it was of my children.

In my dream I stood quietly watching my children fade into the distance as the tuk-tuk slowly motored down the road. 'Wait! Come back!' But I never voiced those words as tears flooded my eyes. Unbeknownst to me, my daughter Sahra kept a journal from the day they left and now, when I look at what she wrote, at the heartbreak in her words, I am filled with emotion. I can't even begin to imagine how hard it must have been for her, and for the rest of the family.

The next morning, I tried to adjust to the conditions. Mon said prisoners were locked in their cells for indefinite periods, some for years. She'd been in the cell for two months and had never once been outside. I could barely comprehend where I was. My mind numbed to the green mildew that grew up each of the four walls of the tiny washroom built into our cell. The ceiling was obscured behind thick cobwebs. I felt nothing but despair as I gazed up at the single light bulb and wondered if there were hidden cameras. The concrete floor rose to a squat style toilet and just to its left, a gaping drain hole opened to the sewage pit below. I stared down into it for a moment before turning to the concrete trough filled with water. Dark green slime coated the base of the trough. A plastic pail lay beside it. All of this was to cater for five or six female prisoners.

Two black plastic buckets stood in the corner. One I presumed was to wash our clothes. The other, I had no idea, but its lid was all that separated me from whatever was thrashing around inside. Slowly, I removed my clothes thinking that I'd feel better after a shower. Only there wasn't any shower, hot water or soap, just a little red pail to rinse off the sweat.

Laos was so hot at this time of year. The heat in the cells became thicker than the air that we breathed. I prayed for morning, when the humidity was not so draining, and when it came, I washed the sweat from my body and did my best to ignore the stench of human waste emanating from the hole in the floor. Mon washed next and as I waited for her return, I sat quietly on the wooden floor and observed the 'Head Prisoners' going about their morning chores. They were all Lao men who were let out early to water the vegetable patch and feed what looked like slimy cat-fish floating in a nearby cluster of rectangular ponds.

'Good morning!' a Lao woman in my cell yelled to the men outside. They responded in unison, 'Good morning.'

Fifteen minutes passed. The guard came and unlocked the cells. Mon said we weren't allowed outside so I sat by the window and watched her make coffee. One of the men from outside carried a black iron kettle filled with steaming hot water.

'Good morning, Madam. I am Bounchan,' he said to me in English, and poured the hot water into a tin flask Mon held through the bars.

'Good morning,' I said, quietly.

Bounchan walked passed several times that day and always caught me crying. He pressed his face to the bars of my window.

He spoke gently. 'Don't cry Madam, we are all suffer same as you.'

I looked at him with despair as I sat cross legged on the wooden floorboards. For a while he just stared at me and said nothing, his brown hands clenching the bars that held me captive.

'You miss your children?' he asked, and I nodded. 'Don't think too much,' he said.

But there was nothing else to do but think as I sat and waited for help to arrive. Perhaps there was no help. I began to wonder if I would be forgotten. Is that what had happened to this man Bounchan?

'Why are you here?' I asked him on one of his frequent walks past. Bounchan moved closer and looked around and back before resting his head against the bars.

'They accuse me of helping people leave Laos,' he said quietly in broken Thai-English.

'But why?' I began.

'Sshh. Don't talk now. Too many people can hear,' he silenced me. 'This place has danger.'

I watched Bounchan limp away to sit under a tree. A long deep scar stretched the length of his leg, broken at his arrest. Panic rose inside of me. What was this place? What had they done with my husband? Why wouldn't they tell me where he was? Why couldn't I see him?

I sat peering through the iron bars of my prison cell. Quietly I thought of my last night of freedom when I had paced the floor of the Lao Immigration Centre and organised getting my children out of the country. I didn't know what was going on. At that stage, I didn't even know where exactly my husband was being kept.

***

It was after the Lao authorities discovered our children were gone that I was transferred to Phonthong Prison. I had no idea if Sahra and Nathan had made it back to Australia, just as I had no idea if my parents were able to fully understand the fact that Kerry had disappeared and my own fate was dangerously uncertain.

I was dragged back to the present by Mon. 'Don't cry Kay,' she whispered behind me. 'Here, come drink coffee.'

A tear slid slowly down my cheek and I brushed it away. Mon made coffee. Her thoughtful, dark brown eyes mirrored the pain in mine. I'd now at least learned that my husband was being held somewhere in the prison. The police had told me as much when they brought me to this place, gloating that I would be joining him. I didn't know where in the prison he was being held, or in what conditions. I'd heard that his legs were blocked in wooden stocks and he'd been beaten, but at least he was still alive. Mon filled me in on everything else I needed to know to get by.

'Why can't we go outside Mon?' I asked.

'Because we must wait for investigation finish,' she said in broken English. 'No problem Kay.'

'How long will it take?' I whispered. 'When can I be with Kerry?'

'I don't know,' she responded. 'Sshh now. Noi coming,' she said.

Mon's face went blank whenever Noi was near. She was convinced the Laotian was a spy for the police, so when she entered the room, Mon turned away and I did too.

'Kay, you okay?' Noi said smiling and walked towards the washroom.

'I want to go home Noi,' I said.

'Kay, I want to go home too, and see my children,' she said.

I wondered if Noi was really going to the toilet, or if she was hoping to catch us talking, which was against the regulations. When she eventually came out of the washroom, she smiled innocently, first at Mon and then at me, and walked outside to sit under a shady tree with Bounchan. Mon and I said nothing for the next hour, just to be safe, but later she told me that many of the 100 prisoners in Phonthong had been locked inside their cells for more than a year. They became like caged tigers, pacing back and forth, driven mad. Frustration tormented me as curious eyes followed my every move. I didn't want to turn out like them, thinking that even their own shadow worked for the police.

Mon's lovely face took on a frown as she rubbed her knees, her long dark hair pulled back into a pony-tail. Muscular paresis was common amongst prisoners because of the poor diet and restricted movement. I heard it became even worse if they blocked your legs because it was virtually impossible to go to the toilet or wash. I thought of my husband and wondered if he knew I was even here. Eventually, when I discovered where they were keeping him, I was able to write messages to Kerry, involving a go-between, and in time, I became a master of secret letters. The first time though, after only a day, I was incredibly scared. I sat near the wall of our cell and began to write. Part of me worried that Kerry wouldn't get my message and the other part worried that the police would. I slipped my note to my secret courier, careful that no-one else saw. I sipped my coffee in silence and waited.

Twenty minutes passed.

All of a sudden one of the head prisoners went to the tree and bashed a metal wheel hanging from it with an iron stick. I put my hands over my ears to block the deafening noise. All the other prisoners did the same until the clanging stopped. Everyone lined up outside our cell block. I got a terrible feeling in the pit of my stomach. Had my courier been caught passing the note to Kerry? Was that what this was all about? I sat with my face pressed against the bars and waited. The head prisoner stood at the top of the concrete stairs, gibbering away in Lao.

'Mon!' I shrieked. 'Look, everyone's in the line. I think there's a problem.' I pointed to the prisoners outside.

Mon turned her head to hear what he was saying.

'It's okay,' Mon laughed. 'He tells them the regulations. Don't worry, Kay,' she smiled.

Every morning, midday and afternoon before each lock up, the regulations were recited so we wouldn't forget how they expected us to behave. I didn't understand much of it because my Lao language skills were limited, but Mon translated. They said that we were supposed to trust the government to know how to make things perfect in Laos.

By 4pm the prisoners allowed out to walk around the prison were lining up outside their cell doors, ready to join me in the stifling heat. Noi stood outside joking with a Thai woman called Toom, whom I'd initially thought was a man. Her dark hair was cut short; she smoked cigarettes, wore men's clothes and even shaved her face. When I found out that Toom was a woman we all laughed at my mistake. Toom was actually really nice.

I often caught her looking at a photograph hanging on the wall near her sleeping place by the door. It was a picture of her sister, a Thai policewoman. Like so many in Phonthong, Toom didn't have a sentence and had never even been to court. She'd spent the last eight years of her life in this hell with no inkling of when she'd ever leave.

I heard the jingle of keys which signalled the arrival of Tan Sombut. He went from cell to cell, locking everyone inside for yet another gruelling night. I listened to the sound of the heavy steel doors slam shut until finally he appeared outside my window. Tan Sombut had a heart blacker than coal, or so the prisoners said. I hid my fear beneath lowered lashes. Pon-Phit, who I recognised from when I first came into the prison, and the others knelt in front of him, their hands raised above their heads as they begged like slaves to be allowed back inside the cell. The prisoners were dogs begging to their master.

Later that night when everyone slept, I examined the picture of the prison compound that was given to me earlier that day in secret. Two prison blocks stood side by side, separated by two large concrete sewage tanks. All the human waste went down the squat-style toilet into the large concrete tanks but the pipes were cracked, so the waste flooded underneath the cells. There were five cells to the front of each block and five cells to the rear. Each held at least six prisoners. Kerry was in the first cell of block two and we were in the third cell of block one, closest to the interrogation room. I worried all the time about going to that evil place. The police took prisoners into that room from time to time and beat them for hours. Even the women were beaten. Sometimes the guards left the door open and we were forced to watch them flog the prisoners with a steel tyre brace.

'Don't listen Kay,' said Mon, and dragged me from the cell window. Quietly she sang in Thai as we lay on the wooden floor staring into each others' eyes. My own filled with fear.

Anouhack had spoken to Kerry and told me that my husband had said he would never let anything bad happen to me if he could prevent it. I tried not to dwell on the 'if' part of his sentence, or that the Lao secret police promised to let us go, if only Kerry would sign a false confession against Gem Mining Laos, the company he was presently involved with through his security business. At last I knew why we were here. They were keeping us hostage, hoping to exchange us for bigger fish—Bjarne and Julie, the company directors of Gem Mining Laos. The media reports said Gem Mining's Bjarne Jeppeson and Julie Bruns were crooks, but that was far from the truth. As security managers we had them checked out through our contacts in the Australian Federal Police. Their story was typical of Lao Government corruption where foreign investors were invited into the country and then, once established, harassed to the point where it became impossible to stay.

The Gem Mining case was unique because they were embroiled in a bitter and public ownership dispute. When Gem Mining hit hard times and needed a cash injection, Bjarne brokered a deal with a group of foreign investors willing to accept the transfer of Gem Mining Laos to a company they'd listed on the stock exchange, Asia

Sapphires Limited. But the deal soured when the foreign investors failed to transfer the agreed Asia Sapphires shares to Bjarne. So Gem Mining remained in the hands of its rightful owners and Asia Sapphires lay dormant without any equity. The Asia Sapphires directors felt unhappy and turned to the secret police's Colonel Bounmaly Vilayvong, front man for Deputy Prime Minister and Minister of Foreign Affairs, Somsavat Lengsavad.

It was on 5 April 2000 that Lengsavad issued an order terminating Gem Mining Laos, citing that it was unproductive in all respects. The Lao Government, however, twice overturned this decision, which then put Gem Mining in Lengsavad's direct line of fire. Bjarne and Julie fled the country following a series of death threats and hand grenades being hurled over their residence wall. Lengsavad couldn't go against the government's decision not to terminate Gem Mining's concession unless he could prove they were somehow lawless. With Bjarne and Julie waging their fight from Thailand, he faced the threat of public exposure. Within a month of Bjarne and Julie's departure from Laos, my Thai SWAT subcontractors had warned that a bounty of US$500,000 had been posted on their heads. I had tried so hard to convince Bjarne to move to a safe house in the Thai province of Kanchanaburi, but he refused. On my request, the Thai SWAT commander issued a 24 hour security detail at Bjarne's house and told the SWAT to shoot anything that came over the wall. Effectively, word had spread throughout the Thai metropolitan police that the Gem Mining Directors were untouchable. It was unlikely Bjarne and Julie would ever relinquish their investment. Bounmaly and his thugs were effectively out manoeuvred. Bjarne and Julie were safe. But where did that leave Kerry and I, seeing as we had provided a security service for them? We'd done nothing wrong and yet that didn't seem to matter. I began to worry even more when I heard the screams at night and wondered if the Embassy even knew we were here.

***

Thanks to our contact with Louise Waugh, they did, and within days the diplomatic wheels started to turn. On 29 December 2000, the Australian Ambassador to Laos, His Excellency Jonathan Thwaites, met with Phongsavath Boupha, vice-minister of Foreign Affairs to hand over a diplomatic note that urgently requested Consular access and a reason for our detention.

The Laos minister understood the Australian Government's concern for early action, but said that the authorities were still investigating. He concluded that Consular access might not be granted until after the New Year and that we had been found guilty, but that he couldn't, as yet, reveal the actual charges. We hadn't had a trial, and the investigation was ongoing, and yet we had been found guilty of crimes they couldn't give any details of. In other words, they were stalling for time.

On 30 December 2000, I hobbled from my cell to the interrogation room. I was surprised when they told me I had been granted a Consular visit at the Immigration Centre. No visitors were allowed to come to the prison, of course, so all prisoners were escorted to Immigration to meet their Embassy, if they were lucky enough to be granted permission.

'What about Kerry?' I asked Anouhack, who walked with me to the room.

'Don't worry. Just go,' he replied.

We stood quietly while the old Lao woman searched me. Tan Sombut warned that I shouldn't say anything to the Embassy about the prison conditions or risk the cancellation of all future Consular visits.

Anouhack translated. 'Kay, follow their instruction carefully. Don't make a problem. You will make problem for Kerry and he already hurt,' he said quietly before adding, 'and tell Louise I need medicine.'

'Okay, okay, you go,' bellowed Tan Sombut.

I walked towards the black door and looked back only once at Anouhack, swinging in his handmade hammock. He'd been here so long he'd somehow made this place his home. I hoped that would not happen to me. He waved goodbye and smiled.

The pedestrian gate noisily swung open to reveal a Toyota pick-up parked nearby. I sat in the front beside the driver, a policeman whose nephew, Hormphan, was a prisoner in Phonthong. My heart pounded, my whole body was shaking. My head spun with thoughts that I couldn't pin down, and then I saw my husband. Kerry walked slowly through the pedestrian gate, surrounded by three armed police. I touched my fingers to the glass window between us, as he climbed to sit on the vinyl bench seat behind me, and whispered, 'I love you,' in between the tears. He told me everything was going to be okay, but just then the police angrily told me to keep my eyes forward. I was not allowed to look at my husband. I was terrified of being alone but at least knowing that Kerry was nearby gave me some peace of mind. I trusted my husband to take care of me. I just tried to hold it all together and not become hysterical.

As the car pulled slowly away, I felt the Prison Commander's black eyes upon me. The red epaulettes on his uniform reminded me that I was under communist control. We drove down the narrow laneway that had first brought me to Phonthong. The rice fields glistened alongside as a water buffalo lazily lifted his head to watch us pass by. We headed through the narrow, dusty roads, past the run-down shacks and simple grass-thatched roofs of poor villages, until we finally reached the infamous Route 13. The road featured prominently in a number of travel warnings due to rebel activity. I secretly hoped we'd be ambushed and liberated by these so-called freedom fighters. But when I saw the grandness of Anousavaree, the Asian-French equivalent of the Arc de Triomphe, signalling our entrance into the city, I felt deflated. We would not be rescued from our nightmare.

Our journey continued forever it seemed. My hands suddenly started to twitch nervously, my breath came in short gasps and I felt like I was having a heart attack. Why couldn't I breathe? I didn't know at the time but this was to be the first of many severe anxiety attacks. I clutched at my chest and looked at the driver, who mumbled something unintelligible. He reached over and turned on the radio. Strangely, this helped. A haunting melody filled the cabin of the car. It was a song that Mon often sang and for a moment I felt relaxed. By the time we reached our destination, however, I began shaking all over again.

The business district of Vientiane was bustling with people. Our office stood just a few buildings down the road. I saw the pale blue shirt and dark blue pants of our security guards who waved at me from the door of the Bangkok Bank. Another waved from across the road at the Malaysian Public Bank. I wondered how they were getting on.

'Go!' the police officer interrupted my thoughts as they took Kerry inside the building first.

I took a deep breath to calm myself and recover from the shock of being transported into the real world. The policemen pushed me from behind. I almost tripped. Life was going on around me. Curious eyes watched me stagger between rows and rows of motorcycles parked outside the Immigration building. The noodle shop was crowded as usual. The old woman who served me countless times before stopped briefly. Her face bore no expression as her dark eyes observed. Inside the Immigration office, I saw a few foreigners filling out visa applications. They ignored me. I wondered how they could be so oblivious to what was going on. Yet I understood that at one time I was just as ignorant as them. Green police uniforms filled every corner of the room. My eyes pleaded for understanding but no-one paid me any attention.

The police escorted me up the narrow stairway to the second floor. As I climbed the dark stairwell I thought of the time before they took me to Phonthong. I thought of the room to the end of the hall with its dirty glass windows that barred my view to Talat Sao, the morning market, and those small wooden school desks that gave no comfort at all as I slept.

'Sit down!' The police officer beckoned me to the small rattan bench seat. I read his name bar on his desk. Mr Khamkit. I quietly thanked him in the little Lao I knew, much to his surprise. He beamed with pleasure as he looked from me to the other police officers seated beside me, complimenting me on my grasp of his language.

'Be patient,' he spoke again, but this time in English.

'Be patient.' I'd heard that already, and would do again many times.

Khamkit walked quietly to the water filter and poured me a glass of deliciously, cool, clean water. I drank slowly and closed my eyes briefly as it quickly quenched my thirst. Slowly the minute hand ticked over until thirty whole minutes passed. Mr Khamkit remained at his desk quietly shuffling papers until a knock at the door disturbed him. A young Laotian police officer entered and announced the arrival of the Australian Embassy. Kerry was nowhere to be seen. We would have our Consular meetings separately it seemed.

'Okay.' Khamkit signalled for me to stand.

I heard the familiar voice of our company lawyer, Bobby, coming down the hall and turned quickly to the door. The Australian Embassy Consul Officer, Louise Waugh, walked beside him. They were smiling as they stepped into the room.

'Hello, my girl,' said Bobby, in his warm Boston tone.

I could hardly control myself as the tears streamed down my face in a mixture of fear and relief. Bobby's huge embrace lifted me off my feet. He told me that things were going to be just fine. I wanted so much to believe him. Yet he never said, 'I'll get you out of here.' He just said, 'I'll do the best I can.'

The First Secretary of the Australian Embassy, Robin Hamilton-Coates, entered the room. I knew Robin from the barbecues at the Australian Embassy Recreation Club.

'Hi Robin,' I said as we embraced, and suddenly I felt less intimidated amongst friends.

'You okay, Kay?' he asked.

I nodded and turned to embrace Louise and tell her that Anouhack needed medicine.

'Okay, tell him I'll bring some to his Consular visit next week,' she said. This was possible because Anouhack was allowed one Consular visit per month, and seeing as his nearest Canadian Embassy was in Bangkok, the burden fell on the shoulders of the Australian Embassy to look after him. He was treated very well by them and was very grateful, but he was also very disappointed that his own Embassy had not once paid him a visit.

A stranger stood before me wearing a dark blue suit and a red silk tie. He was tall, fair-haired, mid-forties and very distinguished-looking.

'Kay, this is the Australian Ambassador to Laos, His Excellency Jonathan Thwaites,' Robin said. The Ambassador's eyes were the colour of a clear blue sky. Suddenly he smiled and enveloped me in strong but comforting arms.

'It's going to be alright,' said the Ambassador, and invited me to call him Jonathan.

Jonathan had been posted at Australian diplomatic missions in Manila, Washington, Moscow and Ottawa. In the latter two, he was the Deputy Head of Mission, Charge d'Affairs and Acting High Commissioner. From October 1994 until July 1998 he had been the Australian Ambassador to Poland and the Czech Republic, resident in Warsaw, and concurrently Ambassador to Slovakia until April 1997. He had been around.

The small tape recorder sat on the table between us as we began our meeting. I felt claustrophobic with the two police officers seated on either side of me. Tan Sombut sat across from me and watched every move I made.

'Are you being treated well?' asked Louise.

I searched my mind. How could I tell them about Phonthong and all I'd already seen? I just wanted them to get us out of there. Tan Sombut's face looked dark and unyielding. I glanced from him to Louise and swallowed nervously, waiting for the words to come. I heard myself saying that I was fine but really I felt trapped and wanted to hit the pause button on the tape recorder.

I wanted to shout and tell them that we were being caged like animals. That screams filled the night and prevented me from sleeping. That images of people being tortured haunted me during the day. But fear kept me silent. Jonathan said he was trying to establish regular Consular access now that the Australian Government had been made fully aware of our detainment.

'Your kids are fine Kay. They're with your parents,' said Louise. I was relieved, but I needed to talk to them, just to make sure.

'Can I telephone them?' I pleaded. Robin spoke fluent Laotian and asked Khamkit, but the answer was no. He said we only had ten minutes to talk. I pressed my palms together in the prayer-like gesture called the *wai*. Khamkit shook his head.

Silently a tear slipped down my cheek as I despaired. My God! Why wouldn't they let me talk to my children? Who on earth was it going to hurt? What difference would it make? I lowered my head trying not to give in to the turmoil I felt building inside.

'Is there anything you need Kay?' Louise asked.

Incredulously I just looked at her. I needed my freedom, to feel safe, I needed my children and to see my husband. But it was impossible to say any of those things. Anouhack had already told me that hysteria would only make things worse.

'Can I have some toiletries please?' I whispered in a defeated tone as Louise wrote in her notepad. 'Kerry has no clothes. He's got ear ache and needs painkillers. Tell our kids we love them. Tell them not to be afraid.' I began to weep.

'Are you able to exercise at all?' asked Louise as she handed me a tissue.

'No,' I uttered in a whisper. 'They won't let us outside.'

'But you are allowed to meet? Once a week in a room aren't you?' Louise asked and flicked through her notes.

'I wish!' I laughed for the first time in ages. 'How can we meet when we're separated the whole time and locked in a 3 X 4 metre cell, twenty-four-seven?'

'Okay, I'll follow up on that one,' said Louise. She made a notation in her book. 'Can you tell us about your room?'

Apparently my mother was driving the Embassy nuts about my living conditions. She wanted to know every single detail. She asked if it was anything like the Bangkok Hilton. Again I laughed. My mum watched too many movies. How could I tell her it was more primitive than that?

'I'm in a tiny cell with no lighting except for a light on the outside veranda that never goes off. There's also a single light bulb in the washroom but that only works when there's no brown outs. There's a squat style toilet that stinks to high heaven and a water trough, but that only holds a few buckets of water to share between the six of us. Sometimes the police turn the water off so we have none.' I watched Louise write everything down.

'How high is the ceiling?' she asked.

'I dunno, I can't reach it,' I said.

I wanted to tell her how filthy and crowded our cell was and that vermin crawled over us at night. That mosquitoes swarmed into the room as dusk fell and all we had to eat was pig fat water soup that they brought us twice a day. But I said nothing. Jonathan confirmed that under Lao law we could be detained for twelve months before they even charged us. I couldn't comprehend how they could keep us for that long. We had done nothing. I wondered how my family would react to that news. My father had already called for all foreign aid to Laos to be cut, believing our

Government should introduce sanctions to secure our release. But Jonathan felt that would only cause problems.

He assured me that the investigations were going to be carried out as quickly as possible. I complained that the prison police weren't passing on our mail. The Embassy said they'd take the matter up with the authorities.

'I just want to hear from my children that they're really okay!' I cried, as the police took me away.

Kerry came down the hall towards me escorted by two police from the prison.

'Hey babe. Don't cry,' he said as we got closer to each other.

The Embassy staff walked into the hall just as the police stood in front of me to prevent me from getting near Kerry. But I side-stepped the officer and landed right in my husband's arms. I clung to him for dear life and sobbed into his neck. Before they prized us apart, Kerry kissed me briefly. I was shoved into a room down the hall where I sat crying, waiting for the minutes to pass.

Twenty minutes later, I was escorted downstairs. My cheeks were still wet with tears as I looked for my husband. But Kerry was already handcuffed and sitting in the rear of the vehicle, surrounded by police.

'Tell my children I love them,' I called over my shoulder to Louise as the officer dragged me away.

Bobby's face was more serious than I had ever seen him. The door slammed shut. The driver reversed into the street and slowly we pulled away. I cried unashamedly as Bobby began to disappear from sight.

'Be patient,' the driver ordered, and turned on the radio to drown out my sobbing.

We travelled for twenty minutes until we reached the familiar Golden Temple of Tat Luang, featured on many picture postcards. We meandered through the quiet dusty roads that flowed through various villages. The journey back seemed far too short. I knew that in a few short minutes we would be back at Phonthong

Prison. I hated the thought of returning. Inside that place I felt so alone, despite the fact that Kerry was there too. If only they would let us see each other, perhaps I wouldn't have found it so difficult to cope. The commander was waiting in the same place as when we departed the prison. I felt hypnotized by his dark stare as he watched Kerry being dragged back inside.

'Go!' Tan Sombut ordered me from the car.

We walked the short distance to the black door. The prison guard looked down on me with his AK rifle slung over his shoulder. I took little notice as I put one foot in front of the other until I stood on the other side of freedom. The police escorted me back to my cell. Kerry's hand stretched out of his but that was all I could see. Mon waited as I slipped off my shoes and put them under the raised floorboards where we slept. I heard the heavy steel door shut behind me as I stepped onto the raised floor. I wanted to read the letters my children had written on their return to Australia, but the police had taken them at the meeting and wouldn't give them to me. So I cried instead as I sat in the middle of the room.

Four agonising days later, they gave me the letters and amongst them was a letter from an American named Bob Anderson, who told me that our story was going throughout the world and that justice would surely be done. I'd never even heard of Bob Anderson and yet he'd heard of us and seemed genuinely concerned that we were in a Lao prison. It was comforting in some small way to realise that people knew we were here.

As the afternoon drew to a close we sat quietly in our cell. I went through the motions of eating the pig fat water soup. It wasn't appetizing and tiny ants floated around the rim of my bowl. I just pushed them aside.

'No thinking home,' Noi said quietly.

I just cried again when I heard the word 'home'. I would never have imagined in a million years what horrors lay ahead.

CHAPTER THREE

Interrogation

'Happy New Year Madam,' Bounchan said smiling. I watched him display a six inch, wooden carving he'd made of a fantail fish. 'What's so happy about it? I responded miserably. Spending Christmas day and New Years in a communist prison camp left me uninspired.

'Perhaps that we are still alive is reason enough to celebrate!' he said softly. I felt ashamed. Bounchan was only trying to cheer me up.

'I'm sorry Bounchan,' I said quietly, and went to the window to admire his fish. 'It's lovely,' I smiled with sincerity.

'Come to the door. I will pass it through,' he said eagerly. It was his gift to Kerry and I.

I crossed the few steps quietly. Mon was busy stirring hot coffee for her brother, Anek, who was detained in the rear cells. Silently, Bounchan opened the door to our cell but waited on the other side. He dared not come in. Mon leaned towards him and smiled, handing him the coffee cup. She asked Bounchan to take it to her young brother. He agreed and said that Anek's health had not improved. I watched the display of anxious expressions flit across Mon's face. Bounchan told her not to worry and took a long sip of the coffee. Smiling, he pronounced it delicious. Seconds later, he reached up and passed the wood carving to me.

'It's beautiful Bounchan. Thank you!' I smiled.

The carving was smooth to touch and intricate in design. The fantail fish itself floated on a love heart shaped base, covered by hundreds of tiny engravings. Each one swirled like waves on the ocean. Bounchan pointed to where he'd carved text on a flat edge, near the fish's face. It read: 'From me for you,' with a little arrow pointing down the structure, and as I followed the tiny arrow's direction, I came to two small fins that jutted out to either side of the fish's body. One had 'Kerry' engraved in it and the other 'Kay'. He'd placed a little white card at the bottom between the two fins that read; 'Happy New Year 2001, Souvenir from Bounchan.'

'Don't think too much,' he said gently before disappearing along the veranda.

I placed the wood carving along the wall where I slept and contemplated what he'd said. Tiny tears sprang to my eyes as I thought of my children, so far away. I barely noticed the silent arrival of a tall male prisoner. He stood peering through our cell window. Mon greeted him. The man moved closer. He casually rested his forehead against the bars.

When he spoke at last, his voice had a deep timbre tone of authority. He looked to be in his late forties, quite handsome, with dark hair cut neatly like a soldier's.

'Kay,' Mon said excitedly, 'This is Suratin from Udon Thani. We call him Phor, which is 'father' in Thai.'

I wiped my tears with the back of my hand and placed my palms together in the traditional Thai greeting.

I spoke respectfully, saying hello, and lowering my head slightly.

Phor had been arrested on spy charges almost a year before. He was a Thai congressman but in Phonthong he was just another prisoner. Phor had a lot of support from his constituents in Udon Thani, a small city about an hour's drive from the Thai-Lao border.

They sent him bananas, pineapples and my favourite, the exotic rambutan.

Phor was generous to the Thais but hated Laotians. He detested the Hmong, the minority group in Laos, even more, and didn't care much for foreigners. Phor smiled but remained quietly still as he watched the emotions flitter across my face. Over the coming days he accepted me as a Thai, because of my friendship with Mon. Every day, he gave us small morsels of food and sometimes tiny pieces of dried fish sent to him by relatives. On rare occasions he got a couple of fresh chicken eggs and although these were considered more valuable than anything, Phor shared them with us. We became good friends in no time. When I felt sad, Phor comforted me in a fatherly Thai way.

Phor prayed to Buddha every day. I watched him through the bars as he walked to the centre of the prison grounds to stop beside what many prisoners called the Bodhee, or holy tree. Phor placed small flowers on one of its limbs and knelt reverently to the ground. He pressed his hands together, prayer-like, to his forehead. Quietly he meditated and when he finished, I watched him walk away to begin a vigorous exercise routine. Phor tied a piece of material around his head that normally held up his pants. He looked like a Muay Thai champion I'd known in Bangkok. 'Boxing Phor,' I called whenever he passed my window.

I longed to be able to go outside too. Sweat dripped from every pore in my body. The day took forever to end. Were we any closer to our freedom? My face pressed against the bars as I watched the prisoners line up outside my cell. Looking at each face I wondered who they really were. Did the eyes gazing back at me wonder the same thing? The speaker continued a Pol Pot style monologue; 'Follow the regulations.' When he finally finished the prisoners were dismissed. Some waved and said they'd see me tomorrow.

It was so hot even with the sun fading, and I was preparing myself for another long, stifling, uneventful night. Suddenly, the black door to Phonthong opened.

'Kay, Bounmaly he come,' whispered Mon, her voice filled with concern.

Within minutes, Tan Sombut shuffled slowly by our cell. A big bunch of keys jangled heavily in his hand. I heard whispers pass from cell to cell that Kerry was about to be interrogated. How did they know?

'He's coming,' a faint whisper called from two cells down.

I saw Bounmaly and several others waiting at the interrogation room. Tan Sombut moved unhurriedly to escort Kerry. I watched him shove my husband from behind then mutter something under his breath. My hands gripped the cell bars as my face pressed against the rusty steel, trying to make eye contact with my husband. He smiled to reassure me, but my heart was beating frantically with fear. At that moment when Kerry walked through the door and I saw Bounmaly pull it closed, I felt as if my whole world disappeared. My hands shook and for the next few hours I sat like a stone staring at the door. I had seen others go inside that same room and come out bloody and broken.

I bit my lower lip, praying my husband would be alright. It was some comfort to know that Kerry had undergone resistance to interrogation training, as a condition of service in the Special Forces. Could he convince them to let us go home? What if he couldn't? What if they came for me? How would I cope with the pain I'd seen them inflict on others? A wave of intense fear suddenly gripped me. I began gnawing on my thumb in anxiety.

'Think Kay. Think!' I said to myself.

Had they delayed our interrogations so they could parade us before our Embassy in good health? Despite the racing of my heart, I tried to remember what Kerry had told me about torture. It was all about control. They'd say things like; 'I'm only going to ask you this one question … but in a hundred different ways.'

But it was difficult to think when all I wanted to do was hide. Pon-Phit called me to eat with her and the other girls, but I couldn't.

I registered the apprehension on their faces but now was not the time to eat. I had to prepare myself for the inevitable. Why couldn't they have just detained us under house arrest? Why did we have to be in this horrid place? I asked Kerry the same thing in one of our secret messages.

He said they were trying to make us feel like we were cut off from what we knew. It must have been working because I felt completely afraid and alone. Being detained in a small cell for days on end only heightened my feelings of helplessness.

Suddenly the door to the interrogation room opened. Bounmaly stepped outside. I watched him slowly bend his dark head to light his cheap Vietnamese cigarette. Silently he paced outside the interrogation room. He appeared frustrated, almost angry. It gave me some comfort to think that they weren't in total control of the situation. Several moments later, Bounmaly re-opened the door and as he did, I caught the briefest glimpse of Kerry sitting on the concrete floor. His hands were cuffed behind him. His ankles were restrained in wooden blocks.

'They put the block on the leg to control the prisoner,' said Noi as we watched in silence.

We heard Bounmaly raise his voice in anger moments after the door shut.

***

The hours passed. I never knew how much my husband had suffered during those hours. I would learn that later. He only ever wrote to tell me how much he loved me and how proud he was of me for staying strong. But the Lao police accused him of spying for the CIA, just like they had accused Phor of spying for the Thai military. They said Kerry's position at Lao Securicor was a cover for intelligence work he was doing for the Australian Military. Neither was true. Sure, Kerry had worked with several intelligence agencies over the years, as special forces do, but he wasn't a spy.

The Chief of the Australian Army granted approval for him to work on accumulated leave. It was an opportunity for Kerry to see if he could make the transition into the corporate sector. He was doing fine up until the day the secret police kidnapped him.

During one of Kerry's interrogations, the police put a plastic bag over his head and almost suffocated him. Another time, they stood on the wooden blocks secured around his ankles and nearly broke them both. When he refused to sign their false statements they beat him. They pushed him to his knees and wrenched his arms up behind him. As soon as Kerry was able to, he informed the Jonathan Thwaites that we were being ill-treated. A complaint was raised by our Foreign Minister to the Lao authorities. But it didn't prevent their police from filling a bucket with dirty fish water, and as two police held Kerry down, another poured the water down his throat. I still remember those faint coughing sounds my husband made. How much pain could he bear? I knew they would never break him. Kerry's motivational strength had gotten him through one of the most difficult Special Forces selection courses in the world. There was no way he would ever succumb to defeat. So where did that leave me? I sat waiting. My hands clenched and unclenched with fear.

'Look Kay,' said Noi excitedly.

A small blue budgerigar perched itself on the bars of our window, inches away from my head.

'A small bird,' Noi smiled, 'Good luck for Kerry,' her eyes widening in surprise.

For a moment we forgot where we were. The little bird whistled contently and I remembered my own blue budgerigar, named Romeo. My neighbours in Australia had offered him a home when we found out we were moving to Laos. It was a bizarre encounter seeing a bird, native to Australia, in Phonthong. Even more incredible that it sat at my window.

'Kay no problem. Kerry okay,' Noi chanted like a child.

Many Asians are superstitious and believe everything is a sign. Noi convinced me that the budgerigar had brought good news and despite the fact that he flew away, I convinced myself she was right.

Kerry emerged from the interrogation room dishevelled but alive. I watched quietly as they escorted him back to his cell. I thought about the little blue bird that gave me hope. Kerry would be fine. But I knew he had suffered by the way he limped back to his cell. For some reason, they didn't interrogate me that night. Bounmaly and the others left almost as silently as they'd arrived. I wondered all night why I had been spared.

'I gave him a valium,' said Anouhack the next morning.

'You're kidding?' I replied, as the young Lao-Canadian stood outside my cell window.

'He got a lot of pain! Too much beating him,' Anouhack smiled, but shook his head as he passed an orange through the bars.

'Thanks Anouhack,' I said quietly and took the fruit. 'Will he be okay?'

'Don't worry Kay, I will take care of him,' he responded.

Kerry must have been hurting to take valium since he rarely took paracetamol. Anouhack said he also complained about having headaches and blood in his urine. I was horrified. What did it mean? Would my husband die?

'The nurse just said be patient. Ha ha, they can do that type of bullshit and then just say be patient. Fuckin' bullshit man,' Anouhack spat.

Late the following afternoon, Bounmaly and the interrogators returned. I watched them push and shove my husband all the way to the interrogation room. A familiar feeling of dread washed over me but fear kept me silent. Each time they took Kerry to the interrogation room, I never knew if it was for the last time. Was Kerry afraid? My fingers clutched the bars as I thought of all the things I wanted to tell him, but it was too late. He was gone and I was left to wonder what they were doing to him.

In fact what they were doing was trying to pressure him into signing a false statement incriminating Gem Mining.

'I agree that I took the sapphires from Gem Mining,' the Lao translator said to Kerry.

'No,' Kerry replied. 'Our company protected the sapphires and gave them back to the Lao officials.'

'You will sign that you took them!' shouted Bounmaly.

'No. You signed the paper to receive them!' Kerry responded calmly.

'You have the key to the safe! You took those sapphire in there,' Bounmaly indicated. He sucked deeply on his cigarette.

'No! I didn't have the combination and you can't open the safe with a key. I told you already that the keys are inside the safe. They are only used to change the combination once the safe is open,' Kerry explained.

'But you have the combination!' accused Bounmaly.

'I never had the combination of the safe. Don't you remember? I was on the telephone to Bjarne that day when you came to seize control of Gem Mining. Bjarne told you to ask him yourself for the combination but you refused,' Kerry stated. The Public Prosecutor, Phonsavane Mingboutha, sat quietly looking from Bounmaly back to Kerry.

'You are responsible for the protection of sapphires,' Bounmaly countered.

Kerry sighed. 'I want to speak to my lawyer!'

'You cannot speak to a lawyer until you cooperate with us. Why do you protect Bjarne and Julie? If you cooperate, sign this statement, then you can go,' Mingboutha explained via the Lao translator.

Kerry continued to request the presence of the Australian Embassy and legal representation but was denied. After four hours Tan Sombut was summoned to the interrogation room to remove the wooden leg blocks from Kerry's ankles. He motioned for Kerry to straighten his clothes and go back to his cell. It gave me another opportunity to see my husband for the second time that day. Tan Sombut pushed Kerry in the back. I waited for my husband to say something, anything that might give me some hope. It seemed like he wasn't going to and I leaned as far into the bars as I could. Finally he said three words, 'Don't sign anything,' and that was it. He was gone.

I knew Tan Sombut would return for me and about ten minutes later, the ominous jangling of keys alerted me to his approach. Panic coursed through my veins as I imagined what horrors were in store for me. My legs shook violently when I left the safety of my cell.

Slowly I put one foot after the other until I found myself walking, almost trance-like, across the dirt clearing. It felt as if I'd walked a mile to the interrogation room when really it was only a short distance away. The door loomed before me, larger than life. I passed through with my fate completely in their hands. Bounmaly invited me to sit on a small wooden bench in the centre of the room. I counted four other men present. Each one was introduced to me by the translator. Prosecutor Mingboutha, sat directly in front of me. On the desk in front of him was a pile of papers. I saw my name on the top of one paper. But most of the others were hidden from my view. Coloured index tabs were placed in sections within the file. I had no idea what these were for or why they would have such a large file. Bounmaly sat to my right. He smiled in such a sinister way that my heart skipped a beat. To my left sat a Laotian wearing a highly-decorated police uniform. His name was Bounyasene, of the Special Investigation Group within the Ministry of Interior. I felt the chill of his contempt as big steely arms crossed in front of his chest. His eyes never left my face. A young man, dressed in black sat next to Bounyasene. He too was an officer in the Special Investigation Group, and he too was unsmiling. The door closed behind me as the translator sat down. I swallowed the fear rising within me and tried to remember to breathe.

Just stay calm Kay. Just stay calm, I thought to myself.

Bounmaly pushed a document in front of me and told me to sign it.

'Your husband has signed the paper already,' he spoke quietly. I thought for a moment what Anouhack told me the day before. He said they'd crushed Kerry's fingers underfoot because he wouldn't sign a false confession.

'I cannot read it,' I said carefully.

I looked from the paper written in Lao to the translator. Thoughts raced through my mind as I listened to him address the prosecutor. Only hours ago I had read Kerry's message that told me to remember, that as afraid as I would become, nothing was worth signing a lie. As the interrogation began it didn't even seem like an interrogation. I actually began to rationalise that they treated me better because I was a woman. A comforting awareness settled over me. They asked me about Gem Mining and what role I played in the Lao Securicor Company.

I was the Administration Manager responsible for client contracts, new business and general administration procedures.

'Do you become involved with the Gem Mining people? What relationship do you have with them?' the translator asked.

'They were our clients and sometimes we met with them socially,' I responded.

'Why do you involve in their business?' he continued.

'I wasn't involved in their business. My job was to liaise with our seventy-five clients. Gem Mining only employed one of our guards to stand at the front door of their administration office. I didn't have much to do with that contract once it was secured,' I explained.

'But you go there to instruct your guards to unlock and lock the doors,' asked Bounmaly.

'No. Our Lao supervisors did that,' I replied.

'So you never see the guards do their job?' Bounmaly asked quickly.

'Well, of course I saw them. Sometimes I told them how to do their job because sometimes they forgot. They'd sleep on the job and other times, they wouldn't even turn up for work,' I concluded.

'Your clients were cheating our government for a long time. Why do you say they are your friends?' asked Bounmaly.

'We're friends with just about every foreign investor in this country. It's how we attract business!'

'You don't care they are cheating Laos?' he asked.

'I didn't know if they were cheating. I was never involved in their company,' I replied.

'But your husband was involved. He signed the paper to accept responsibility as representative of Gem Mining,' Bounmaly countered.

'He signed but his appointment was rejected,' I responded.

'If you know that, then you know more than you are telling us,' said the prosecutor.

I waited for the translation.

'No. My husband told me about it and then the law firm representing Gem Mining took the responsibility for them,' I replied.

I began to relax. As long as I continued to tell the truth I felt that everything would be okay. My father had always told me that if you tell the truth you have nothing to worry about. I hoped he was right. They asked me the same questions over and over. Each time I answered truthfully. It was exhausting and nonsensical but they kept it up. Mingboutha wrote in Lao while Bounmaly and Bounyasene moved behind me. Subtly the mood of the room changed. I couldn't understand their questions that came thick and fast. Were they trying to confuse me? I sat patiently hoping they'd stop. Then Bounyasene shoved me hard from behind.

'You lie!' he spat.

'You stole sapphires!' Bounmaly accused.

'No I didn't,' I replied with an edge of frustration.

Bounyasene grabbed my right arm and squeezed it hard. His face reddened with anger. I turned away. The interrogation continued for another hour until they finally pushed the document in front of me a second time.

'I can't read it,' I said exasperated.

'Sign!' Mingboutha barked.

I took a deep breath and told him I couldn't sign it, which of course, only made Bounyasene angry. My ear throbbed from his bellowing.

'Sign! Sign!' he shouted.

Suddenly, I felt like I'd been hit with a rock in the back of my head. It stunned me. The prosecutor said something in Lao but all I felt was dizzy. When I turned my head slightly I saw him backing away towards the door. My head hurt.

'You are not afraid?' the translator asked me.

I turned my eyes to him and tried to focus on what he was saying. He repeated his question. Did I answer him? What was Bounyasene doing? I felt a tremor course through me. Did they know how afraid I was? My hands trembled so visibly that I decided to sit on them.

'We can do anything to you and nobody can care,' said Bounmaly. I swallowed to find my voice.

'You should sign, Madam Kay Danes,' Bounmaly said. 'Give the problem to your husband. He is the man. Sign and we let you go home to your children.'

'But I can't read it. Please let my Embassy and my lawyer visit and then I will be able to sign,' I cried, finally finding my voice.

'Your Embassy cannot help you! Your country does not care about you! Laos has good friendship with Australia,' they said. 'Your government does not care about you. If they care then why do they give the money to Lao … huh? Fifty years friendship, now you are alone.'

The sound of male laughter filled the small room. I began to wonder why they were so desperate for us to sign a confession if they were already convinced of our guilt.

'Your husband took the sapphires and give to you, so you can give your client in Thailand,' the translator said.

'No!'

'What business you are doing in Thailand?' Bounmaly asked.

I told them everything there was to tell about my bodyguard company in Thailand. I told them exactly the breakdown and structure of my company and that my brother-in-law Leslie Danes was engaged as a consultant.

'What is your brother do there?' the translator asked.

'He's Kerry's brother actually. He's a security consultant in my company. I pay him US$4,500 a month from the contract to make sure the client is happy with our service.'

'That is a lot of money for one man,' said Bounmaly. 'Who pay the tax on that money?'

'The tax is paid in Thailand,' I replied.

'Why you have so much money at the Friendship Bridge when we arrest you?' Bounmaly asked.

'I've already explained that to you at the bridge, Bounmaly.'

'Explain again!' he stated.

'The money was a payroll for my subcontractors in Thailand, the Thai SWAT,' I explained. 'You can check my bank records. That money is earned legitimately. According to the decree made by the Governor of the Bank of the Lao PDR, foreigners don't have to declare any amounts of foreign currency taken out of Laos. The government made the change to assist investors by making it easier to do business,' I responded.

'How do you know our law?' questioned Bounmaly. 'Are you a lawyer too?'

'No! But I made myself familiar with your law,' I responded. 'Why don't you understand me?' I asked. 'I can't sign your documents because I can't read them. I didn't steal any sapphires and I haven't broken the law.'

'You lie!' Bounmaly interjected hotly. 'We have witnesses that say you destroy the computer data of Gem Mining.'

'That's not true!' I replied. 'I told you already that we only moved their computer to our office to secure the data.'

'You not afraid?' Bounyasene asked, through the translator, and walked behind me.

I kept my head lowered, hoping he would not hit me again. 'If I die, I die and can do nothing,' I said, clasping my hands together in prayer. 'I'm telling you the truth!'

'What about your husband?' Bounmaly asked. The Public Prosecutor looked at me. My eyes lowered from his to the dimples in his cheeks. Was he amused?

'If you kill my husband then he will die. I cannot change that,' I responded. I felt something press hard against the back of my head. I couldn't breathe. A male voice laughed behind me. Those in front of me wore an expressionless mask.

'Stop it!'

I wanted to shout the words but they were trapped in my throat. God help me! Again I felt something hard press to the back of my head. Bounyasene stood directly behind me. 'I didn't do anything,' I cried out. The silence stretched. My heart pounded in my ears as the sweat dripped down the small of my back.

Click!

I wasn't sure what had happened exactly but I knew that Bounyasene had a gun. I felt the room swim as a wave of warm numbness seeped over me.

I couldn't recall how long I was drifting away for, but when I felt the blood rush into my head with the force of a tidal wave, I wished that I could have been elsewhere. My head throbbed. I barely heard the door open as Bounyasene came back inside and sat down beside me. His steely gaze bore right through me, his face stained red with anger. 'We can come back in the night,' Bounmaly warned. I felt my heart accelerate.

'You will not know when,' he whispered behind my ear. 'We can take you somewhere and no-one will find you. No one will care,' he threatened.

I swallowed the saliva rising in my throat as the images flashed before me. The room was so quiet for the next few seconds that I was sure they could hear my heart beating.

'Kerry will suffer in front of you and you will suffer in front of him,' Bounmaly said as he walked quietly around me. 'Then we will shoot him in the head.'

Fear gripped me.

'And leave you in Phonthong forever,' he finished.

I barely had time to absorb the full impact of his words when Mingboutha interrupted. I listened to the translator who asked for explanations about things I'd already explained. Bounyasene jumped up from his chair and I almost fell off mine. 'Sign! Sign! Sign!' he shouted, inches from my face.

'I can't,' I cried as I felt his hot breath on my cheeks.

His face stained dark red as he pushed the document in front of me again. He slammed a silver pen down hard on the table. I muttered something about the Geneva Convention although I didn't really know what I meant.

'You have no rights. You are in Laos,' Bounmaly shouted. 'We don't follow Western law here. We will tell you what you can and cannot do. You cannot speak human rights. You are in Laos!'

This attitude to human rights issues made everyone laugh with scorn as they explained that a Communist state could and would do anything it wanted. My country could do nothing. Neither the UN nor the rest of the world could interfere in the sovereignty of the Lao People's Democratic Republic. I was told again and again that the United Nations had no power over Laos.

'Would your Government give me a Lao lawyer, if I was in your country?' Mingboutha asked.

'Of course they would. At least one to work with your appointed lawyer! In my country, everyone is entitled to a lawyer and a translator if they need. It's called ...' I lowered my gaze, '... human rights.'

At this, Mingboutha smiled and said, 'You are a good liar Madam Kay Danes.'

He signalled to the prison police that the 'interview' was finished. I was taken back to my cell where Mon waited anxiously. When the police left us alone, I fell on the blanket that Mon laid out next to hers. She whispered that I keep quiet. I was beyond talking anyway and closed my eyes. Mon quietly sang to me in Thai.

***

Despite the physical and mental abuse, Kerry and I continually refused to sign any documents written in English or Lao. We continued to request the presence of an Embassy official and legal representative, but were refused. The prisoners were agitated that our interrogations were conducted at night. Some complained to the Prison Commander that life was hard enough without having late-night interrogations. They were told to be patient. Interrogations were only supposed to be conducted between 10am and 3pm. Never at night. However, we were always interrogated outside 'normal hours'. It was unheard of for officials to be involved in the interrogations, yet they were present at our every one, unlike the translator, who had disappeared after the first occasion and was no longer deemed necessary.

Meanwhile, the Lao Foreign Minister, Somsavat Lengsavad, crucified us to the media. There was nothing we could do to stop the lies being told. Who would ever know the truth?

The investigation team kept returning. Kerry was escorted from his cell to the interrogation room. His hands were shackled behind him and when he entered the room, they pushed him to the floor. I saw a policeman lock his legs into the wooden blocks. They pushed a document in front of him and assured him that it had been checked by the Australian Embassy. I watched my husband shake his head in refusal.

***

One question put to me haunted me the entire time we were detained: 'Why do your employers not rush to your defence? After all, they are the Joint Venture partners with the Ministry of Interior, are they not?'

I didn't know the full details at the time, so I couldn't really answer. Our position within the multinational Securicor company had always been clear—make the dangerous environment for high-paying foreign investors in Laos appear safe. It had never been an easy undertaking, but Securicor had repeatedly reassured us that we had their full support as they had ours. Surely if we were being accused of failing to secure our clients' assets, then the matter could be resolved through proper investigation. But at this stage, I didn't know what help I was going to get from them.

The Laos Government took that as a sign that Jardine Securicor hadn't any confidence in the integrity of their own managers. The more I thought about it, the more I worried. Where would this leave us?

'Don't think too much,' Mon said as I lay beside her in our cell that night, but I couldn't help thinking about it, and as the hours crept by I couldn't help but wish that this nightmare would end.

CHAPTER FOUR

Innocence Lost

The night passed slowly in Phonthong Prison and I eventually slept through sheer exhaustion. My final thought was that in the morning, I would focus on other things and not relive those terrible hours in the interrogation room. I would try to forget and simply concentrate on staying alive. In Phonthong Prison, everyone had their own horror story to tell, except there was no way of telling it. The conditions were dreadful and many prisoners had no idea if they would ever go to court, let alone return home.

'Sometimes people stay forever Kay, not lucky to have Embassy and people to fight for them,' one prisoner said in passing.

Of course, I had no way of knowing if my Embassy had made progress since they could not communicate with us unless given permission by the prison, and after our first visit we were suddenly refused any more contact. Other prisoners who had access to outside information said the Australian Government had sought an immediate response from the Laos Government as to why it had reversed its decision in granting twice-weekly Consular access, but we were still denied Consular access for several weeks, keeping us completely in the dark as to what was happening with our case, and effectively preventing us from coordinating a defence.

A Ministry of Interior official advised that there was no reason for the sudden change, other than that it followed a meeting between officials of the Ministry of Interior and the Ministry of Foreign Affairs.

'Your Ambassador goes to speak with the Ministry of Foreign Affairs, Mr Xindavong,' said Anouhack as he passed an orange through the bars of my window.

'What did he say?' I asked anxiously.

'He said he knew nothing of course. Don't worry. Your Ambassador will try to get another meeting.'

'Great,' I said despondently.

'No Kay, your Ambassador talks a lot to the Laos Government. I heard your case is very high profile. Your government wants to know what made Laos go back on its agreement,' he said seriously.

'Really?' I asked.

'Yes and the Lao Government request your Embassy to keep the media under control,' said Anouhack, looking around. 'Here give me that magazine,' he pointed.

I leaned over my bedding, pushed against the wall and got a magazine I'd found on the floor, left by another prisoner lucky enough to get a trip to their Embassy and receive some reading material to relieve the boredom.

'You don't worry Kay. You and Kerry make a big problem for the Laos Government,' he laughed, and took the magazine that I slipped between the bars. 'I'll talk to you later,' he said, and walked away.

I sat hoping that Jonathan would make the Lao Government understand what a big mistake it had made. The Embassy submitted a third person note to the Ministry of Foreign Affairs requesting regular Consular access. The Ministry of Interior, however, refused the number of visits they had requested. It was no surprise to learn that the officer-in-charge was none other than

Bounyasene, the man who, along with Bounmaly, had tortured and terrorised me.

They wouldn't allow telephone calls to our children or digital photographs of us to be taken. They would at last allow letters from our family but these would be subject to strict censorship, and we didn't always get them. The first letters from my children were still withheld. Anouhack said we were lucky, but I did not feel it. How was it lucky to be a hostage? Every moment of the day, I longed to be somewhere else, and didn't appreciate others being happy that we were in Phonthong.

Even as the days and weeks went on, I still couldn't ever get over how hopeless the situation was for some people, and how they had come to accept that they were at the mercy of the justice system and Lao government. I couldn't accept that we were being left here to rot.

A Thai male prisoner, Pooperk, found himself arrested on 2 July 1999. He was one of the lucky ones because he had been to court and sentenced to two years.

'They want money from me,' he laughed.

'Does your Embassy even know that you are here?' I asked him one afternoon.

'They know, but can do nothing,' he responded in annoyance at the system that had taken his freedom. 'My release is now three months gone over.'

'Why?' I asked, unable to believe that no one was doing anything.

'Because even when you finish you must be patient,' he said in defeat.

I felt sad for Pooperk. He wore the same old clothing every day because he had nothing else, and nobody to support him. How he managed to smile after all this time amazed me. He used to sit outside my cell near the shady tree and talk loud enough for me to hear. He was very good at making me see that we were all in a similar situation. One day he came to stand by my window.

'Good morning,' he smiled and passed me a small woodcarving. It was a bizarre carving with words inscribed: UFO, Happiness, Peace, and Harmony. It was the most unusual handicraft I had ever seen. He insisted I keep it with me as a reminder of his existence, just in case he did not make it beyond the black door of the prison. He leaned closer, 'Last night, I heard the police talk about your case for a long time. You don't worry okay!'

***

From behind the bars of my cell window I sat and watched life unfold. Over the next few days and nights, Kerry and I were interrogated a total of six times each. Each time was more intense. I began to question whether we would survive.

They told me so many bad things would happen if I did not confess. They said they would take me to the 'dark room', and force me to sign a false confession. I had no idea where Phonthong's dark room was and I did not particularly want to know. The mere mention of it brought instant fear. Would I die in Phonthong? I found out that the dark room was actually at Phontan Domestic Jail and not Phonthong, but our cells could easily convert to dark rooms. But they were not the same as the tiny one-metre-wide cells of horror I had heard so much about. Some prisoners claimed the dark rooms were possessed with the souls of prisoners who had died there. They said their spirits remained trapped in the four walls and forever tormented its occupants.

During interrogations, I encouraged myself with words of hope from my fellow prisoners who told me to be strong. They had all endured similar or worse treatment and said, 'Never give up hope, even when it seems hopeless.' I held onto these words and prayed harder than I ever had as a child at Sunday school. I distracted myself by thinking how remarkable my new friends were. They put aside their own concerns to support us in our most desperate hours. When I was almost overwhelmed with fear,

I tried to remember the Lord's Prayer I would recite as a child each night before I slept, to bring back that feeling of safety and warmth I had always felt at home.

Bounmaly said his police would take my husband and I from Phonthong because we would not sign a false confession against our client. He threatened that we would never see each other again and each time I was dragged back to my cell following an interrogation, I was reminded that my future could change at a moment's notice. I began to fear them kidnapping us and wondered if I would ever feel safe again.

'Mon, please don't let them take me,' I cried to her one night. The others in our room were sleeping.

'Sshh Kay. Go sleep,' she whispered and held my hand as I tried to push the fear from my mind.

Sleep evaded me and the heat became unbearable. I quietly crept to the tiny washroom and squatted Asian-style on the grimy concrete floor. Resting my head in my hands, I quietly sang an old Elvis Presley song that my Dad used to sing when I was a very young girl: 'Hear my cry, hear my call, and hold my hand lest I fall.'

The night passed and with the morning our usual routine began, with the communist chants, aimed at teaching us how to live. The prisoners allowed to leave the cell to line up did so, and when we were alone in our cell, I told Mon that Bounmaly said he was going to move Kerry and I. Four hours later, the black door opened to Phonthong. Mon was the first to see it and turned to me almost frantic.

'Kay! Bounmaly, he come,' she called.

I ran to the door to see for myself as he made his way towards the interrogation room with a group of police. I began wringing my hands together. Mon suddenly gripped my arms and forced me to look at her.

'You do not let them see you are scared Kay,' she said.

They were coming for me. How would I survive? They had labelled me a criminal just as they labelled the other innocent prisoners as criminals and the ethnic minorities as rebels.

'You come,' the police officer called to me. His voice dripped with hatred.

Bounmaly and three other police waited for me to go outside before they entered our tiny cell. They told Mon to sit in the corner as they searched everything and everywhere in the room. Pon-Phit lifted my bedding. I had no idea what they were looking for.

'Where are the sapphires?' Bounmaly asked her.

She looked perplexed. Since Pon-Phit had searched me upon my arrival to Phonthong, she knew there were no sapphires in my possession or for that matter, inside Phonthong.

Anouhack watched from nearby and laughed quietly when Bounmaly announced I had smuggled sapphires into the prison. He wanted to know who I had given them to. I could not understand why he persisted with the lie. The police grabbed my arm and pointed me in the direction of the interrogation room. I looked to my friend Mon as I turned, not knowing if I would see her again. Other prisoners stood quietly and watched. Their faces bore no expression as their eyes followed my course towards the interrogation room. I was grateful when they did not shut the door or close the shutters. For what seemed like ages but must have only been a few minutes, I sat on the floor looking as disinterested as I could.

'You be like Thai people Kay, no fear.' Mon's words echoed in my head giving me an inner strength to fight whatever demons would come at me. Mon had become like an older sister and I had faith enough to believe her when she said I'd get through this, no problem.

At least twenty police surrounded me. I could smell the aroma of a familiar Vietnamese cigarette behind me and knew that it was Bounmaly. They placed my small blue rucksack on the table in front of me. Bounmaly went through all my belongings, slowly and methodically. He said nothing. Then carefully he replaced them and told the police to lock the bag in the storeroom. He began talking to the police in the room, telling them I was a terrible person, 'Mafia', and had stolen many sapphires. I was an enemy of Laos and for ten long minutes, he rambled and raved until I was sick of hearing his lies. I spat at him under my breath, calling him a liar in Lao.

The young police officer standing to my right heard and announced that I could speak their language. The room fell silent. Bounmaly stood just a breath away from me, puffing on his cheap cigarette. The smoke almost choked my lungs. I could feel the tiny hairs on the back of my neck stand on end. The young police officer started yelling at me repeatedly, 'You speak Lao,' as he pointed his finger a centimetre from my nose.

'I don't understand,' I said quietly. Bounmaly laughed and told them not to bother with me.

I sat in silence for what seemed an eternity and waited for them to start intimidating me again. However, to my surprise they took me back to my cell. Kerry's face pressed into the bars of his cell window so I could get a glimpse of him. I forced a fake smile so he would know things were okay. Bounmaly and the police left after that and I discovered that they were looking for a small telephone that Bounmaly said I had hidden in my cell, along with the sapphires.

Pon-Phit knew it was all nonsense. She laughed aloud as she walked away, saying that Officer Bounmaly was very crazy. However, it really was not a laughing matter. Bounmaly was getting desperate for failing to implicate Gem Mining in illegal activity. That night I awoke suddenly. 'Sshh, go back to sleep,' Mon whispered in the dark.

'What was it?' I asked quietly.

'Nothing, sleep now,' she said. I heard the same blood-chilling scream twice more that night. The sound came from the thick wall behind our cell.

The morning came and with it the same old reminder of the regulations. The political prisoners said the communists had done it that way since long before their arrests. They detained many of them arbitrarily for up to 18 years.

'Every day the same,' one political prisoner had told me. His face revealed only a bored expression as I watched him in the line.

'Follow the regulations and all will be perfect in Laos,' or, 'Trust the Lao Government, they know the perfect way!'

'They're such hypocrites,' I said to Anouhack after the morning roll call. He laughed aloud.

'Yes,' he said with a smile. 'They say we are foreign bandits and are here to learn how to be good.'

'They're the fucking bandits Anouhack.' I spat the words under my breath.

The prison police locked everyone in the cells at 4pm so they could sneak around like stray dogs and steal the few vegetables the prisoner's grew. I hated it that they could just take whatever they wanted. I suppose there was no one who could say, 'No you can't eat my food!' Some police were not all bad. Like Tan Peng who suffered mouth ulcers and constantly complained that no one had any medicine. I began to hope that through police like Tan Peng, I might better understand their way of thinking.

They believed that if you were in a bad place then you must have set your feet purposefully on a particular path to get there. You must then do many good deeds in order to find another path to take you to a better place. I was not quite sure how they could rationalise that way but I suppose it was because they witnessed suffering on a daily basis from birth. They knew that war had ravished their country because men sought power and wealth. They witnessed corruption that had become an integral part of their existence. Innocence was lost in Laos. In its need to survive, the new generation was fuelled by corruption. What fuelled those who came to torture us? Usually when they arrived, some prison police, like Tan Peng, went to the far end of the prison, or waited outside. I guess he did not like the screams either. Tan Sombut never went outside. He always sat near the doorway and listened. Sometimes he would eat his lunch and ignore some poor soul copping a beating. Sombut was cruel. Sometimes he beat prisoners for no reason at all. For a long time I just couldn't understand him.

'He is poor too Kay. His family have no money, no house like some rich police. Look, he does not even have any shoes,' one of the prisoners explained to me.

As the days passed, I noticed the other younger prison police wore black shoes whereas Tan Sombut wore dirty old flip-flops. For some reason I began to change my mind about him, thinking that perhaps there might be a good person underneath his hard exterior.

There was only one way to find out. To treat him as a human and not as he treated us, as dogs. I gave Tan Sombut my black work shoes that afternoon as he shuffled towards our door to lock us all inside. He was literally taken aback as he looked at the shoes and then at me. 'For you,' I said simply in English. I heard Noi translate for me.

'Why?' he asked, as the shiny black shoes dangled in my hand through the bars of the heavy steel doorway.

Tan Sombut was shocked at my generosity. He did not say thank-you and I did not expect him to. He shuffled along the dirty track towards the black door, carrying the shiny black shoes in his hands. He looked at them the whole time he scuffed away.

'Why you give him your shoes Kay?' called one of the prisoners.

'He does not have any and I do not need them here do I?' I responded.

I heard soft chuckles as they said I was crazy.

***

I did not dare write and tell Kerry what I had done because I knew he hated Tan Sombut. However, my instincts told me that I had done the right thing. I was determined that I would never lose my sense of humanity.

I would not let their system break my spirit or my compassion for others. Tan Sombut wore my black shoes the next day. He still shuffled in his usual lazy gait, but it seemed he walked a little taller.

Pon-Phit, Noi and Toom all left the room that morning as I waited with Mon to see if anything different would happen. As our door began to close, I began thinking that I had been foolish in dreaming that my gesture would affect Tan Sombut. He walked away to unlock the next cell, ignoring me.

'Madam,' Tan Sombut turned back. His eyes held mine and for the first time since my imprisonment, I did not lower my eyes to the ground.

'Thank you!' he said in English.

It was the first time he had ever spoken to me as a person. The prisoners who heard smiled and took their place in the line waiting for the regulations. I smiled too as Tan Sombut turned and walked away.

'Very good Kay,' whispered Mon, who was obviously just as surprised as I was. It was a small gesture on both our parts, but I hoped it would help change the guards' view of me, and vice versa. I hoped they would at least offer me a little more freedom and let me out of my cell.

The suffering in Laos was not restricted to Phonthong. The country itself was a giant prison and despite the fact that those like Tan Sombut had a certain degree of freedom, their quality of life was not much better than ours. The regime made all the rules and only in its favour. Human Rights meant 'you have the right to die.' And die they did.

A Frenchman by the name of Francis Phetdum Prasak died soon after a Consular access visit. He collapsed holding his chest.

We begged the police to take him to the hospital but they refused. We screamed all night until they yielded but it was too late. I watched them load Francis into the back of a tuk-tuk. He was dead. The message was shockingly clear to all of us. Life in Laos was cheap.

CHAPTER FIVE

The Smuggled Letter

It reminded me how vulnerable we were when no one mourned the death of the Frenchman, Francis Phetdum Prasak. I was still shocked when we went to Immigration that afternoon to meet Jonathan Thwaites. Louise Waugh, the Consular Officer, and our lawyer Bobby Allen accompanied him. The Embassy was still trying to get regular Consular access but the authorities insisted that twice-weekly access was unrealistic. The good news was that they had quashed the ridiculous rumour of Kerry being a spy. Now all they were accusing us of was stealing sapphires from the safe of one of our clients. Anouhack's warning reverberated in my mind: 'Be careful what you say Kay or you will never speak to your children again!'

The Lao Prosecutor, Phonsavane Mingboutha, complicated my possible release by pressuring the Bank of Lao into disregarding the new law that allowed me to take money out of Laos legally. He insisted they follow an out of date law and the Bank of Lao agreed.

'Can they do that?' My eyes opened wide with shock as I posed the question to Bobby.

'They do whatever they like but that doesn't mean it's legal!' said Bobby. 'Many foreign investors do what you did because Laos lacks any adequate banking infrastructure. We'll just have to be patient and hope things will get resolved.'

'What about our employers? What is Jardine Securicor doing to help us?' I asked.

I was sure that the great corporate giant would be on their way to negotiate our release. They were one of the most respected security firms in the world. However, I began to feel uneasy when Bobby looked away. His eyes flashed to Louise, who sat quietly.

'What is it?' I asked anxiously looking from Bobby to Louise. 'Tell me!' I demanded. Bobby fell silent.

'Kay, I spoke with the Director of Security for Jardine Securicor in Hong Kong yesterday about your employer paying for the legal representation for you both,' Louise began.

'And are they going to?' I asked, puzzled as to where this conversation was heading.

'Well, at first they said they would meet all legal costs and provide whatever legal support is necessary. When I mentioned that Bobby may have to withdraw because of the pressure from the Government and that we didn't know anyone else suitably qualified in Laos, your employers said they would only pay for services provided locally,' she concluded.

'What? Their joint venture partners are the ones detaining us!' I immediately responded. 'Surely they could come and negotiate around a boardroom table and get us the hell out of here!'

'They said they'd get back to us but I was informed that the company was keen to put blue water between them and yourselves. Meaning they want to separate the issues.'

'What are we supposed to do when Bobby leaves?' I asked.

'Kay, don't worry about it. I'll keep trying,' said Bobby, taking my hand and rubbing it gently to console my obvious distress.

I could barely comprehend anything they were telling me. This was a huge concern to me.

'Let's just take one step at a time and leave Securicor to me,' Bobby responded flatly. In the end I was glad we did leave it to

Bobby. Though I couldn't know about it while locked up in prison, I'm sure he was influential in persuading Securicor to pay for our legal representation in the end, seeing as they were not going to fight the case for us.

'Time finish,' said Mr Khamkit, ending our meeting.

I clung to Bobby for as long as I could. He told me not to worry but I did. Tears soaked my cheeks as I walked from the room into the hallway and saw the familiar figure of my husband coming towards me.

'Kerry!' I cried, rushing into his arms, and buried my face in his neck. The police tried to prise us apart but we resisted.

'It's alright love,' he said to comfort me.

'I want to go home,' I cried.

'Okay babe. It's okay,' he repeated, when eventually the police forced us apart.

'Get her out of here, Bobby, whatever it takes!' I heard Kerry shout before I disappeared into the room next door.

The wait was like an eternity. Two Lao police officers sat opposite me reading a paper and did not care that I was emotionally distraught. My hands covered my face and silently I sobbed. The minutes ticked slowly by until we were saying goodbye to Jonathan and Bobby.

***

The next week when we returned to the Immigration building for another Consular meeting, I saw the Australian Broadcasting Corporation's Foreign Correspondent, Geoff Thompson, standing at the roadside with his camera pointed to our approach. He looked sun tanned as if he had spent weeks on the beaches of Phuket. I wanted to shout to the world that we were innocent, but fear kept me silent. When we neared, one of the police officers escorting me lifted his clipboard to block the camera's view. As I walked past my fellow Australian, I could have easily reached out and touched the dark blue shirt he wore. Soon it would be too late to say anything. The entrance of the Immigration Centre was just beyond the rows of motorcycles to my left. My heart pounded in my chest, daring me to risk the consequences, whatever they might be. My lips felt dry as I moistened them with my tongue and my skin slowly burned as the beads of sweat formed on my brow. At the final second, I turned my head and over my shoulder, I said the first thing that came into my head.

'I love my children. I've never broken the law.'

I did not even know if he heard me but I missed my children so much that it was enough for me to have been able to say those words aloud. The police rushed me through the door.

'No English,' the police officer said angrily. We mounted the dark stairwell that led to Mr Khamkit's office.

Geoff Thompson's footage featured on prime time television that evening. Kerry looked annoyed and defiant as three armed police officers escorted him to Immigration. Apparently Kerry told the journalist to tell our family that he was well and when Geoff asked Kerry about the allegations, Kerry responded by telling him they were all lies. Geoff Thompson also reported the first words I uttered to the world outside since my arrest: 'I love my children. I've never broken the law.'

My sister wrote the following week, and I was obviously relieved we were now allowed to receive letters, even if they were censored, although we still hadn't received the first letters written by my children. These were a vital contact with the outside world, with our family, and our children. She said they had taped the footage so the kids could watch it repeatedly. Nathan sat for hours looking at my image frozen on the screen.

'I want to give Mummy a kiss,' he said, hugging the television. In many ways, our children suffered more than we did. We could not change what was happening any more than we could protect them from the lies told.

Bounmaly reported that the key for the entrance door of Gem Mining was in Kerry's control. It was ludicrous to suggest that with over 75 clients, Kerry would have all their keys on his belt. Bounmaly said Kerry broke the Lao law when he had acted on his client's instruction to direct the transfer of two Gem Mining computers and some office furniture to the Lao Securicor storage room for safekeeping.

Bounmaly complained that Kerry did not get permission from the Lao Government to move the Gem Mining assets. However, at the time, the Lao Government had not seized control of Gem Mining. Therefore, Kerry was under no obligation to report to anyone other than his client. Why would he? Bounmaly created a mass of confusion, to make every action look suspicious. Although the Gem Mining storage room held 1.7 tonne of sapphires, Bounmaly said Kerry was responsible for the loss of the contents of the Gem Mining safe. He claimed 130 kilograms of partially processed stones were missing from the safe, then changed those figures to 265 items of jewellery. Yet the Lao Securicor memorandum clearly stated that the contents of the safe were the responsibility of Bjarne and Julie alone. Furthermore, Bjarne and Julie had already signed a statement confirming that they had directed their Lao Manager to remove the jewellery from the safe and deliver it to them in Thailand. There really was no case to answer.

The ABC Foreign Correspondent, Geoff Thompson, obviously gained an impression that the Lao Government had already decided our guilt when he asked Bounmaly if the matter was not for a court to decide. In his response, Bounmaly said he did not know if it was.

It became clear that the Lao Foreign Minister and Deputy Prime Minister Lengsavad had formed an opinion of our guilt when he made a statement to the ABC Foreign Correspondent:

'According to the investigations and inspection conducted by the Lao authorities, there is strong evidence and proof that the

Danes family are responsible for the loss of property within the company,' said Lengsavad.

However, as Thompson so rightly pointed out, the jewellery allegedly missing was not a Gem Mining asset. The Lao Government had no right to claim it. It was obvious to everyone involved in the case that Bounmaly was setting us up to take the fall for Gem Mining Laos.

The media reported so many different versions of the so-called events that the cast of characters began to unfold like a Hollywood movie. The confusion that surrounded our case was a ploy to distract people from understanding what was really going on. It was a deliberate and calculating plan devised by Bounmaly, whose mishandling of the Gem Mining nationalisation had exposed the Foreign Affairs Minister and created instability in the investment community. The foreign investors of Asia Sapphires also sought to use our detainment to fuel their case against Gem Mining. They made damning accusations against Kerry and wrote letters to the Australian Prime Minister and Foreign Affairs Minister, seeking to convince them that we were unworthy of their concern. Our Government disregarded the claims. After this, Bounmaly suggested that the Lao Government might be prepared to trade us for Bjarne and Julie. Effectively, he had confirmed that we were hostages!

Australian Government sources revealed that Bounmaly had detained several Lao employees of Gem Mining, exactly one a week after my detainment at the Lao-Thai border. One of them, a former Lao police officer, had been carrying a large quantity of sapphires at the time.

***

In the prison the following day, I received a message from Kerry telling me that he had informed the Ambassador of our nightly interrogations. Four days later, the police finally gave me the letters from my children they had been keeping from me. I sat in the corner of my cell and quietly read each one, starting with Sahra's.

The tears slipped unchecked down my cheeks as I thought of my little Sahra pouring her heart out on the pristine white pages before me. The second letter was from our son Nathan who was only seven years old and had to rely on my sister Karen, to type his. Our eldest daughter Jess also wrote, and it was really difficult to see her trying to hold the family together in our absence.

My father carried an enormous burden as he endeavoured to come to terms with our detainment. He had to make impossible decisions without knowing exactly who was who and what was what. Nevertheless, as fathers do, he did everything short of moving mountains to try to protect me. My father's persistence pulled him from pillar to post as the media frenzy took hold. It ignited a flood of support from a number of people including Kerry's uncle, Geoff Spiller, who recommended my parents engage a man called Peter Church, an international lawyer and Director of ASEAN Focus Group, on our behalf. Church had extensive contacts in Laos and had recently interviewed the Laos Prime Minister for his forthcoming book on the life stories of the Presidents and Prime Ministers of the ASEAN countries.

As an author of several historical works, Geoff was a meticulous researcher and more importantly, was objective. He saw straight away that we were in trouble and that this involved much more than any alleged crimes on our part.

The Embassy told us too that he had offered financial support to our children and was willing to take care of the practical arrangements of paying telephone bills and school fees. His generosity certainly came as no surprise to Kerry and I, who had always known how kind he was.

In the meantime, the Lao authorities informed the Embassy that Kerry and I enjoyed intimate time together and went outside our cells for exercise. I might have found the nightmare easier to bear if only that were true.

Somewhere deep within, I found the courage to write my first letter to our children. As I gripped the pen, I paused briefly to stop my hand from shaking. What could I say?

I worried about what might happen if they caught me smuggling a letter outside but I wanted to tell my family that I was afraid. How could I tell them about all the horrors I had seen? I breathed deeply and lay quietly trying to think. My body turned to face the dirty, concrete cell wall that separated my sleeping space from the tiny washroom we all shared. My cell mates also lay still on the wooden floorboards that kept us a foot off the concrete floor below. The police forced us to lie quietly for two hours every day. They said the silence would help us maintain control but at times, I felt as if they were slowly driving me insane. I convinced myself I could hear the tiny footsteps of the ants crawling below us. Nevertheless, the silence was my friend too. It meant I could hear the guards coming closer on their regular patrol. I closed my eyes pretending to sleep, hiding the pen in my lap. I knew they would lock my legs in the wooden blocks or put me in solitude for an indefinite period if they caught me writing. I also knew that the risk of trying to smuggle a letter out of the prison could result in the cancellation of future Consular visits, but I was desperate.

When left alone again with only the sound of the ants to disturb the silence, I painstakingly scrawled the tiniest of text on a single sheet of borrowed toilet paper. I told them how much I loved them and missed them, and urged them to be strong, and to keep believing that we would be home soon. It was all I could do, all I could think to say.

By some miracle, I smuggled that tiny letter out of the prison. I was careful to fold it small enough to conceal it under the two end fingers of my right hand. When Tan Sombut ordered Pon-Phit to search me prior to our departure to the office of Immigration for our next Consular visit, I began my distraction by buttoning up the blue prison jacket that all prisoners wore. I desperately hoped he would not notice how my fingers shook as they curled around the tiny paper. However, Tan Sombut seemed more interested in my pockets and shoes. I was relieved when he did not ask me to open my hands for inspection. I guess he probably thought I could not button and conceal at the same time. I was lucky that day but I knew I had a lot to learn if I was ever going to attempt smuggling letters again.

We travelled by car along the dusty streets that took us into the city. It was hot, and my palms became wet when the sun hit my skin through the glass. I worried about the tiny letter and hoped it would not become an unreadable, splotchy bundle of ink and tissue. I thought for a moment about traffickers and the risks they took to smuggle drugs throughout South East Asia. Though mine was only a letter, I imagined the nervous apprehension was the same, as the letter became a dead weight under my fingers.

The afternoon heat sapped away my energy as I left the car to enter the Immigration building for our Consular visit. I had only twenty minutes to wait before the Embassy Staff arrived. I passed the time wondering how I was going to transfer my letter to them. It was a great relief when the door to Mr Khamkit's office opened to admit Jonathan and Louise.

'Hi Kay, how are you?' he said smiling warmly.

I could not explain how I truly felt, so I half-smiled back at him and said I was fine.

Our meeting went by in a whirlwind rush as it always did on a Thursday. The Embassy staff prepared to leave and still I had not given Louise my letter. A thousand eyes watched my every move, or so it seemed to me. My heart pounded as the moisture in my palms increased. Sensing my distress, Louise gave me a handful of tissues for my tears and gently said goodbye. 'Hang in there Kay,' she said from the door.

They were leaving! My eyes darted from the police and then to the back of Louise who was by now disappearing down the hallway.

'Shit!' I muttered under my breath. I would have to wait another week before I could try to pass the letter on again. Another week before my children could hear from me.

'Come we go,' the police officer said, to my utter relief. There was still time.

'Okay I'm coming,' I said louder than I really needed to. I hoped that Louise would hear me and slow her departure so I could catch up.

For the first time I hurried to leave the building, not because I wanted to return to Phonthong, but because I wanted to make sure our children had some word from us. I quickened my pace, and crossed the dirty linoleum ground floor in no time. Louise was about to open the door of the Embassy car parked in view. Luckily, she turned around. I mouthed the words 'come here'. With the police directly behind me, I swallowed my fear and stretched my hands towards her. Louise looked puzzled. My eyes pleaded for her to follow my lead.

'You can have your tissues back,' I smiled, pressing them firmly into her hand. To add further distraction to what I was doing I added in Lao language, 'Sok dee, sok dee,' hoping to fool the police into thinking that I was merely wishing her good luck.

Louise told me the next week that she had almost thrown the tissues in the trash, except when she shook them the little letter fell on to her lap. She said it gave our children tremendous hope.

***

We had been detained for just over a month when a Sri Lankan prisoner known as Mr Kylie became seriously ill with dengue fever. It was no surprise because the mosquitoes swarmed our cells both day and night. We watched for several days as Kylie lay at death's door in an overheated cell not far from mine. His temperature was dangerously high but despite this, the police commander refused him medical care. During the week, we heard the insistent screams from the male prisoners shouting for the guards to come quickly. However, the police refused. I feared for Kylie.

In the early hours of the morning the prison nurse finally came and merely gave Kylie a couple of out-of-date tablets containing paracetamol. He said as they always said, 'Be patient.' A few hours later, the male prisoners took Kylie to the makeshift infirmary. Of course, this was just a small room with a window that overlooked an even larger sewage pond.

The prisoners placed Kylie's limp body on the wooden table that sat in the middle of the room. Above him hung an old green ceiling fan that looked as if it had been broken for years. Kylie didn't know where he was and suffered a seizure moments after they placed him on the table. The prisoners panicked. They began shouting for help but no one came. I watched helplessly from my cell, wondering what to do. I was not supposed to leave the room but as I looked towards the cell door, I noticed it was unlocked. Fear rather than locks kept the prisoners in their cells. Kylie's body convulsed and thrashed back and forth on the table. The men tried to hold him down. Their faces revealed their own fear at not knowing what to do. I couldn't just stand there and watch this man suffer. Throwing caution to the wind, I opened the door and ran to him. When I got to them, ten male prisoners were fanning Kylie's sweat-drenched body. The convulsions had stopped. Kylie lay limp under a heavy woollen blanket.

'Kylie,' I called to him, pushing my way through the crowd. I touched my hand to his dark forehead and felt him burn with fever. Slowly I lifted his heavy eyelids in turn with the soft pad of my thumb. His eyes glazed over. His dark pupils rolled back into his head revealing only the whites of his eyes. I had no way of knowing his actual temperature but I knew it was far too high and he was gravely ill.

'Bring me a bucket with some water!' I demanded to the male prisoners who quickly flew into action.

They tossed a green bucket outside to the others milling by the window and told them to waste no time filling it. When it was full, the bucket was passed back through the window and brought to where I stood beside Kylie. I found an old red rag in a cupboard in the corner of the room. I dipped it in the water and pressed it to Kylie's forehead. Quietly I assured him that everything would be alright. I was surprised at how hot the rag became when I ran it over his dark skin. I dipped it in the water repeatedly to try to cool him. It didn't matter that the water was contaminated because we had all been bathing in diluted sewage water every night anyway. All that mattered at that moment was reducing his body heat.

'Quickly, everyone, we need to get his temperature down,' I said, urgently.

The male prisoners fanned him while I continued to bathe him. It seemed an eternity before Kylie's temperature lowered, but eventually it did. He stopped thrashing.

'It's okay Kylie. Can you hear me?' I asked, but got no response.

I felt so helpless. Finally, a female nurse came to the room and was surprised that I was attending to Kylie. In fact, she seemed more interested in me than she did in Kylie. I searched for compassion in her light brown eyes and saw with sadness that there was none. Suddenly the prisoners fell silent at the arrival of Tan Sombut. I think I must have felt his presence before I actually noticed him standing just inside the doorway. His dark eyes pierced mine. I swallowed nervously and bit my bottom lip, silently pleading with him not to be angry. Tan Sombut watched my every expression. His eyes roamed my face and rested briefly on my lower lip caught between my teeth. I stood like a ghost waiting for what seemed like death to pass by me. His eyes lowered to where my hand gripped the wet red rag, and then to Kylie. The female nurse muttered something to Tan Sombut and for a moment he was distracted.

The room filled with silence, broken only by the beating of my heart.

I felt so sorry for Kylie. He did not deserve to die in this place. Two years and still he had never been to court. How was it that he was responsible for his friend's leaving town without paying a US$300 telephone bill? How was it that despite the fact he had agreed to pay, they would not let him telephone his family for the money? The sad reality of Laos was that people were arrested all the time, and some for very little reason.

'Kylie, Kylie, can you hear me? Kylie you are okay, they will take you to the doctor. Please don't worry,' I said to comfort him.

'Officer Sombut, can Kylie go to hospital?' I cried, in broken Lao.

Moments passed and Tan Sombut said nothing. He just stood looking at me with my hands raised prayer-like. With a flick of his head, the male prisoners rushed to Kylie and began preparing him for the journey to the hospital. As they carried him away, I touched my hand to his head and spoke quietly: 'Kylie please be okay!'

Without further delay, I ran quickly to my cell to tell Mon what was going on. She worried so much that I had left the room. As I made my way back to my cell, I noticed Kerry crouched at his cell window. I could just make out his face.

'I think he'll croak,' I called out to him in Australian slang.

Kerry stretched his arm through the bars towards me but with more than thirty feet between us there was no way I could reach him. Tan Sombut was about to come out of the infirmary so I quickly blew a kiss in Kerry's direction before hurrying back to my cell.

Four hours later, we were all surprised when Kylie returned semi-conscious. The prisoners carried him to his cell. They said he was too weak and would probably die. That same afternoon, they took Kylie out of the prison and we never saw him again. The police said he had returned to Sri Lanka but we did not believe them for a minute.

Anouhack told me that the Ministry of Interior was the only department that could approve hospital transfers but it was practically unheard of. We were all doomed if we got sick.

'Hey Kay good news for you,' Anouhack said, as he handed me a small piece of apple.

'What is it? What did you hear?' I asked pressing my face against the cell bars. The rust stains marked my face but I was far from caring about my appearance.

'Your Government talk a lot last night. Mr Downer in charge of the Foreign Affairs in Australia sent a letter to Foreign Minister Lengsavad. Good news hey?' he said joyfully.

'My God,' was all I could say.

'Don't think too much,' Bounchan interrupted my thoughts. 'Your Embassy is working hard for you.'

'I know Bounchan. I just miss my children!' I replied softly.

'Be grateful you hear from them because many prisoners here cannot,' he spoke gently. 'Did you know that this prison was built in 1994 to be a refugee centre? Technically, we are all refugees waiting for the boat to freedom huh?' he laughed.

Too bad Laos was a landlocked country, I thought.

CHAPTER SIX

Legal Wrangling

As Anouhack had said, the Australian Foreign Minister had sent a letter to Lengsavad detailing the Australian Government's concerns for our well-being and continued detainment. It was diplomatic and polite, full of praise for the close ties formed between Australia and Laos, and full of apologies for my father's outbursts over the internet, which were full of condemnation for the country of Laos. It said nothing the Laos Government did not already know, lamenting 'the continued separation of Mr and Mrs Danes from their young children, on grounds that have not been fully explained,' that 'has been the cause of particular distress for their families,' and urging a quick resolution to 'this unhappy incident in an otherwise constructive bilateral relationship.'

Lengsavad failed to even respond to Downer, which got everyone in Phonthong prison talking.

'You see Kay, the communist laugh at the western governments,' said one prisoner. I could only sit there hoping that Downer would demand a response, and one that would be powerful enough to silence the tongues that constantly flagged the weaknesses of our government!

***

Our locally based American lawyer, Bobby Allen, passed me two power of attorney documents at our next Consular meeting. In the first, I formally appointed Kerry's older brother, Leslie, as Managing Director to my Thai bodyguard business, Pacific Security Services, which was a completely separate operation run by myself. The second retained an Australian lawyer named Ted Tzovaras to represent us. At the same time, though we didn't know it, the lawyer Peter Church contacted my father to inform him that the Director of Security for Jardine Securicor had heard we had already appointed a lawyer. The Director said he did not know who it was or how we came to such a decision but that Jardine Securicor were also considering their corporate position in Laos, and might require representation. They asked Church to stay in touch with them.

Bobby explained that the legal case against Gem Mining was progressing slowly because the Lao authorities were trying to pressure former employees to make statements against the directors. Rumours circulated throughout Vientiane that court proceedings would be held in Bjarne and Julie's absence. Ultimately, it was a foregone conclusion that they would be convicted of a criminal offence despite the fact that they continued to refute the allegations against them. Julie signed a declaration in front of the New Zealand Ambassador in Bangkok confirming that she had asked the jewellery to be removed, and that it wasn't an asset of the company anyway. Even though it was hers, Julie agreed to surrender the jewellery, if by doing so it would secure our release.

This had a deflating impact on Bounmaly and diminished his credibility but it was unlikely that this would end our detainment. Bounmaly had lost face. He had become desperate and without our confession for a crime we absolutely did not do, there was a good chance that the Laos Government would send him far away to a re-education camp.

Our visiting time was almost at an end and I knew that soon they would escort me to the room next door.

'Now, don't be upset if I'm not here next week Kay,' Bobby spoke in a muffled tone.

'Why?' I cried, afraid my lifeline was about to be severed.

'Okay, finish,' Mr Khamkit interrupted.

Bobby stood up and I walked into his waiting arms. 'I don't know how long I can hang around given the heat and besides, your new lawyer is coming,' he whispered, as he hugged me goodbye. I suddenly felt anxious that Bobby might be leaving sooner than expected. I did not know that the Lao Government had shut down the law firm Dirksen, Flipse, Doran and Le (DFDL) where Bobby worked. 'Okay Bobby,' I said quietly.

I searched for the words to express my gratitude for all he had ever tried to do for us. Somehow, words seemed inadequate as I squeezed him tighter, almost afraid to let go.

'Don't worry Kay,' he assured me. However, his soft blue eyes looked anything but confident.

'Just stay strong. We will manage. Don't worry about a thing,' he half smiled.

It was just a phrase: 'Don't worry about a thing,' and yet we all worried. Our family worried too. They were just as much in the dark about our situation as we were. I thought about them as I sat in the next room waiting for Kerry to conclude his meeting with the Embassy and Bobby. There was never enough time to say all the things I wanted to say. 'Tell my children I love them.' 'Tell them not to be afraid.' 'Tell them not to worry.'

If only the Lao authorities would allow Kerry and I to meet at the Embassy together. However, they said we could not because our investigation was ongoing. They were probably afraid that we would share secrets despite the fact we did not have any. I just wanted to hold my husband and have him tell me everything would be okay. Being apart from my children was bad enough but that they separated us from each other was just another form of torture they seemed to delight in. My family had sent letters, a few basic food supplies, and a small bottle of mouthwash. We kept the mouthwash only because Tan Peng had escorted us that day and we had promised it to him. However, they took our food supplies and letters. They took every opportunity to assert their control and as humiliating as it was to beg, I knew that I would as soon as we arrived back at the prison.

'Those bastards can't even read bloody English, why can't we just have them?' I complained to Anouhack, who said he would ask again for the letters.

The hours passed slowly in Phonthong as I thought I would go mad waiting for news outside. Tan Peng, I noticed, went to Kerry's cell a lot and when he walked passed my cell, he smiled.

'He got mouthwash from Kerry,' explained Anouhack. Over the week, the mouthwash ran out and Tan Peng came for my supply, but it was all gone.

I tried to help the other prisoners as much as they were helping me. One of the women developed mouth ulcers and begged me to help her.

'You have salt?' I asked her, but she didn't understand, and started to cry.

'Pang!' I called to the American-Hmong woman who was about to walk by.

'Do you have salt?' I asked.

'What's wrong?' she asked quietly, coming to stand outside my cell.

'Nang has mouth ulcers and I can fix them with some salt,' I explained to her slowly, as Nang opened her mouth wide for Pang.

'Sure, okay,' Pang said, and went next door to her cell.

When Pang returned, I explained through her to Nang how to mix the salt with warm water and gargle. She thanked me profusely, calling me 'Sister Kay'.

Word soon spread throughout the prison that my magic had cured Nang's mouth ulcers. A few days later, Tan Peng returned and Nang showed him how to make the saltwater rinse. He was as happy as if he had won the lottery. After a few successes, they promoted me to Doctor.

***

'Kay, I am going soon to visit with the Embassy,' said Anouhack. He was dressed smartly and was smiling from ear to ear. I could not help but be excited for him to be going.

'I will get to see my wife, Phaiwan,' he smiled. His face glowed with happiness.

'Please try and find out what's going on,' I begged him. I watched him walk through the black door until it closed behind him. I strained my ear to hear the car pull away from the prison, knowing it would take Anouhack on that same ten-minute journey that connected us with the outside world. When Anouhack returned to Phonthong, his arms were laden with food supplies. He beamed and looked happier than I had ever seen him. Even the reality of returning to the prison did nothing to dampen his joy. I wondered if I would ever feel that way.

'Kay, here some fruit for you,' he said as he passed the small bag of rambutans through the bars and then even more quietly whispered: 'I spoke with Louise.' I smiled at him as I took the bag and passed it to Mon. 'What did she say?' I asked quickly.

'She said your lawyer has a meeting with the prosecutor and then is going to Thailand to collect the information for your case,' he replied.

'And?' I asked.

'That's it,' he laughed. 'I don't know why they don't tell me anything more than that. They don't understand this place,' he responded, shaking his head.

'Well, it's good news anyway. Thanks.' I tried hard to hide my disappointment.

'Yeah. It's good news for you at least. My case still difficult because they want too much money to release me,' he said, frustrated.

'How much now?' I questioned, knowing that Anouhack was just as much a hostage as we were.

'Oh. Now is US$350,000,' he said.

'Bullshit!' I almost choked.

'Yeah bullshit alright! Where can I get that sort of money in here?' he laughed aloud as he waved his arms around to survey his surroundings.

'I better go Kay. I'll tell Kerry.' He said goodbye before the 'spy police', the informants, could approach.

I did not know how Anouhack managed to remain so positive when he was facing a similar situation to us. The Canadian Embassy had not even commenced any formal negotiations. He had over-stayed his sentence by more than six months and the United Nations, for whom he had worked as a Project Manager, had clearly abandoned him along with their project.

***

We had been hostages of the regime for almost three whole months at this stage, and yet it seemed much longer. How could they continue to detain us in the absence of a crime, let alone in the absence of an arrest warrant? Kerry remained confined to his cell despite repeated requests from the Australian Embassy. I was luckier. Noi asked Tan Sombut if I could go outside to cut her hair, having discovered I had once been a hairdresser. He agreed.

'You want to come outside Mon?' I joked, knowing that she could not.

'No can sister Kay. I must make coffee for my young brother,' she said as she smiled in the same joking manner.

I felt frustrated having to communicate in another language. English was not encouraged. In fact, it caused problems more often than not because the guards felt stupid for not being able to speak it. It was just as well that Kerry and I both spoke Thai. Most Laotians could understand the Thai language because they often listen to Thai TV or radio and because the two cultures are similar.

I was glad to be out of my cell-like sauna but distressed when Kerry remained trapped in his. He swore and cursed the guards and despite the fact that he swore in English, 'Get fucked' was easily understood in anyone's language. Though I knew my husband was suffering I still found his aggression amusing.

'Kay, cut slowly,' said Noi.

The Laotian sat on a wooden chair just outside our door. It was a tremendous feeling to be on the other side of the bars. I looked occasionally to the tall trees dotting the horizon beyond the prison wall and wished I were there and not here. A big black crow squawked in the distance. Mon sang happily from our cell and for the next fifteen minutes, I smiled and snipped away at Noi's short brown hair with scissors on loan from the police.

'You can forget everything sometimes Kay, when you let your mind be still,' Noi spoke quietly.

I smiled, and wished that Kerry could have seen me smiling. The next day began with the same routine but this time the Thai girl Malivan wanted her hair cut. She boldly moved the chair from the veranda to the flat ground where the prisoners lined up. I stood at our doorway and watched her signal me.

'Kay come,' she called. I looked at the police officer sitting ten metres away to her left. What would he say if I went so far from my cell? Malivan called again and told me not to be afraid.

'It's okay,' she smiled, waving her hand at me to join her. I left my cell filled with anxiety that my freedom was to be short-lived but it wasn't so. The police ignored me as I walked quietly down the five concrete stairs to Malivan. She had been arrested simply for being at a pro-democracy student rally. She was one of the lucky ones. The alleged leaders of the demonstration were taken away and never heard from again.

'Don't worry Kay. Look Kerry,' she said pointing to his cell.

I was almost too afraid to look but when I did, I saw Kerry's hand waving through the bars. He was in the first cell of block two, about fifteen metres away. Anouhack sat on the veranda talking to him. I expect Kerry was grateful for his company just as I was glad that finally my husband could see me. The next day, Nang wanted a haircut and so the police told the prisoners I could stay out of the cell until midday lock-up. They told me where I could and could not walk. Fear was the silent barrier that kept everyone controlled. I soon became part of their routine. Kerry sat behind the bars of his cell while other pairs of eyes watched me watching him. Occasionally I would wave while pretending to stretch my arms. Kerry smiled and though we still weren't together, we were at least able to see each other from a distance.

I asked every day if my Thai friend Mon could come outside but every day the police refused. It made me feel guilty leaving her alone, but still I cherished my morning time outside.

***

Days passed. The women in the prison were happy to keep me company but also careful not to talk too much. Over time, I began to learn more about each female prisoner. Nang had suffered more than mouth ulcers according to Anouhack. She felt she needed to have an operation to remove a copper intrauterine device she had fitted long before her arrival at Phonthong. Consistent with the side effects of the contraceptive device, Nang experienced lower back and abdominal pain, as well as fever. She worried that it hadn't been checked in over two years. There was a risk that she would develop more serious side effects. Nevertheless, the police had no knowledge of contraceptive devices and insisted she was simply seeking ways out of detainment.

Like many of the women in Phonthong, Nang had no money and no family support. If she got sick then she got sick. There was no going to hospital or calling a doctor. If she died, she died. Life was cruel in Phonthong and the more I saw how they denied others their basic human rights, the more I began to understand the real dangers of my situation.

Anouhack lay quietly in a hammock tied to a tree that stood at the edge of the fishponds. I sat nearby on an old wooden chair.

We quietly discussed the taboo subject of politics, but were interrupted by a tall, skinny man who came to talk with Anouhack. He was terribly under-nourished. His hair, though probably once black, was cut short and heavily speckled with grey. His face was kind as his eyes twinkled with a strange combination of humour and shadows of despair.

'I want to tell you my story but we must talk quickly,' he said with quite good English.

'Sure,' I said softly, waiting for him to sit down on the wooden bench. He introduced himself as Mr Joy, and his story had a huge effect on me.

He told me about how his family had fled Laos as members of the persecuted Hmong minority, and ended up in a Thai refugee camp waiting for repatriation to the United States. The US Immigration and Nationalised Services rejected his application for political asylum, submitted in 1986. They said it was because the communists had educated him. Friends in the United States tried to petition the INS to accept him but the repatriation program had begun. Mr Joy fled the refugee camp in 1993 and sought shelter in a Hmong-Thai village. They deported him in 1994 because he could not afford the bribes that the village chief asked for in order to keep him safe. Upon his return to Laos, the authorities arrested Mr Joy. They detained him without trial or charge. I was both entranced and shocked that such a thing could happen but Mr Joy said that it was a common occurrence. Many of his compatriots had been driven from Laos and even decades later, continued to be persecuted, simply because they were Hmong, the children and children's children of those who helped the US in the Vietnam War. Despite everything, he remained optimistic. 'One day things will be different and I will wait even if I am an old man,' he said quietly.

'When you are free, don't be afraid to tell the world what you have seen in here in this hell. How they can treat other human beings worse than the dog? You must ask the United Nations and Western Governments and the Foreign Aid Donors to take action, to make this regime uphold the human rights of the people in all the prisons in Laos and in the country-side, and don't ever forget everything you have learned in here, on your journey to freedom!'

'Mr Joy, you better not get too excited hey!' cautioned Anouhack.

'Just remember Madam,' he smiled.

***

Perhaps the saddest story I had ever heard in Phonthong was Noi's. Mon said Noi had returned to Laos when the authorities arrested her Thai husband. They invited her to bring him medical supplies and food. The police didn't say why they were detaining him. But thinking she had nothing to fear, Noi gathered their two small children aged five and three and began the journey from her village to another in Phontan. There she could safely leave her children in the care of the local women and make her way to the jail. Upon her arrival at the prison, the police arrested her and sent her to a political prison known as Somkhe. They didn't say why.

Noi's husband, who was well into his fifties, died of a heart attack some months later. Noi learned of his death from a prisoner who had transferred from Phontan to Somkhe. Instead of releasing Noi to her children, the police forgot about her. Eventually they transferred her to Phonthong Prison. At night, I heard Noi crying. She sat staring out the window to the black door, quietly rocking back and forth.

'What happened to your children Noi?' I whispered as I went to sit beside her.

'I don't know. I wait and wait but much time pass now,' Noi whispered in the still of the night.

'How long Noi?' I questioned.

'Twelve years,' she whispered.

Noi's dark eyes welled with tears. I saw the pain etched in every line of her once youthful face. No wonder she was always sad. Twelve years was an incredibly long time to wonder what might have happened to your children. I had no idea how I would have coped had that been me. Noi said Kerry and I were lucky that they didn't send us to the domestic jails where conditions were far worse than Phonthong. She and Toom had spent many years in Somkhe as political prisoners. She said the police filled their cells with forty to fifty women at a time. They didn't have the typical Asian style toilets, just a small hole in the ground at the end of the cell. At least we had a small concrete washroom despite the fact that it was a daily chore keeping it slime free.

We also had the added luxury of a single light bulb hanging from the ceiling of the tiny washroom which would otherwise plunge us into complete darkness, even during the day. We didn't have much else, but what we did have we treasured. A toothbrush, a pail to wash the sweat and grime from our bodies, or a plain bar of soap was all one needed to remain human. My new friends had lived in places far worse than I could ever imagine, so it didn't surprise me each night to find one of them staring at the black door. Memories haunted them—memories of loved ones they'd probably never see again.

'Tell me about Toom,' I asked Mon one night when we were supposed to be sleeping.

'Toom not like to talk about her case,' Mon said quietly as we lay on our blankets and took turns fanning each other from the heat. 'She go to the jail in 1993. Long time now. Maybe a little bit crazy,' Mon said seriously. She pinched her two fingers together to show just how much Toom was crazy.

'You think so?' I asked, watching Toom standing by the doorway smoking a cigarette. She was careful not to let the smoke drift our way, holding her hand towards the tiny vents cut into the wall a foot below ceiling height. She certainly didn't act crazy.

'She has a sister in Udon Thani and miss her too much,' she whispered. Toom looked in our direction and smiled.

I was later told in secret what she had allegedly done, but I found it difficult to imagine Toom knifing two Lao police to death. But then I didn't really know her. We often see only what others want us to see. Certainly, I preferred to think of her as Anouhack described, a woman defending herself from a rape attack. It was far easier to share a cell with a victim as opposed to a murderer. Mon insisted that Toom hadn't done the terrible things they accused her of doing.

'Yeah, well you won't get any argument from me Mon,' I replied.

Of course, there were prisoners who deserved to be in Phonthong. To say otherwise would be naïve. There were prisoners who'd admitted smuggling drugs for money. How many young lives had they destroyed in the process of their activities? But did they deserve to be tortured? I gave up casting judgements, and in the quietness of Phonthong Prison, cared less about why people were there, as opposed to them simply being there. Kerry and I hadn't broken any laws and yet we had become prisoners of the regime. They labelled us criminals and like so many detained alongside us, were yet to be formally charged.

***

On 8 February 2001, they took us by unmarked car to the Immigration building. I went up to Mr Khamkit's office and waited until I was invited into the room where, much to my surprise, the Embassy staff were waiting. I looked at Louise who stood immediately and came towards me with her usual friendly embrace. To my disappointment, Bobby who had been both my lawyer and my friend was not there. He had left Laos. Ambassador Thwaites greeted me with a warm embrace that always made me feel safe. I was sure it was not protocol for an Ambassador to hug a prisoner so I was tremendously relieved that he did not think of me as a criminal. Tears sprang to my eyes at his compassionate gesture, but I quickly blinked them away.

'Kay I want you to meet someone,' said Louise as we moved to sit down. It was then I noticed a stranger in our midst. He introduced himself as Ted Tzovaras. He was to be our new lawyer.

'Hi Kay, it is good to finally meet you,' he said with a warm smile. I listened as he confirmed that he was taking over legal representation from Bobby who had left Laos shortly after our last Consular meeting. He did not explain who had approached him on our behalf so I assumed it had been my father. He was dressed in what looked like a dark navy Giorgio Armani suit, and tiny square shaped gold cuff links glistened when he leaned forward to shake my hand.

He assured me that our case would never get as far as court. He submitted to us a letter that outlined his strategies in brief. He said our best chance of release was through diplomatic negotiations and not through legal proceedings, and hinted that the Lao court was not transparent and would not allow us to challenge it. No foreigner had ever been found innocent in a Lao court. With so little time left to discuss our case, I asked about my family. Our lawyer was now the face-to-face link to them and I was desperate to get a message back to my father.

'My Dad's pretty upset at the moment. Can you help him not to offend anyone else in Laos?' I asked. I knew he meant well and was showing his outrage at the treatment of his daughter, but his good intentions were stirring things up in Laos. Frankly, I did not care that he had called them corrupt bastards. It was what I would have called them. The Embassy however, advised that his comments had not helped their diplomatic approach and virtually suggested a gag order on my father.

'Following this meeting Kay, I'll be travelling back to Sydney via Brisbane and I'll personally meet your father and explain everything,' he said calmly.

'I can't have him come here. I cannot control what they … what might happen,' I said, letting my voice trail off rather than explain the number of fearful possibilities.

'Yes well, I do have a plan of approach but this is not the appropriate forum to discuss those details. As a contingency, in case our first angle doesn't work, I have a plan B that will involve putting a legal team together of some very high profile lawyers. They will focus mostly on the legal aspects of your case. Don't worry!' he responded.

'You just concentrate on getting through this. Just concentrate on staying positive Kay. You're both receiving remarkable support from the Australian Government and Foreign Minister Downer has already written to his counterpart in Laos calling for your immediate release,' he encouraged.

I half smiled at Jonathan, who sat quietly observing our meeting. Without his continued support, no one would have paid us much attention. Jonathan smiled back sincerely and for a few brief moments, I felt calmed. Until of course, the Lao authorities told us to end our meeting. Our fifteen minutes had come and gone too quickly. My heart began pounding in my chest as I turned to leave.

As I stood up and hugged Louise goodbye, I slipped a tiny note into her hand. It was my second letter to our children, urging them to stay strong, and reminding them that we loved and missed them dearly. I told them about the blue budgie I had seen that gave me momentary respite from the horror of my surroundings.

I wish I could have told them how the blue budgie had distracted me from their father's interrogation, but it would have terrified them. As I made way to leave the room, our new lawyer stood before me and held both my hands in his, forcing me to look him straight in the eye.

'I'll have you out of here Kay, as soon as possible.'

I was convinced I would be freed immediately.

'See you next week Kay,' said Jonathan.

As I made my way down the dimly lit passageway, I anxiously fixed my eyes upon the door opening slowly.

'Hey babe,' Kerry smiled to me as the police escorted him down the hall towards me.

'I wanta go home!' I pleaded, voicing my torment aloud.

Tears rolled down my cheeks despite my earlier promise to myself that I would not let Kerry see me cry.

'It's alright babe, hang in there,' he soothed. Kerry's gaze penetrated the barrier between us, urging me to be strong. However, I was not strong. My lips quivered as my body shook. I tried to push my way through the police but they were equally determined to keep us apart.

'It's alright babe,' Kerry said.

'I love you!' I cried back to him as they took me down the hall. I tried to look back over my shoulder but the police pulled me along until I was alone in the room where Kerry had been.

'Be patient Madam,' the young officer said and motioned me to sit on the chair next to the wall. I sat waiting for Kerry's meeting to finish and did my best to recall my own meeting. Then, what our lawyer said suddenly registered. He would get us out. Guaranteed.

The weight of all I had endured suddenly lifted from my shoulders. It was going to be alright. I was going home at last. I wiped my tears with the back of my hand. I was going to be free of this nightmare and then in just a little while, Kerry would be home too. We would eventually return to Thailand with the kids and move into my penthouse apartment in Sukhumvit. Sahra and Nathan would go to the International School where I had enrolled them during my last visit to Thailand. I would run my bodyguard business myself and life would be good again. My mind filled with hope and expectation.

I did not know how our lawyer would manage to secure my release. All that mattered was that I would soon see my children and everything would be okay. I stared at the clock ticking on the wall and blocked all logical thoughts from my mind. I composed myself and felt less anxious. I was going home and the thought of going home consumed me. Going back to the prison did not seem as bad since, as I thought, it was only temporary.

By the time we reached the prison, I was thoroughly convinced that the Embassy would be sending a car for me at four o'clock. I walked through the black door as Anouhack had done that day he had returned from the Embassy with his arms laden with food supplies. His smile had stretched from ear to ear and now so did mine.

'Mon. I go home,' I whispered to her.

'Good Kay. Good,' she said excitedly.

When the afternoon came and went, I found myself still locked in the cell. Perhaps they were coming later. I closed my eyes and forced myself to believe that.

In the morning, I woke earlier than usual and waited for the police to come. They eventually came at 7am but they did not let me out. At 8 am, the police came to unlock the cells but when they got to ours, they said nothing. We quietly left the room to line up for morning roll call and Pol Pot monologue, and I kept looking over my shoulder towards the black door thinking, 'any minute now'. All morning I sat underneath a tree watching and waiting for the black door to open. By midday, they locked us back inside the cells for our forced nap. There was no way I could sleep as I strained my ear to hear any sign of them coming for me. By the afternoon, they let us out again and I took up the same position under my tree. I only went to the toilet once because I thought if I left my post then perhaps I might have missed the police coming for me.

'Kay. They not come. Why?' said Mon. She watched me slowly sink into despair when all my hopes were shattered. I looked at her and said nothing. Tears welled in my eyes. The pain of reality engulfed me. I wanted to scream aloud my torment but felt suffocated. I could not breathe. Silently I stared at Kerry who sat ten metres away on the other side of barred windows, plastered in sweat. Despite the extreme heat, he somehow managed a smile. My eyes pleaded to know what was going on outside in the world but fear kept me silent.

'I want to go home!' I threw back my head, closed my eyes and shouted the words into the air.

My heart was broken. Soon it would be time to go back inside the cell. I wanted to disappear but where could I go? There was nowhere to hide in Phonthong. I sat thinking about our children and wondered if they were okay. I felt so sorry that I had not been able to prevent what was happening. My mind kept tormenting me with memories of them detaining me at the Friendship Bridge on the Laos -Thai border. As hard as I tried, I could not quite shake free the images of fear on Sahra and Nathan's innocent young faces that haunted me repeatedly. I felt I had failed them as a mother by not protecting them from a trauma they should never have endured.

The heat of the sun made my head ache but I imagined that thinking of my children made it ache even worse. I clutched my head in my hands and closed my eyes, trying to stop the images flooding my mind. If our lawyer told my family he had secured my release, would they be feeling the same elation I felt yesterday and now the despair I felt today? I cried silently as my thoughts tormented me.

A young Laotian who passed me a small note from Kerry interrupted my thoughts. It was just before lock up so I would have to reply the next day. I stood quietly under a tree. The guard in the tower along the southern wall stood rigid in his usual pose—his AK assault rifle pointed in our direction until lock up was complete. In my mind, I followed the other Lao police officer moving to the rear of our cell block. The keys jangled noisily as he began locking down the five cells housing 25 male prisoners. His path took him along the rear of Kerry's cell block where he locked up another twenty-five prisoners into five cells. Madam Gin-Gin was locked in the rear cell in isolation because the police felt she could not get along with the other prisoners. She was just an old Chinese woman who spoke a strange mountain dialect, which made it almost impossible to communicate with her. By ten minutes, the officer would be rounding the corner of the cell block where a further twenty-six prisoners would be waiting to be crammed back into their tiny sauna-like cells. The guard never hurried because none of us was going anywhere. Each minute outside the room was a welcome relief so I did not care how long he took.

Silently I watched the officer move towards Kerry's cell. All six male prisoners were already locked inside. They had been all day and every day since they arrived in Phonthong. The guard checked the locks on the heavy steel door. Then as he neared, coming closer and closer, I waved to Kerry and quickly made my way to stand with the other girls outside my cell. According to the regulations, we always had to be lower than the guards were. Only I could not get down in that typical Asian squat that the other girls had mastered.

Aside from that, I refused out of principal to kneel before these men. I complained that compared to the Asians, I was too fat to get back up again. That provided them some amusement so I managed to get away with it. The heavy steel door closed behind us. I removed the rubber flip-flops from my feet, a present from the Embassy, and climbed onto the wooden floorboards to sit with the other women. The black door opened and the guard left. I took that as my cue to slip into the washroom to read Kerry's message.

'Hey Babe. I love you heaps and I am so proud of you for staying so strong. Do not worry about everything. It'll be all right. Try and get some sleep tonight and not think too much about what's happening. You are stronger than any man or woman I know… even most men in the SAS. I love you with all my heart. Love Kerry. xxxx.'

I re-read his message about five times before finally tearing it up and washing it down the hole in the concrete floor to the sewage below. His words were etched in my memory.

I would write a response in the morning telling him that I too had told our lawyer to find out why our children had been searched prior to their departure from Laos, and why a bank cheque and mobile phone were taken from my daughter. That cheque worth US$98,000 was my savings I had earned over the past two years. I had given it to Sahra the day before she left Laos and told her to tell my mother to bank it. If our lawyer did not do something soon, the Lao authorities would discover the money still linked to my account. Perhaps they had already.

Our new lawyer Tzovaras left Laos immediately after our first Consular meeting on 8 February 2001 and began negotiating with Jardine Securicor to pay his fees. We wanted Securicor to support us in our case, but were still unsure if they would pay for our legal defence at this stage. It was going to cost a lot of money.

It was later that I found out it was actually the Gem Mining Director, Bjarne Jeppeson and not my father, who had retained Tzovaras on our behalf. It was so difficult to keep informed when we were stuck behind bars, and I wished we were able to be more aware of what was going on behind the scenes.

***

The next morning arrived with a promise of more extreme temperatures. Our Canadian friend Anouhack came to my cell with the latest news report.

'Hello Mr CNN,' I called him. 'What riveting news did we get last night?' I asked dryly.

'Oh Kay,' he leaned towards the bars. 'Last night they talk about your client, Gem Mining. The Laos Government gave them a sentence of 20 years and said they must pay US$59 million compensation.'

Anouhack's eyes widened. No one had ever been fined so much for allegedly stealing their own assets. No one for that matter had ever been fined so much at all, for anything.

'Actually Anouhack it was only US$30 million!' I repeated the figures that the Embassy gave us.

'Oh well. What's an extra twenty million hey?' he laughed. I laughed too. It was as hilarious as it was outrageous.

'Your lawyer was talking last night. He's Australian right?' Anouhack asked quickly.

'Yeah,' I replied.

'He said now they got the conviction against Bjarne and Julie, you and Kerry can probably go free.'

'Yeah like that's gonna happen!' I responded dryly.

'Ha ha. I don't think so either,' Anouhack laughed again and waved goodbye. 'I go tell Kerry.'

The news reports came in from other prisoners throughout the day and with each report, the details of Gem Mining's sentence and fine increased. Our own trial was pending. Meanwhile, the Laos Foreign Minister Lengsavad officially appointed the Vice-Minister Phongsavath Boupha, to deal with our case. He instructed that our Consular access was for Embassy staff alone and that our lawyer should not involve himself in any future meetings. The Public Prosecutor continued to reject any meeting between his office and our lawyer. Vice-Minister Boupha told Jonathan that no date had been set for our trial because the investigation was continuing and in accordance with Lao law, may continue for a further twelve months.

So our lawyer couldn't meet with the prosecutor, and couldn't meet with us at Consular appointments, and they hadn't even decided when they were going to sentence us for a crime we didn't commit.

There was no end in sight.

CHAPTER SEVEN

The Hmong

The prisoners of Phonthong were not at all what you would expect to find in an ordinary detention centre. Then again, Phonthong was anything but ordinary and those around me were barely surviving. They lived in hope. However, hope was not enough to prevent some from dying. People die. It is a fact. Nevertheless, they should not die needlessly when governments like that of Laos sign agreements promising to safeguard human rights and to prevent ill-treatment and torture. My Hmong friend, Mr Joy, was one of those unique individuals that the average person on the street would never meet. He had endured unimaginable suffering in the most appalling conditions in places hidden from the rest of the world, but he retained his dignity, grace and humour.

Mr Joy inspired many prisoners. He believed everyone was born equal and at the very least, was deserving of human dignity. He believed that governments were obliged to uphold agreements they sign, particularly when it might prevent the mass genocide of those outcast in Laos. He taught me a lot about his people. Their once quiet rural existence was shattered in the early 1960s by the arrival of the Vietnam War. That war destroyed the peaceful land of Laos. The Lao King and Queen died in a death camp alongside tens of thousands of others who dared to oppose communism. Simple mountain villagers and peasants with no written language and no formal education were willing to help the Americans and allied forces to restore democracy to their homeland and drive the communists away forever. However, it was not to be.

'Many American soldiers were saved by my people,' Mr Joy said.

'Are they the Freedom Fighters?' I asked.

'Some are and some are not. Many just want to live in peace. They are hunted as the descendants of those 35,000 soldiers who died for democracy promised by America. Women and small children who were never involved in the war must now pay the price,' he concluded.

Suddenly a commotion at the gate startled us as a swarm of Lao police marched purposefully through the black door.

'What the hell?' I looked anxiously at Anouhack who quickly sprang from his hammock.

The police barked orders in Lao language as they went from cell to cell. I could not understand a word.

'What is it Anouhack?' I asked.

Had someone reported us for talking about democracy? It was not as if we were about to take up arms against the communist regime. We were merely expressing our views. Why was that so wrong? Long moments followed as I waited for Anouhack to tell me what was going on.

'It's okay,' he said quickly. 'The commander has ordered all the prisoners to change cells.'

'Kay, Kay quickly,' Mon called from our cell. I ran to her immediately. 'Where are you going Mon?' I asked as I watched her walk from our cell with her bedding.

'We separate,' she cried. 'I go now.'

'No!' I declared and grabbed her arm. Frantically I looked at the commotion that had seized the veranda outside our cells.

Prisoners were responding to the police who barked at them. Pushing and shoving. Chaos consumed our block.

'Kay, come with me,' said Mon.

But I didn't go with Mon to cell number two because I was afraid. In such a short time, I had become familiar with the routine of those I lived with. I begged Mon to stay with me but she insisted that cell number two was better. She didn't listen to Noi and the others who said that it was more dangerous. I didn't know what to do. I was confused. Noi kept telling me that the Hmong-Americans, Pang and Sue, were not to be trusted. She said they worked for the police and Mon was making a big mistake moving in with them. I couldn't understand why Mon wouldn't listen.

'Don't go Mon, they are spy police,' I whispered. The tears cascaded down my cheeks as I watched my beautiful Thai friend walk away. The seconds passed. Mon paused at the doorway. I held my breath waiting for her to defy the guard's orders. Her almond shaped eyes glistened with tears as they glanced back at me. And then quietly, without a word, she was gone. I was devastated. It felt as if they had taken her far away to the northern jails of Sam Neua. Mon was closer to me than any sister could have been. She had sung me to sleep in soft muted Thai tones and kept the nightmares away. Her smile made me feel secure. Her words encouraged me to face all the fears that came in and out of my new life. But for some reason I doubted her judgement. Now I was alone and miserable.

'No problem Kay. We have more room now,' said Noi, trying to keep my spirits alive.

Pon-Phit, Noi, Toom and I were the only four to occupy our cell. The police decided to leave us alone at Pon-Phit's insistence. We each slept in a corner of the room but I missed Mon more than ever. With her gone I would have no one to talk to. Pon-Phit spoke only Lao and refused to speak Thai because she hated them. Noi spoke broken English but frequently misunderstood me and Toom just stood at the window and smoked.

'What are you doing?' I called to Mon at night, and when there was no answer from her my sense of loneliness hit me hard and in the quiet of the night, I realised my mistake by not going with her.

When the third morning came, Tan Sombut unlocked our cell and insisted I move my things next door. I was so ecstatic I almost hugged him! Toom moved in with us too. Tan Sombut ordered Noi and Pon-Phit to cell number one with Malivan and Nang. The men from cell number one moved to the rear cells. Madam Gin-Gin moved to the cell we vacated, number three. I think she was much happier being next to the women. So many nights she had woken us with her screams. I guessed she just wanted to go home too.

'And I just scrubbed our washroom yesterday trying to get some of that green slime off the walls. Now Gin-Gin got a nice cell to live in,' I laughed.

'You really think we are spy police?' asked Pang sadly. Mon had told her why I didn't change rooms that day. Both she and Sue were hurt.

'I did,' I responded sheepishly. We all had a good laugh about it later.

The Lao court had sentenced Pang and Sue to five years for drug related offences. Pang began telling me her story. 'Sue went shopping at the market and bought the most beautiful Hmong skirts. If you saw them you would say how beautiful they are too.'

'So what happened?' I asked. Pang continued to stitch each tiny cross-stitch into some black cloth as we talked.

'She was back at the hotel when I returned. The police came and arrested us together. They said we did the drug smuggling in the skirts. But Kay, I didn't know anything about that,' she looked at me with her eyes wide and innocent.

'Did Sue know?' I asked.

'No Kay. She just wanted to buy them to take home to America. They are so beautiful,' she said, wetting the new thread with the tip of her tongue before feeding it carefully through the eye of the needle.

'So what happened?' I asked curiously.

'They sent Sue here and sent me to Somkhe because I would not sign the confession to traffic the drug they said was soaked in the skirt material,' she confessed. 'I went there for four months.'

'Did you confess?' I asked.

'After I nearly died in that hell Kay, I confessed, but I didn't do it.' She put her hand over her heart and pleaded with her eyes for me to believe her.

'They told me if I signed then Sue and I would be released. But they sent me to Phonthong and then to court. We got five years sentence. I almost had a heart attack when the judge said that,' she said quietly, reliving the moment. I watched as she stitched each delicate thread into the beautiful skirt. It was ironic that the authorities imprisoned her for desiring the very thing she was now making.

'They take forever to make Kay,' she said, agreeing that it was crazy. 'But so beautiful when finished,' she smiled back at me, almost childlike.

Many prisoners would have died without her help so who was I to judge? Pang and Sue went to the Immigration building just as we did but only got Consular access to the US Embassy once every three months. They had missed a visit once and were told they would have to wait for the next one.

'That will be seven months Kay. We could be dead by then.' Pang wiped the tears from her eyes. We sat quietly absorbing her words as Sue paced back and forth in the cell, fanning herself from the heat that threatened to kill us all.

'Somehow we must survive this hell,' Pang spoke quietly.

'How can we survive if no-one knows what goes on in here?' I said absently.

'Kay when you go home, you will tell them,' Pang whispered as she leaned closer. I looked at the sadness in her eyes that reflected the sorrow of so many prisoners in that hell. Prisoners without money or certain connections were doomed. If they survived the torture and even if they served their sentence or were acquitted, which few ever were, then still they might not be released until money was paid to the police.

***

In Phonthong, the days were endless and blended into each other. I did everything to stop thinking of home. One of the more popular ways we would stop ourselves from thinking was to sing. We would sing in the morning, afternoon and just before we slept. It seemed that while we were singing we forgot our surroundings and just enjoyed the rare moment of happiness. Mon liked to sing a lot and had such a beautiful voice that she could have easily sung professionally. Mon also liked to make clothes and cut up my blue trousers to make me a mini skirt and tank top to wear at night. I had lost so much weight from the heat inside the cell. It was like living constantly in a sauna.

'Now you will not be so hot Kay,' she said, holding the scraps of material up in front of her to admire her intricate stitches.

Mon was the loveliest person I knew. When I felt like crying, she started singing and dancing like a belly dancer and we'd all laugh together. She taught me to sing the Thai National Anthem, much to the delight of the Thai prisoners and to the annoyance of others. We sang frequently to pass the hours that seemed endless.

It was not so much that I had become another person in Phonthong but I think I evolved in many new ways. I no longer thought like a Westerner. Without realising, I began to think differently. I was submerged in automatic responses in either Thai or Lao language. I wasn't even aware of when I began making that significant transition. I think some inner survival mechanism took control of my consciousness.

As I listened to the stories of those around me, I came to realise that I had come from quite a different world than them. It was hard to imagine that the misery surrounding us was actually real and for the first time in my life, I saw cruelty like no other. I found no escape from the evil that tormented us night and day. No one could stop the screams coming from the interrogation room. I tried to cover my ears but my hands trembled and never quite blocked out those torturous sounds of anguish. I watched and waited for the brown wooden door of the interrogation room to open and when it did, I wished I were somewhere else. Beatings were frequent. Prisoners suffered dental fractures, broken bones, or both. Some prisoners were literally starving to death. The police didn't care. It was the foreigner's prison after all and everyone knew that foreigners were the wealthiest people in the world. I couldn't imagine any place worse than where we were.

At least the notorious 'Bangkok Hilton' allowed visitors, even if it meant you had to shout to the prisoner through a wire cage. Phonthong prisoners were isolated behind a wall of secrecy. Outsiders never came inside. Very few prisoners had contact with their loved ones, yet Laos had agreed to the UN Declaration of Human Rights and told the world they did not ill-treat anyone or deny people their human rights. The Lao authorities were liars but more than that, they carelessly destroyed lives. Young men sat staring blankly into the nothingness of their minds, day in, day out. It frightened me to think about what they had endured. But I began to understand what our interrogators had meant when they said, 'Your country can do nothing.' Questions of morality were irrelevant in Phonthong when it became obvious with each passing day that the Laos Government treated human beings so appallingly. Did my Government know what went on behind these walls? Did they even care? My mind became plagued with unanswered questions. Most of the time I rarely felt safe or in control. I never knew when it would be my turn to go back into that interrogation room or whether they would drag my husband off to the mountain caves of Sam Neua, as they threatened to do.

My days and nights were filled with constant fear because I was living in an uncertain dream. But there were prisoners in Phonthong who had never put their face to the sun as I had, or felt the soft green leaves of the trees brush against their skin. Our captors locked some prisoners away in darkness for indefinite periods. Time, it seemed, had no relevance in these small cells (0.5 m X 1 metres) they called the 'Dark Room'. Every prison in Laos had at least one dark room and those who went there barely survived, or if they did, were never the same again. The dark room was a place where wills were broken.

Bounmaly Vilayvong threatened Kerry with the dark room and there he would become insane. As much as I was afraid for my husband, I feared being left alone even more. At least knowing that my husband was nearby was enough to give me courage. But if they took him away from me, then how would I survive? The fear of losing something or someone that you depend on is torture. I never felt safe in Phonthong but I did not let them ever see my fear.

I learned so much in Phonthong Prison that I would never have learnt on the outside. The secret genocide of the Hmong was something no one ever mentioned. In fact, most Laotians we had worked with had never so much as even mentioned the word 'Hmong'. I sat with political prisoners who allegedly did not exist, and yet they lived and breathed the same foul air I did. I learned from them things I never knew before. One told me that he carried his younger brother on his back for miles when the communists invaded Laos in 1975. The man was a victim of the bombing and the chemical 'Agent Orange' that burnt the young flesh from his body. He did not know his brother was dead as his legs hung limp from either side of his frame.

I sat quietly and listened as another prisoner told me that he had dug the graves of 150 Hmong. He claimed the police tied them together with barbed wire and left them to swelter under the midday sun. Tin sheeting covered their bodies and eventually they fried. With tears in his eyes, he recalled those times when they forced him to push each limp body into a shallow grave. There was nothing to mark their previous existence on the earth. They were lost forever.

I began to realise how my journey through Phonthong Prison was a small part in a much bigger picture. The political prisoners said that it was a destiny to be prisoners of the regime. The torture and suffering of the people and those forgotten in Phonthong would be revealed to the world.

I befriended another young Hmong called Onchan, serving a ten-year sentence as a political prisoner. His family lived in a northern province of Laos and nearly all of them had been incarcerated in various Lao jails. Looking at Onchan playing guitar, I did not see the freedom fighter in him at all. His manner was gentle and his face an open book. He could have been everything the police said he was but in Phonthong, he was just another prisoner. So what if he had once fought against the regime? Had it not seized his homeland illegally and by force?

Onchan loved to sing and was like some comic musical performer as he swayed in time with the music past each cell. 'Sing with me Madam,' he called and strummed the old guitar. Onchan sang haunting melodies that I never understood until he explained the far-off look in his eyes was for his young son and daughter he'd known only as babies.

'I just hope to see them again one day Madam,' he said quietly.

I formed many special relationships with the prisoners and in particular, the Hmong. Their dialect was difficult to understand but surprisingly, they spoke impeccable English by comparison to

Lao standards. That evening we sat sweating in our cells when five new prisoners arrived.

'Who come?' called Toom to the room next door.

'Look like all men,' Noi responded.

We watched as the group were escorted to the interrogation room and made to kneel before the police. After about an hour passed, we saw them coming from the room.

'They come,' Toom whispered and we all raced to the window to see them. As the men neared, we could see they were Hmong. Sue and Pang called out to them in their Hmong language. 'Good afternoon!' They smiled but said nothing.

'Hello!' other prisoners called out. But still they said nothing.

Whenever a Hmong person came to Phonthong, their chances of surviving were greater than elsewhere. This new group was lucky even though they didn't know it at the time. Over the coming days, we were curious about them and whenever possible, I would go look at them.

'You take this food,' I said, handing the one they called Chao a piece of fruit.

'Thank you Madam,' he said quietly, then scurried like a frightened mouse to the dark corner of his tiny cell.

I soon became friends with Chao, a forty-two year old Hmong man. He told me how they arrested his group while they were visiting relatives in a province north of Vientiane.

'The Laos Government said we can return but after we return, then seven days, the authorities come to arrest us. They say we are talking about democracy to the people. They show us the tape with the message on it but it is in Lao language. If it were true, we would not speak the Lao language to our people. We speak Hmong so they can understand but in any case, we do not come to talk about democracy,' he confessed. It sounded like they were set up.

I sat with my back to his cell window and quietly listened to him talk about all the things he had seen since his arrest in 1999, and the horrific conditions he had been kept in.

'I want to call you Mai Kue Yang,' he said one day. 'Because you are my sister, you should have the Hmong name.'

I smiled as I spoke his strange mountain dialect back to him: 'Thank you older brother Chao.'

Chao laughed as he heard me speak the Hmong language. I only learnt a few short phrases because it was such a difficult language, but I loved using it.

'I don't know how long I can survive Mai Kue. Fifteen years is too long. Mr Her has the sentence of twenty years because they said he was the leader of our group,' he said.

'But Mr Her looks like he can barely swat a fly,' I replied.

I was astonished that the police thought Mr Her was the ringleader of the rebel group. He shared Kerry's cell and was afraid of everything.

Every day Chao stayed quietly in the room waiting patiently and hoping that he might be allowed outside for even a few minutes to stretch his legs. And every day, just as I had done with Mon, I begged the police to release him. Of course, they always refused. One time I even went to his cell door and crouched low to the ground. As the police came to unlock his room I begged for him to be let outside the cell. Raising my hand, I spoke quietly. 'Please let Chao come outside the room.'

I wasn't sure if I'd said it correctly but the police officer knew what I was trying to say. He shook his head as he looked down on me, squatting.

'Cannot!' he said and walked on to the next cell. In the Phonthong gulag, there was no strict rule as to who could leave their cell and who couldn't after a while. It was up to the prison officer and depended on the day and how he felt. If he decided you weren't coming out, you weren't coming out.

I smiled at Chao and told him to be patient. He stood dressed in a white singlet top like the one Phor wore and a pair of bright red shorts, which looked so out of place in this lunatic asylum. Chao smiled at me and fanned himself from the intense heat.

***

There was a rumour circulating the prison that I was going to be released the following week with Phor. Phor told me that since his arrest on 29 March 2000, he was told three times that he was going to be released. Now that the Gem Mining case had finished, the way was clear for us to go home, or so they said.

'I give everything to the prisoner and even my underwear,' he laughed. 'This time, I keep the underwear.'

I followed Phor to the Bodhee tree, the holy tree. We didn't have any incense to burn. We didn't even have a Buddha. Phor said it didn't matter. We would just approach the holy tree with kind and beautiful thoughts. He found a clump of tiny purple flowers growing near the edge of a fishpond. I watched him place them in the main fork of the tree. Phor explained that the flowers were symbolic of the impermanence of this life. They help us to remember about the change taking place all around us.

'We are like the flower, always changing,' he said. From his pocket, he took a tiny orange candle, lit it, and then put it in the centre of the purple flowers. I watched mesmerised.

'So we can see the wisdom of Buddha and remind us not to remain in darkness,' he said. Phor placed some sticky rice next to the candle and the flowers. He explained that offerings of food were an expression of thankfulness and gratitude.

'Some time we give fruit and vegetables or sweet cakes for special occasions,' Phor told me quietly as I stood beside him. 'Here, you give some too,' he said, handing me a small portion of the rice.

As I placed the rice beside the flowers and the candle, I cleared my mind of all troubled thoughts. I followed Phor's example as he pressed his hands together, prayer-like, raising them to his forehead. I listened respectfully as he quietly prayed in Thai and closed my eyes to feel the peacefulness of the moment wash over me.

Phor was a very spiritual man who was always meditating or reading about Buddha. I respected his faith, just as I respected the faith of other prisoners who often prayed to Allah and Jesus. In my heart, I prayed for freedom not just for me, but also for Phor, Chao, Mr Joy, and all the others who were suffering in Phonthong and all over Laos. It seemed after long moments beside the Bodhee tree my fears subsided and for the time I stood with Phor, I didn't worry so much about our situation.

On many occasions, I began my morning exercising with Phor. He was able to run laps around the perimeter whereas I could only run about fifty meters back and forth. And because I was so unfit, I could only keep going for ten minutes. Phor would encourage me to keep going while Mon would yell out to me that I was crazy to run in the sun. The police didn't bother about me so much anymore. I still had to be careful, so I didn't go beyond the boundaries they set. Actually I felt as if they were beginning to understand me, and I them. I tried to show them the person I was and not what they thought I was. But whether they believed I was genuine or not was another thing.

I wasn't set free and neither was Phor. But as time passed, some of the prison police began to be less strict and whenever Kerry and I travelled to Immigration, they let us sit in the same vehicle, though not together.

Had they heard on the radio that our Foreign Minister Alexander Downer had sent a follow up letter to his counterpart Somsavat Lengsavad, requesting an appointment for the Australian Ambassador? Our case certainly had everyone talking. The Lao police often asked other prisoners why the Australian Government was so concerned about us. One thing was obvious, in that whatever happened to us also had a significant impact on the other prisoners. The support given to us by the Australian Embassy and Australian Government started others thinking. Pang and Sue, my two American-Hmong cell mates, began to question why their Embassy didn't do the same for them.

'Your Embassy cares about you so much Kay. I've never seen anyone here have such good luck like you and Kerry,' said Pang.

We travelled back to Phonthong together following a joint Consular visit. It was wonderful that our visit had coincided with theirs. It was as if we were going on a special outing. We laughed, joked, and said that we'd been out touring the city courtesy of Lengsavad. We recounted our make-believe adventures and embellished that we'd drunk Lao beer and danced at Tat Luang. All the prisoners nearby laughed knowing it wasn't true. But for a while we enjoyed being silly. In the back of my mind, I held on to one single thought; with our Embassy and Government standing firmly in support we would somehow endure this nightmare!

I felt too that it was now doubly important for me to get out of here in one piece—not only for my family's sake, but also to tell the world exactly what was going on in these prisons where dignity was ignored and human rights were non-existent.

CHAPTER EIGHT

Souya

Our lawyer engaged the Laos Foreign Minister in a legal debate, but Lengsavad was not interested in the traumatic effects of our continued detention. He had already nationalised Gem Mining Laos. But our detainment continued to raise strong criticisms of Laos from otherwise sympathetic governments that contributed foreign capital and aid. Denmark was amongst the first to withhold its foreign aid, influenced by the Gem Mining Directors.

The Australian Foreign Minister Downer repeatedly cautioned that our detainment would affect the existing good relations between Australia and Laos. Downer viewed it as contrary to the legal principles of international human rights and made this statement repeatedly. The Lao Government however, showed no obvious concern that its authorities had breeched the Universal Declaration of Human Rights, which they had signed on 7 December 2000. It looked like they didn't really care what foreign governments thought of their actions.

But whereas diplomacy meant governments had to be tactful, the media did not, and our detainment made news headlines across the world. My Dad received a letter from a well-known Senator in the White House in Washington DC, and thought it was only a matter of time before the US President himself stood up to save us. But DC was a long way from Phonthong and there were no oil reserves in Laos to spark any US intervention.

In the meantime, our embassy continued to give us support. They gave us Chinese New Year calendars in February and at first I didn't understand why until Kerry sent me a tiny message telling me to look closely at the dates on the calendar.

'My God,' I whispered quietly.

The others in the room didn't hear me because Toom was taking a shower and Pang was singing aloud as she sewed the delicate cross-stitches of her Hmong skirt. Sue was talking to the Burmese girl called Lek, who had arrived a few days earlier.

'What is it?' Mon whispered curiously.

'Look at this Mon,' I said rolling over on my blanket to where she was lying.

In the top right hand corner of the square for each day, a letter appeared. It was cleverly disguised to match the black ink of the Chinese lettering. As I connected the letters with my index finger I read the words from the Embassy.

'Hang in there… working hard for you.'

'Very good Kay,' Mon cried. 'Your Embassy very good!'

I lay on my blanket and felt a smile spread across my face. As night fell, I began to hope that before too long we would go home and that I would be able to see my children again.

**

Inside the cell, we had learned to adjust to the familiarity of routine as the only way to feel any sense of security. Every action followed a sequence. There was a time for showering, a time for eating, a time for sleeping, for singing, for playing and a time for sitting quietly. There was a place where I would hang my towel and Mon would hang hers. Or where I would put my coffee cup and Toom would put her coffee cup. Everyone learned to keep out of everyone else's personal space, which was incredible when you thought about how little space we had. Everything had an order; who would shower first in the morning and who would shower second. A new prisoner had the ability to change everything. But a new prisoner also meant that there was another mouth to feed and as it was, food was in short supply.

A group of Chinese prisoners arrived one day—a woman and three men. Everyone in our cell quietly wondered where the police would put the female prisoner. But the odds were in our favour that she'd go next door because we already had six in our cell whereas they only had five. And indeed, she did. Her husband went into Kerry's cell. The young one called Souya, a North Korean, went into the cell with my Hmong friend Chao. The Chinese man went into the next cell down from his.

'Why does that old woman cry so much?' I asked Mon as the night wore on.

Hardly anyone slept that night because the Chinese woman was inconsolable. Pon-Phit did her best to keep her calm but it sounded like she'd never shut her up. Toom stood by our door smoking a cigarette. She could hear Pon-Phit translating Chinese to Thai so that the others could understand why the woman was so distressed.

Their group had left North Korea because like in Laos, the people suffer the same hunger, disease, and brutal oppression by its cruel, totalitarian regime. They trekked for four months across the Tumen River into China, hoping to reach an embassy or get assistance from refugee activists known to be operating illegally on Chinese soil. It was their intention to enter Laos and purchase illegal travel documents, or failing that, present themselves at the South Korean Consulate requesting political asylum. What gave them even more incentive was the generous financial package promised to refugees in support of the South Korean Government's political statement about its wealth and generosity compared to the impoverished North. Each head of household could receive the equivalent of AU$32,000 paid in three instalments and their dependants, an additional AU$6,500 each. They could receive subsidised housing in public rental apartments, support for education and further vocational training and job placement.

The young boy in the group was terribly distressed because his parents died along the way. He had to go ahead without them. When they crossed into Laos, the police arrested them, claiming they were anti-revolutionary elements, opposed to Kim Jong Il's succession. The Laos police said that in three days time, the North Korean authorities would take them away for execution.

'Sshh. Police coming. Go sleep Kay!' Mon lay down beside me as the police began their patrol.

We closed our eyes and waited for the police to pass by. When they got to the next cell, they yelled angrily for the old woman to shut up. She argued that she had not committed treason and that she was of Chinese origin despite the fact that she had married a North Korean and settled there. She begged the Lao police to understand her dilemma but they didn't care. The mere fact that she had left North Korea only confirmed to them that she was a criminal. This act of treason would result in execution according to North Korea's penal code. The Lao police threatened that if she didn't maintain some control they would take her to the dark room. For the rest of the night she remained quiet.

In the morning, I followed Mon outside the cell as usual to take our place in the line. I saw the young boy, Souya, sitting by the window in Chao's cell. He looked sad. There were no secrets in Phonthong and the details of their plight had passed between the cells quickly. When they dismissed us from the line, everyone went about his or her usual routine. Some washed their clothes with water that dripped from an old broken tap, a few feet from the so-called infirmary. Others went to toil their makeshift garden plots and soaked them with the raw sewage they collected from the open sewage tanks next to our cell block. I waited for my chance to speak to Chao who remained locked in the cell with the young North Korean boy.

'He cried a lot last night, Mai Kue,' Chao whispered, using my Hmong name.

I stared quietly at the young boy who looked about twelve years old. He put his index finger to his throat and moved it slowly from left to right. In anyone's language 'death' translated the same.

'No, no, Souya. Not you! It's okay!' I said to comfort him.

He shook his head but smiled. At that time, he seemed much older than I did at thirty-three. I passed a piece of bread through the bars to Chao and left as suddenly as I arrived. It was too dangerous to talk for long to those locked inside the cells. Over the next three days, after line up, I sat quietly under a tree, five or so metres in front of Chao's cell. Young Souya came to the window each day and sat staring out at me. His small round face revealed nothing of the turmoil he must have endured before arriving in Phonthong. Chao said at night that Souya sobbed quietly. He was such a small boy in such a terrible place and caused us to think of our own children. Noi cried thinking of hers, still somewhere in a village where she'd left them twelve years ago. Chao cried thinking of his five children left in a refugee camp in Thailand. And I cried silently in my mind, thinking of ours, wondering if we'd ever get home. When the police came on the third day, Mon and I gathered as much food as we could for the group's journey. We got a towel, some fruit, and a warm jacket for Souya.

'Take it. You might get cold,' I ordered him, though the temperatures were still in the high 40s Celsius.

Souya smiled and somehow held back his tears. I thought him incredibly brave as I held his hand briefly, pressing a tiny piece of paper into his palm. It was a scripture written in North Korean. 'The Lord is my shepherd'. I tore it from a bible that I received from the Australian Embassy.

I hoped that Souya would survive and if he didn't, I hoped that he would find peace. I hugged him goodbye as if he were my own son. Tan Phet did nothing to stop me as the tears welled in my eyes. I wanted to keep Souya safe but no one could do that. At best, he would end up in a forced labour camp where he would face cruel, inhuman, and degrading treatment. More than likely, he would be killed. I tried not to think of that reality.

There was nothing I could say to Souya to make things better. All I could hope to do was make sure I told his story upon my release, to show him as a brave and noble young man, older than his years due to the traumas he had suffered. His suffering, his tragic story, would not be in vain. I vowed to expose the cruelty of these regimes.

I marched Souya to where the police and his group were waiting for him outside the interrogation room. I saw the woman from the cell next to ours hug Malivan and Nang goodbye. As I neared the others, Souya walked ahead of me and stopped next to the Chinese man who'd been in the cell next to his. I walked over and handed the supplies we'd gathered to the old Korean man from Kerry's cell.

'For you,' I whispered.

'Thank you. God bless you,' he said in broken English, much to my astonishment.

The police motioned them to the black door. Souya remained brave. I stood in the middle of the clearing between the interrogation room and the fishponds and watched the small boy slowly walk away. His dark eyes never left my face, not even for a single moment. We forced ourselves to smile the whole time, until finally; he was gone.

'Goodbye Souya,' I shouted to him.

My voice carried over the prison walls. I didn't care that it was against the regulations to shout. My heart was breaking. Not a single eye was dry as we cried. Even the men milling around a shady tree nearby cried. Souya had brought a glimmer of happiness to our lives, albeit for the briefest moments. The sweet twelve-year-old boy, who reminded Chao of his sons and me of my Nathan, was gone! A feeling of dread washed over me—would I ever see my own children again? How was it possible to live in a world where this kind of thing could happen to families?

***

At 2pm, the police came back through the black door and told Kerry and I to prepare for a Consular visit. It was 1 March 2001, our ninth Consular visit with the Australian Embassy. As we travelled by car to Immigration, I tried not to think of the events of that morning. Ambassador Thwaites was waiting for us when we arrived. He looked puzzled by the redness in my eyes. It was obvious to everyone that I'd been crying but I said nothing as I threw my arms around his neck. I longed to go home.

'Are you okay?' he asked gently.

'Sure,' I whispered and slowly stepped back. My eyes filled with despair as they rested briefly on his. 'It's been a tough morning,' I said but didn't elaborate.

By some miracle, the Embassy staff had gained permission from the Lao authorities for me to call our children. It was a shock to find out that today of all days I would speak to my children. I was still reeling from the loss of Souya.

'What?' I replied, barely able to believe what I heard.

'They've given you permission … but only five minutes,' he responded.

I watched Louise dial the number on her small cellular phone. I was finally going to speak to my children. My God, had it really been three months since I waved goodbye to them that day? Where had the time gone? And yet it felt to me as if a lifetime had passed as I endured each day without ever knowing if our kids were okay, truly okay. My hand shook as I took the phone from Louise. My heart pounded in my chest.

'It's Jess,' Louise said.

'Hello Jess.' I swallowed hard. My world spun as I heard our eldest daughter's voice for the first time in months.

'Hey Mum,' said Jess.

I listened to the heartbreak in my childrens' voices as they took turns to tell me how they were. I listened and I cried because they cried. Mr Khamkit watched in concern as the tears ran like a torrent down my cheeks. I wanted to tell my family everything I'd seen and endured. I wanted them to know that they locked us in cages, mocking us through the bars. I wanted to tell them about Souya leaving, Mr Kylie dying, and the endless suffering that filled my days. I wanted to tell them that the blue sky shone above me when they let me outside my cell, but the birds that flew overhead only reminded me of how much I longed to be free.

'Nathan … don't cry … please don't cry,' I sobbed through the line. My seven-year-old son wailed my name in anguish. I felt helpless against his pain. His small voice broke my heart. But no matter how much I wanted to, I couldn't reach out to comfort him. I wanted to wrap my protective arms around him as any mother would, and tell him it had all just been a bad dream. But that was impossible. My son was thousands of miles away.

'Don't cry, Nathan. It's okay,' I said, but I couldn't tell if he could hear me.

The phone passed to my youngest daughter Sahra. I tried to pull myself together, feeling the guilt wash over me. I'd failed to fool my children into thinking that I was okay.

'Mum … you sound so funny,' Sahra whimpered.

'I … I have a cold … and … my nose is blocked,' I lied.

'Oh… when are you coming home? Where's Dad?' she spoke softly.

'I … I don't know Sahra … just be brave … and take care of your brother … I'm sorry I can't talk more. They won't let me. I've got to go. I love you!' I said quickly.

'Finish,' said Mr Khamkit.

'I love you all. Tell Nathan not to cry. It's okay, I'm so happy to hear from you,' I whispered through the tears before handing the cell phone back to Louise.

'My God Louise that was hard! Nathan was crying so much.' I turned to Jonathan. (I no longer called him Ambassador). His face mirrored much of the anguish I was feeling. My own was wet from tears.

'It's okay,' he said and squeezed my arm gently.

'I'm just so frustrated with everything. Why can't they understand that we haven't done anything wrong? What if they take us to court and sentence us on trumped up charges? They can't see the truth for the bullshit lies Bounmaly tells them!' I stammered as fresh tears fell.

I had become hysterical as my breath caught in my throat. As I fought to regain some composure, Jonathan and Louise did their best to console me. They smiled but I could see the uncertainty in their eyes. When our meeting was over, Louise and Jonathan walked me to the car. I hugged them both as if it would be the last time.

'Please ring my kids and tell them I'm so sorry I made them cry,' I said through my tears.

'It's okay,' Louise said softly. She rubbed my back gently in comfort, 'You're allowed to cry.'

'Come!' the police officer ordered. He took hold of my arm and led me away to the car. Seated in the front, I let my tears fall again. The Lao policeman driving the car tried to comfort me.

'Hey juck noy,' he said. It meant `a moment', and made me cry even more.

When we finally arrived back to Phonthong, I took a few deep breaths and walked back through the black door. Everyone knew I'd been crying and made fun of me to lighten the tension in the prison.

'Oh, you cry Madam?' they laughed. 'You got eyes of the vampire.'

'Dracula come to Phonthong,' Noi called.

I walked the path that led to my cell and cried some more. I didn't really care who saw me. 'I spoke to my children on the telephone,' I said simply, and wiped my eyes with the back of my sleeve.

'Too much sadness today, Madam is not good,' said one of the prisoners passing.

'Yeah ...' I whispered and looked to the cell two down from mine. Chao was sitting in silence. The sadness was etched deep on his face as he thought of the young Korean boy, Souya.

'He's gone,' Chao cried.

'I know,' I spoke softly, and at once felt both the deepest sympathy for him and a desperate hope that I would soon be reunited with my own family.

CHAPTER NINE

More Legal Obstacles

According to a report from the Lao authorities, we were still going to be responsible for the loss of 265 pieces of jewellery despite the fact that Gem Mining were found guilty in absentia for taking it. This meant they were charging two different sets of people with the same crime. Jonathan Thwaites argued that Kerry's only responsibility in the matter was to secure the premises of Gem Mining in his capacity as a Manager of Lao Securicor. It was in his contract. Further, Julie had presented the jewellery to the New Zealand Ambassador in Bangkok and accounted for it in a statutory declaration that it was her personal property and not an asset of Gem Mining. Therefore, nothing had been stolen, which meant there actually was no crime. Lengsavad did not appear to know any of this. Jonathan stated that 1.7 tonne of unfinished rough sapphires were delivered in its entirety, to the Lao authorities. This was not challenged. He concluded that it was difficult to see what was left for us to be responsible for.

Our lawyer met with members of the Lao Legal Department, whose main issue now seemed to be that we 'did not cooperate when investigated.' They went so far as to say that they didn't think I was involved, the first time in months that anyone in the Lao ministry came close to admitting I was innocent. Our lawyer constantly reminded them that there was absolutely no basis for my continued detainment. The only complaint involved a sum of money found in my possession, the source of which had already been proved as the payroll for my Thai Subcontractors in Bangkok. Tzovaras surmised that if the case rested solely upon Kerry's role in representing Gem Mining Laos, it could be dealt with. He knew that it was all merely a face saving exercise to the Lao authorities. They couldn't say they had made a mistake, so he hoped to give them the out they needed.

'You should understand that the Lao Law does not provide for adversarial proceedings,' we were warned, 'and we would lose if we went to court.'

The fact that our Lao lawyer, Mr Phasith Phommarack, held the privileged title of Chairman of the Inspection Committee of the Lao Bar Association meant nothing. Phasith submitted his statement and plea on our behalf to the Deputy Prime Minister of Laos, citing both the huge amount of doubt surrounding our guilt and the extreme hardship and damage caused by our imprisonment and prolonged separation from our children. However, like our Australian lawyer, he too advised that we should pursue a resolution through diplomatic, not legal means. Was there even such a thing as justice in Laos? I pushed aside my troubled thoughts to see who was coming through the black door to Phonthong.

'Kay… Bounmaly …he come,' said Mon. She pointed to the interrogation room.

'No way,' I cried, clutching at the tree that shaded me from the hot afternoon sun. But it wasn't Bounmaly. My heart missed a beat. It was Mingboutha, the Public Prosecutor.

'Kay. Go!' called Oudai.

I walked to the interrogation room with a sea of eyes watching me.

'Good afternoon Madam,' the translator announced at my arrival. I faked a smile as I took my usual seat on the rickety bench. To my surprise, Bounmaly and Bounyasene were nowhere in sight.

It was just the translator and the Prosecutor who attended. For the next two hours, I answered their questions. They tried to make a deal with me. If I signed a confession stating that my husband stole the sapphires, they would take me to the Lao Plaza and we could celebrate my freedom by drinking vodka as they said they did in Russia.

'I can't sign. My husband didn't do that, but I'm happy to go and drink vodka with you,' I smiled. I watched the Prosecutor sigh and collect his papers. Carefully he picked up the unsigned confession and pushed it into his leather briefcase. The buckle clicked the case shut. His brown eyes were serious as he picked up his pen and clipped it to the inside of his pocket. I watched him straighten his yellow tie. Quietly he leaned towards me, his face inches away. The dimples in his cheeks stood out as he smiled. I looked at him questioningly.

'I haven't done anything. Please let me go home to my children,' I begged one last time.

'Madam, I am happy to say that this will be the very last time you will ever see us again,' he said, rising to his feet. 'And Bounmaly sends you his regards!' he spoke in perfect English.

The shock that he could speak English registered on my face and he laughed aloud. Brief flashes of past interrogations sped through my mind. All the times I had agonised, trying to defend my innocence in a way they could understand, when all the while they were laughing at me. As I quietly walked to the tree where Anouhack was sitting I barely noticed my husband walk to the interrogation room. 'They can speak English very well Anouhack!' I said.

'They lie all the time Madam,' replied Mr Joy, watching me as I sat down. 'This regime only knows how to tell the lie.'

I looked at him and then to Anouhack who was nodding in agreement. Kerry stayed in the room with them for three hours. When he came out again he was laughing. The Prosecutor left

Phonthong and the big black door to freedom slammed shut behind him.

'What is it Kerry?' said Anouhack, almost falling out of his hammock to ask the question. The police hadn't even bothered to escort Kerry back to his cell because he automatically began walking in that direction and threw over his shoulder to them a hearty, 'Fuck off.'

'They want me to go to Thailand and kidnap Bjarne and Julie for them. Evidently it's a condition of our release.'

Anouhack bellowed with laughter.

'Hey Kerry, are you going to become Lao police?' laughed Pang. Anouhack quickly translated out loud for the political prisoners to hear and anyone else who cared to listen. They all laughed heartily that Kerry had been offered a free trip out of Phonthong to Thailand, and turned it down.

'They can go get fucked!' Kerry said as usual. This was it; they had finally made the situation so outrageous that it had become unbelievable. It was a farce, and everybody knew it. I yelled to the blue sky above, releasing all my frustrations: 'Corruption of Lao country!' Tan Sombut leaned casually by the window, watching us from the interrogation room, but said nothing.

It was an act of treason to say such things but what did I care? We were already their political hostages. What more could they do to me that they hadn't done already? My heart pounded in my chest as the adrenalin flooded my veins. The political prisoners laughed. Some of them had been arrested for merely thinking that Laos was corrupt. Fourteen, fifteen years had passed and still they had no idea when they would go to court, if indeed they would ever go. Rage stirred deep inside me.

★★★

Foreign Minister Downer wrote a second letter on 6 March 2001 to Deputy Prime Minister Lengsavad, again stressing the Australian Government's concern at our continued detention. Still Lengsavad didn't reply. Then a report was released on the Lao news that we had been found guilty under article 101 of the Penal Code. It carried a three to seven year sentence. Ambassador Thwaites said that the news report was false, and that the station had misreported the Lao Prosecutor who said what could happen and not what had actually happened.

Tzovaras continued to be so optimistic that it was hard not to believe him. Perhaps things weren't as bad as we had imagined. Perhaps, we would be home soon. I just wished they'd hurry up!

Our Lao and Australian lawyers met with the Deputy Prosecutor but the meeting did not begin well since the Deputy Prosecutor would not recognise Tzovaras' authority to act on our behalf. Furthermore, he would not recognise our Lao lawyer either because we hadn't signed a power of attorney for him to represent us. Tzovaras stated that he was in the process of that undertaking. The Deputy Prosecutor said that he did not want to talk to him, but as he thought Tzovaras had met with the Lao Foreign Minister, Lengsavad, he was willing to discuss our case in brief. The tension in the room crackled while Tzovaras listened as our Lao lawyer translated.

The Deputy Prosecutor said he had heard rumours that staff from the Public Prosecutor's office were accused of behaving improperly during our interrogations.

'I was at the interrogations. The rumours are not true,' he lied. In fact, he was never at the interrogations, just as he never went to Phonthong Prison. The Lao officer sitting to his left took notes while the other sat and cracked his knuckles. It was clear that our lawyer's letter to the Lao Deputy Prime Minister regarding the conduct of the interrogations had caused them problems.

'Perhaps incorrect perceptions easily occur when there are language and cultural differences?' Tzovaras responded.

'Perhaps,' the Deputy Prosecutor agreed.

Our lawyer drew on facts gained from Consular meetings and from the Securicor lawyer who had assisted in the writing of the Memorandum of Understanding, to secure the 1.7 tonne of sapphires at Gem Mining.

'Kerry Danes is a man of great integrity. He has an impeccable record in serving his country with honour and excellence. He condemns dishonourable conduct,' he stated convincingly. The Deputy Prosecutor listened but said nothing. The silence indicated to our lawyer that he hadn't yet understood his point.

'Hypothetically, if Jeppeson and Bruns wanted to have gemstones taken out of the country, why would they ask someone they had only known for one year?' he asked.

'I do not know, why?' the Deputy Prosecutor responded dryly.

'Why not ask someone they had known for a long period of time?' our lawyer responded.

'If I believed that Kerry had any involvement in missing gemstones then I would handle this case differently.'

'How?' asked the Deputy Prosecutor.

'Well for a start, under article 2 of the Lao Penal code, I would have Kerry make a full confession and not allow him to aggravate the matter by telling lies upon lies.'

'But what about the jewellery that was missing from the safe?' the Deputy Prosecutor demanded.

'The responsibility of the safe fell on Julie Bruns and Bjarne Jeppeson, not Kerry Danes!' replied our lawyer. A long silence followed. The Lao officer's pencil paused on the paper.

'He controlled the security so he must be responsible,' the Deputy Prosecutor demanded stubbornly.

Tzovaras shuffled the papers in front of him and wondered how he was going to make the Deputy Prosecutor understand. He cleared his throat and put forward a suggestion:

'It would be better if the Danes were placed under house arrest so that I can access my clients to resolve this matter. It would make a good impression.'

Rising from his chair, the Deputy Prosecutor walked to the door and opened it.

'First you must have Mr Phasith appointed properly in accordance with the Lao law. Then we shall see,' he concluded with finality, motioning them to the door. Phasith gathered his brown weatherworn briefcase and made polite responses as he and our Australian lawyer prepared to leave.

'Thank you,' he said as he offered his hand.

'No problem,' replied the Deputy Prosecutor, as, unsmiling, he shook his hand and acknowledged Phasith with a brief nod. The hallway creaked as the two men walked quietly in retreat. The following week, the Lao Government released more propaganda to the international media waiting to lap it up.

'He committed some wrongful acts,' said Lengsavad. 'It's not like we had no just cause to arrest him. He definitely committed some crimes,' he added.

The foreign press accused the Lao regime of holding us as scapegoats after failing to stop the original owners of Gem Mining Lao from fleeing the country. Arguably, Laos had become an unsafe environment for foreigner investors. Some Australian mining multinationals were eager to invest in copper and gold mines but decided to wait, partly because of our case and partly because they had found it difficult to raise money for such investments from foreign bankers because of our case.

Our Foreign Minister hoped to get better outcomes in terms of the management of our case by the Lao authorities. He said we were 'being very stoic and determined in a very difficult situation.'

The Lao authorities were stalling to build a case against us and we were certain that we would be going to trial sooner rather than later. The only uncertainty was what exactly they would find us guilty of since we hadn't committed any crimes.

'No-one can leave Laos innocent Madam. You will go to court and you will be convicted. That way, when you leave here no-one will ever believe what you say about the conditions we must endure,' said one political prisoner who had been listening to my conversation with Anouhack.

'Yes, that's true Kay. Even if you are innocent it doesn't matter,' Anouhack agreed. 'We are all guilty,' he said glumly.

'Well, I hope they hurry up and convict us,' I replied angrily.

Mr Joy spoke up: 'Last night I hear them say that Australian Foreign Minister said that he is very concerned about you and Kerry. He wants you to keep up your spirit and to know your Government do everything they can. They are unhappy with the way you are treated by the Laos authorities.'

'Everyone it seems is taking a great interest in our case,' I said quietly to Mr Joy.

'Yes madam, because your case can open the eye of the world to Laos,' he replied with a smile.

'The Australian Government have told the people not to come to Laos,' said an older man sitting beside Anouhack.

'They should tell them all to stay away for good,' I replied and everyone laughed.

***

While they detained us in the filthy squalor of Phonthong Prison, bombings and other security incidents continued to occur in Laos, mainly in the capital city of Vientiane. There was a lot of unrest and the fight for freedom was far from being crushed by the communist regime. We heard a bomb go off not far from the prison and another one, they said, created minor damage at the Lao-Thai Friendship Bridge.

I wondered how our staff were managing our seventy-five clients without us in this still hostile environment. Maintaining security was not only a high priority for the Lao government, it was a serious position we undertook on a daily basis to protect both our clients and our reputation as a security provider. Even the

Lao government had once acknowledged our services as vital to the community. Who could they turn to for help now?

'Maybe they need Lao Securicor?' Anouhack laughed.

'They should let you and Kerry outside to protect Laos,' laughed Mr Joy.

'Yeah and who's gonna stop those bastards working for Somsavat Lengsavad that are robbing all the foreign investors?' I responded.

'Yeah there is a lot of talk about your case. They say that 135 kilograms of sapphire were missing from the Gem Mining office. Then change that amount to 3.5 kilograms,' said Mr Joy.

'Madam, what is that letter that Kerry signed for the Gem Mining? Do you think that is why they arrest him?' asked an old man detained as a former member of the Royal Lao Air force.

'No I don't. That letter was dated 8 June 2000 and we were arrested six months later. It explained everything about Bounmaly's harassment of Gem Mining and was not an attack on the Government!' I concluded.

'Why did Kerry sign it?' Anouhack asked.

'Our company lawyer told him to sign for Jeppeson,' I responded. 'You know Laos, they've got to have a signature and a stamp on everything to make it official.'

The letter wasn't an issue. They were just throwing it up now because they had nothing on us.

'They unlawfully detained us when they couldn't kidnap Bjarne and Julie in Thailand,' I confided in Anouhack. 'Bounmaly's goons put a bounty on their heads but my Thai friend out-manoeuvred him. That's why he's pissed at us,' I said.

The Embassy confirmed that a senior Lao official had told them that the current enquiry was focussing on the involvement of the Lao Gem Mining staff arrested at the Laos-Thai border exactly one week following my detainment. The investigative committee had also visited our office, Lao Securicor.

Our former operations manager confirmed that the committee requested him to sign a false statement, which he refused, claiming Lao Securicor was responsible for all Gem Mining's assets.

Our employers still hadn't come to Laos to defend us outright. Tzovaras said that he was concerned they might withdraw their legal funding because of these developments. Then in an even more bizarre twist, a journalist printed an article alleging that Kerry was involved in the murder of an Australian lawyer, Max Green, in Cambodia. Kerry provided both a statement and alibi to satisfy an enquiry from the Australian Federal Police. At the time Max Green had checked into a Cambodian hotel and was found bludgeoned to death with a brick, Kerry was serving his country in Kuwait on 'Operation Pollard'.

On 29 March 2001, we again met with the Australian Embassy, Tzovaras, and Lao Lawyer Phasith, now officially appointed by us.

'I'm afraid the news is not good,' Tzovaras began and leaned closer.

'Is it ever?' I grimaced and noticed that Jonathan wasn't smiling.

'They are insisting that Kerry confess to embezzlement and compensate the State for stolen gems,' he said quietly.

'They want what?' I hissed.

Tzovaras raised his hand to stop me from saying any more. Jonathan placed his hand on my arm.

'It's okay,' Jonathan said reassuringly.

'I will say to you what I'll say to Kerry when I meet with him after our discussions. Do not sign their confessions. They are holding you both in violation of the Lao law and to the International agreements they have signed with the United Nations,' he counselled strongly.

'I'm not signing anything,' I declared.

'I don't want you to worry about a thing. Everything is in place and I'm hoping that very soon this will all be over,' he encouraged.

'God I hope so,' I said. I looked at the Ambassador for some confirmation but Jonathan never gave false hopes. I began to realise that despite whatever anyone else ever said, Jonathan would always tell me the truth, even if I didn't like what I was hearing.

'Mr Downer will be meeting with Foreign Minister Somsavat Lengsavad in Santiago, Chile at noon on Friday, 30 March 2001,' said Jonathan.

'Is that good?' I asked.

'Well it is expected to be a fairly substantive meeting as both parties have now been fully briefed on where we stand. The Australian Government will not let the matter rest if positive news is not forthcoming,' Jonathan replied.

His response was not lost on the ears of the Lao listeners as their interpreter wrote frantically on the writing pad before him. Tzovaras told us both that if nothing positive came from the meeting in Santiago he had numerous measures in mind, which would bring pressure to bear on the Lao authorities. He said the evidence he held was convincing proof of our innocence and the suggestion that a confession be a condition of our release was an outrage.

'I will remain here in Vientiane at least until we know the outcome of the meeting in Santiago, which will determine further action,' he stated.

'Just get me out of here … please!' I begged.

'Kay it will all be over soon. Don't worry about a thing,' he promised.

Our lawyer bid me farewell and promised that everything would be okay. I left the room feeling that things were far from okay, but hoping he would do as he said. Following Kerry's meeting with the Embassy and lawyer, we returned to Phonthong.

***

That night, I sat by the window of my cell and thought over everything. My business had taken me to the most interesting places, where I had the pleasure of meeting royalty, VIPs, corporate executives of multi-million dollar companies and heirs to billion dollar fortunes. I rubbed shoulders with CIA operatives, shared conversations with Crown Princes and margaritas with shipping magnates, and drank thousand dollar bottles of champagne with hoteliers.

Now, I was sitting in a gulag. If the Lao authorities hadn't detained me at the Lao-Thai Friendship Bridge, I would have been sitting in my new office in Sukhumvit, managing my own company, and not sitting in Phonthong wondering what the hell was happening to it in my absence.

Our Lao lawyer Phasith met with the Lao Public Prosecutors' office who declared that our Australian lawyer's legal submission did not conform to their requirements and added that the matter could only be resolved diplomatically. Kerry would have to confess in writing to embezzlement of state assets and compensate the State for the loss of gemstones and jewels. It was put to Phasith, both explicitly and implicitly, that we would be released if we signed statements (confessions) and paid compensation. Although they did not declare the amount of compensation sought, it was clear that an extremely large amount would be required. Such actions by the Lao PDR authorities could only amount to extortion and were clearly contrary to international law and decency.

From Santiago, Foreign Minister Downer emphasised that our imprisonment without charges amounted to a denial of justice. His counterpart gave a confusing account of our case. The Lao Foreign Minister argued that we had not been arrested arbitrarily because we had committed offences and yet he couldn't provide any evidence to support the allegations. The Prosecutor had not established a case that would stand up in a court of law. Just because gems were allegedly missing, if indeed they were, did not mean that we took them.

'I am particularly worried about the welfare of Mrs Danes and the impact her detention is having on her young family. Her ongoing detention is simply not fair and I think the matter has to be resolved quickly,' Downer concluded, echoing earlier concerns.

Meanwhile, we baked. It was so hot in Laos that I truly thought I would die. I would go to the washroom and pour water over my head to cool down but within minutes sweat would start to bead on my forehead.

'Look Kay. The police take Kerry out the room,' said Mon standing at the doorway, her hands gripping the bars as she looked out.

I ran to the window and jammed my face hard against the bars, looking to the right side of the prison where I knew his cell was. It was out of my sight of course, but I could just see Kerry walking towards the kitchen.

'He's outside Mon,' I responded joyfully.

'Where he go?' she spoke wistfully. We craned our necks to see.

'Kay. Kerry go out,' called Oudai. He smiled too as we all became excited that Kerry was finally out of the room after almost five months of confinement.

A police officer sat at the far end of the kitchen and watched Kerry as he walked back and forth along the length of the building. I stretched my arm through the bars and held it there for him to see. Kerry waved his arms to and fro, stretching and secretly waving to me. I was thrilled that his moment of freedom had finally arrived. Our routine continued with me going outside from 8am to midday and then Kerry going out from 1.30pm to 4pm. As excited as we both were with our new found freedom, we were both worried about the heat. Kerry told Anouhack to get permission for us to switch our exercise periods. The police agreed. When the afternoon came, I walked to the Bodhee tree with Phor and together we placed flowers at its base. Though I felt guilty that Kerry suffered because of me, I was extremely relieved to be outside and thankful that he always put me first.

CHAPTER TEN

A Diplomatic Envoy

Pi Mai, the Lao New Year held between 13 and 16 April, is also known as the Water Festival, and is the biggest traditional festival throughout the country. It begins with an early morning merit making, food offerings to Buddhist monks, and the release of caged birds. Citizens remove Buddha images from the temples throughout the city, cleaning each one with scented water before taking the water to the streets to dowse one another. Laotians believe that the water will wash away all the bad luck of the previous year.

My mind went back to happier times before we were taken hostage in this hell, to a happier Pi Mai scene shared with my husband and two youngest children, and for a while I got so lost in my thoughts of that day that I completely forgot I was in Phonthong prison. I came back to reality with a sigh.

There were rumours that the police would lock everyone inside the cells for three days. This prompted everyone to reschedule the annual festive holiday of Pi Mai. I sat under my tree watching the girls race around with coloured pails, drenching anyone who crossed their path. We didn't have any temples in the prison and there was no place for anyone to worship their God, nor did we have any images of Buddha. But what we lacked in physical resources we made up for with our vivid imaginations. The Bodhee tree standing in the centre of the compound became our holy place.

Approaching the festival, we started to get in the mood, dressing in our mismatched clothes, and painting our faces with whatever lipsticks and eye shadows we could scrape together from gifts given to me at Embassy visits. We even painted the men's faces and tied their hair in tiny ribbons. We threw pails and pails of dirty fish water at each other, pretending it had been cleansed at the Holy Place. We thought nothing of the rash we would develop later as we drenched each other to rid ourselves of all the bad luck.

We laughed hysterically and soon forgot all about the pain and suffering that was etched in every grain of our prison lives. We stopped thinking that we had families on the outside who worried about whether we would survive to see our freedom. We simply existed for the moment because the moments were all we had. It was just too painful to think beyond that. It was the only way to survive in this place.

Many prisoners watched with envy as we played. They sat hour after hour staring through their barred windows, longing to be on the other side like us. Our freedom was just another reminder of their lack of freedom. It became yet another torture. But we could not change the situation; all we could do was make the best of it. Anouhack escaped the water for a while but eventually the girls tracked him down. He squealed so loud that we thought the whole of Vientiane could hear him. Surely, the Commander would get angry, we thought, but he didn't. Perhaps he was too drunk, like the prison police outside that we heard singing and playing guitar.

Bounchan, Homparn and Chanlee sang a variety of Lao and Thai songs and for a couple of hours we danced to entertain those prisoners locked in their cells. Kerry ignored us and he kept running back and forth, as part of his usual fitness regime. What he didn't see was the girl Malivan crouching by the fishpond, watching him. Slowly Kerry made his way to the front of the cells. He made a u-turn just before the clearing where the police had told him not to cross. I stood ten feet away, watching my husband. It was comforting to me that we were able to make eye contact but we dared not speak for fear we would be reported.

Suddenly, without warning, Malivan lunged from behind a tree and threw the entire contents of her pail in Kerry's direction. He was caught completely by surprise and stopped dead in his tracks to wipe his face free of the sewage water that dripped from his head to his feet. Everyone laughed but soon that laughter turned to a roar when Kerry chased Malivan across the prison grounds.

'No Kerry no!' she squealed.

Effortlessly he scooped the young Thai girl high in his arms and seconds later, dunked her unceremoniously in the middle of the dirty fishpond. The prisoners inside the cells clapped their hands loudly. Malivan screamed when the slimy catfish made contact with her body. It was hilarious. Kerry reached out his hand and pulled her to the dry side of the bank.

'Oh Kerry you got me,' she laughed and we were all surprised that Kerry didn't get locked in the wooden blocks for enjoying the moment.

Too soon, the clanging of the steel tyre brace signalled the four o'clock line-up. It reminded us that try as we might, we could never escape the reality of our imprisonment. Quietly the prisoners stood in line and listened to the regulations and further claims that the western world was corrupt.

'Trust the Government to know the way to be perfect for the future! Follow their wisdom to see the way forward. Do not question their knowledge or the way they do everything because they defeated the Americans in the war, alongside our Vietnamese brothers. The Lao Government is all-powerful and knows all things to bring peace, prosperity, unity, and harmony to the people. Follow the regulations and you will be redeemed!'

Quietly I absorbed his words and gave up trying to argue with their logic that was as illogical to me as my ideals were to them. It was pointless to think that I could undo years of indoctrination, particularly when I silently agreed that America had no right to kill so many innocent people in that crazy war. Pon-Phit said that in those days, she saw a young boy of nine or ten lying on the ground with a ball bearing stuck in his skull, his mother grieving nearby. She said the millions of tonnes of bombs the US dropped during those war days were still creating as much damage to life and limb today as they did when she was a young girl.

In the quiet of the night I re-read a letter from our lawyer that talked about our detainment and the things he was doing to push our case along. He assured me that 'the support expressed by the Australian government and the Australian people in various ways was overwhelming,' and that diplomatic procedures had been stepped up, with Prime Minister John Howard now demanding our release from the Lao PM. He also told me how the media had taken on the story with the result that foreign investment in Laos was seriously affected. His final words gave some comfort and some hope: 'You can be sure that neither the Australian Government nor the Australian people will rest until you are released.' For now, I just had to sit tight and, as we were constantly told here in Laos, 'be patient'.

By the following week it was the official beginning of Pi Mai and everyone who was allowed out of their cells was called to a meeting in the kitchen area. The commander said that all prisoners would be locked in their cells for three days. Some would be allowed out in the morning and they would rotate with others who would come out for the afternoon. I felt my spirits deflate, thinking of whether or not Kerry would be let out. As it happened, the Commander lied. Everyone in Phonthong was locked inside their cell for eight days. Everyone that is, except the five Lao head prisoners, the two kitchen staff prisoners and nine female prisoners, thankfully including myself.

April was the hottest month in Laos. It was so hot that you couldn't even touch the steel bars that kept us captive. They were like iron stokers straight out of the fire. Prisoners were dry retching from the lack of airflow to the cells. Some succumbed to severe dehydration. Bounmy got sick and fainted. Pang paid the prison nurse money from her account book to put him on an IV drip. We didn't know if Bounmy would survive another day because he appeared so frail, almost ghost-like. Then to make matters worse, someone turned off the water to the cells. After a few hours, the concrete troughs in each cell would be empty. Somehow, we had to find a way to fill them.

'Get a bucket!' I called to the girls. We carted water from cell to cell. The prisoners locked inside scooped the water through the bars with whatever they could find. None of us ever understood why the water was shut off but we suspected it was just another ploy to assert dominance over us.

The guards in the towers watched and reported everything we did to the Commander. Several times, racked with frustration, I wanted to scream at them, 'Fuck off,' but I didn't. I was too afraid they'd lock me in the cell like those other poor bastards.

***

Our Consular visits were cancelled for the next two weeks because the actual Pi Mai celebrations had begun across the country. All food deliveries from the outside to the prison were cancelled and we resigned ourselves to eating only the pig fat water soup and sticky rice again, with nothing in the way of fresh food to supplement our diet. The Muslims starved. It was as if someone had stopped time altogether and I wondered how our children were coping. But thinking of them only brought me pain.

We were simply being left to our own devices at times, to find and cook food, even when the guards knew there wasn't much to find. Homparn cooked ten skewered toads over an open fire.

Their tiny bodies were charred black. He smiled when he saw me approach.

'Madam, do you know how to tell when the toad is cooked?' he asked.

'Do I want to know?' I replied.

'The insides become the outsides,' he laughed. It was a ghastly sight to watch their insides bubble to the outside. Homparn tested one and slowly turned the others over the open flame. The crunchy sound brought a murmur of satisfaction as he passed one to me.

'You eat?' he asked.

'Oh I'm full. I already ate the river rat,' I said quickly and left the cooking area. He just laughed.

As midday approached, the heat became unbearable as the humidity rose to the high fifties. Kerry sat in his underwear, sweltering in his cell. Anouhack sat outside trying to keep him company.

By the time the official Pi Mai festival passed, the police gave permission for Kerry and a few other prisoners to come outside the cell. They practically fell out when the door opened. Kerry was told that so long as we stayed away from each other, he could come out morning and afternoon. It was a small compromise and naturally, we agreed. What choice did we have after all?

A small rattan shack sat by the prison kitchen about seventy metres from the cell blocks. During the week, Kerry would go there with Anouhack and drink tea. Afterwards, he'd stretch and begin his rigorous exercise regime. We heard from 'Mr CNN', Anouhack, that our Foreign Minister, had written again to Lengsavad, asking him to consider the implications of our case and the effect it was having on bilateral relations.

'Charge them or release them,' said Downer.

I would have much preferred it if he just said 'release them'.

Having previously complained and protested several times through our Embassy that we were not always given our mail, and having been in the prison for several long months, some of the rules were relaxed a little, allowing us to read letters from home, though they were still prone to censorship. My sister Karen knew how much I loved poetry and sent us several verses from my favourite poets. She also included poems that she had written herself, which touched me greatly. I read them aloud as the big orange sun set low on the horizon.

'Your sister write very nice poem,' said Mon. 'Maybe one day I can meet her.'

'One day I hope you do!' I replied. I folded the poems and tucked them carefully back inside the Embassy envelope. I quietly wrote to my family and told them how much I was missing them. I told them how intolerable the conditions were becoming, but I couldn't tell them everything, and in the end finished by repeating how much I missed them all.

Before Kerry and I came to Phonthong there was no badminton played in the prison. But I grovelled to the police and soon our 'Olympic' tournaments were in full swing. Mon's family sent racquets and the prisoners made a net from fishing line. We got a packet of shuttlecocks from the Embassy. A makeshift court was soon scratched out of dirt and we got down to some serious fun.

We were in the middle of a very fast badminton tournament when the police shouted at me to get ready to be taken to the Immigration for an Embassy visit. I didn't even have time to wash off the sweat.

'Go!' they called again. 'Embassy.'

At the Consular visit, we were informed that the Australian Prime Minister had again intervened in our case in an attempt to try to force Laos to release us. He wrote to the new Lao Prime Minister Bounyang Vorachit, congratulating him on his appointment and warned that Australia could no longer accept our detention.

'In the absence of a clear case they should be released,' Howard wrote. Foreign Minister Downer hardened the diplomatic language and described our continued detention as quite disgraceful.

Evidently, the Lao Ambassador in Canberra was hauled before Australian officials. Our case reached a crucial stage when a final report from the Lao Prosecutors was handed to the Foreign Minister Lengsavad. Downer began an official letter writing campaign calling for our release. He also called upon the Australian Governor General, His Excellency Sir William Deane, to write to the President of the Lao PDR in support of our release.

'What else did they say?' Anouhack asked, following our return from Immigration.

'They said that Mr Downer will send a special envoy to Laos to talk about our case with the high officials,' I responded.

Word spread quickly that the Australian Prime Minister himself was coming to Laos. I didn't want to disappoint anyone so I kept quiet and let them all believe that Laos was about to get its arse kicked. The Governor General of Australia took up the fight to protect us.

Sir William Deane asked General Siphandone to use his considerable influence in Laos to have us released immediately. He also called for us to be moved from Phonthong to a secure location where our health and well-being could be monitored more closely.

It was confirmed that a high profile Australian diplomat, John McCarthy, was coming to Laos to seek a resolution to our case. Not only had he enjoyed an illustrious career as Head of Missions to the South East Asia region but he was also a barrister at law. McCarthy would convey the difficulties of maintaining the bilateral relationship with Laos in its current form, worth AU$20 million, if justice was not at least seen to be done. Meanwhile, the Australian Federal opposition leader, Kim Beazley began campaigning in earnest.

'The Government should do everything it can to secure the couple's release,' he said as he took to the floor at parliament house in our nation's capital.

But while our Government called for our immediate release, the media reported that charges were expected to be laid against us by the end of the month. The political prisoners said that it was inevitable that the court would find us guilty. No one ever left Laos innocent, they said. In my letters to our children, I decided not to dwell on such things but instead began telling them what little I could about those detained with us. I told them about Mon and that she took such care of me. I told them about Anouhack and Mr Joy and how everyone was waiting to go home. I told them about Mr Mai, who was aged somewhere between fifty and sixty with thick black hair that always parted to one side and exposed stark white roots. He had been kind to me and to Kerry. Mai was taller than most Laotians I knew and his skin was much whiter. Anouhack said Mr Mai got into trouble with Lao police after he had provided translation services for a Cameroon moneyman. It all revolved around a magic box that transformed black paper into millions in US currency. The cost of the black box was a mere fifty thousand dollars but when the trick failed, the Lao investor had his police friends arrest Mr Mai. He told them Mai's family had lots of money. He didn't tell them that Mai's family didn't want anything to do with him. He wanted his fifty thousand dollars back and although Mr Mai only ever received 2,000 baht (US$50) for his translation services, the Lao businessman said he did not mind waiting however long it took Mr Mai to reimburse him. The economic police visited Phonthong frequently to demand money from Mr Mai, who of course had none. The few dollars he did get from the Embassy each month would hardly buy his freedom.

Mr Mai was doomed but he was good company. He said that Kerry and I were like the sugar cane in the elephant's mouth.

'Almost impossible to get out unless you kill the beast,' he laughed.

I don't know why he found that so amusing but he did. As the weeks passed, I began to think that Mr Mai was right and that we were, well and truly trapped inside the elephant's mouth. But who would kill the beast to set us free?

The Australian Government said that we were hostages but the SAS Hostage Rescue Team would not be coming to our rescue. I sat with my Thai friend Mon under a shady tree and tried to fathom why that was. After all, my husband had trained the SAS specifically in the role of hostage rescue.

Slowly the black door creaked open and Mr Mai returned from his Embassy visit. He walked towards me with a brown paper bag in his hand and a huge smile on his face.

'Here Madam. Something to make you smile,' he said. I squealed with excitement as I looked inside.

'Oh, thank you Mr Mai,' I said and turned to grab Mon's hand. 'Come on!' we ran to our cell. I reached inside and pulled out a small tub of ice cold, creamy, chocolate ice cream.

'Ooohh,' Mon said, licking her lips. We sat cross-legged on the wooden floorboards and slowly savoured each tiny mouthful. There were too few moments like that in Phonthong. Most of the time, we were surrounded by endless despair and when something bad came along, we feared it. But when something good happened, we cherished it and were grateful.

***

As we approached May 2001, two young African boys in their early twenties were arrested and brought to the prison. The Lao police said they were members of a black money gang; a magic box scam just like the one Mr Mai had been caught up in. I stood and watched the police beat the young men, Willy and then Karim, in the interrogation room. It didn't matter that we saw. They even left the windows wide open.

Willy had to be dragged from the interrogation room. He couldn't walk. The police refused to remove the heavy wooden blocks from his legs. For several long minutes the prisoners stood still, just watching, and waiting for him to fall. The police laughed and did nothing as Willy inched one foot after another.

'My God, someone help him!' I called out. But even the prisoners who had been detained for twenty years were rooted to their spot. They dared not interfere, as stipulated in the regulations that we were all supposed to follow without question. An eternity passed. Willy almost fell over a number of times and then he gave up moving altogether. The prison went quiet as everyone waited, holding their breath. And then something unbelievable happened. Kerry ran towards Willy and as he moved closer, I heard him say, 'Trust me.'

Kerry hoisted Willy onto his back in one smooth motion and carried him all the way back to his cell. The prisoners stood stunned until I began clapping my hands at my husband's show of bravery. He was lucky he didn't get locked in isolation for defying the regulations, but I suppose Kerry just didn't care.

A week later, the black door opened to the prison and twenty-five police congregated in the interrogation room. They were an awesome sight as they carried television cameras on their shoulders, video cameras and small hand cameras. There were police from different departments. We could tell by the uniforms they wore and the different insignias. I joked with Anouhack and said they were coming for the magic show because moments later, they sent for Willy and Karim.

The two African boys walked slowly to the sound of our quiet chuckles. When they entered the room, we tried to edge closer to see what had caused such a fuss. An hour later, they were still entertaining the police with their magic trick. Two weeks later, they left the prison. When Kerry and I went to our Consular visit that Thursday afternoon, we saw Willy and Karim waiting outside Mr Khamkit's office. Oddly, the police didn't mind us talking to them. Nor did they say anything about Kerry and I standing together in the hallway.

'We were all worried about you,' I smiled as I kissed both the boys on each cheek.

'No problem. They saw the trick, took the box and I reckon now they're probably gonna make their own money with it,' laughed Willy.

'Yeah. We're just picking up our passports and then heading back to Thailand,' Karim declared.

'You mean they're letting you go?' I asked surprised.

'Sure are!' Willy responded. His smile filled his face.

As we waited, we talked with the Africans and told them to contact the Australian Embassy in Bangkok when they arrived, and to get a message back to us that they'd actually made it. No one trusted the Lao Government when it came to letting people go. Usually they said people went home when actually they ended up elsewhere, either in a seminar camp, or thrown off the back of a truck bound for the mountain caves in Phonsali.

We were told that, for the first time, we could have our Consular meeting together. This was a huge relief to both of us and breathed hope into my heart that slowly, things were changing. Our Lao lawyer, Phasith smiled warmly as he sat down next to me. His old brown leather briefcase rested on his bony knees.

'How are you Madam?' he questioned sincerely.

'I'm fine Mr Phasith,' I lied.

Louise passed us both emails and faxes from my family and a letter from a dear friend that kept my spirits up, reminding me that people had not forgotten me.

'Do you want to speak with your children?' Louise asked, though she already knew the answer. She dialled the number on her cell phone. This time I was fully composed. After speaking to my children, who were relieved they were no longer separating us for our meetings, the visit ended.

***

The next day, I watched a Frenchman they called 'Joe Hay' walk the perimeter of the prison. They said he'd lost his mind during an interrogation seven years ago when he was arrested in the south of Laos.

'What did he do?' I asked Anouhack.

'Who knows? The other Frenchman, Francis Phetdum Prasak, said they injected Joe with some mind-altering drug during an interrogation. The police said he was a spy,' Anouhack replied.

'Yeah right, and I'm James Bond,' I said as Joe Hay came closer.

'Excuse me. Do you know James Bond?' he asked seriously.

'Hey Joe! Are you American?' asked Anouhack. The tall blonde haired man with the big nose and skinny pale blue eyes smiled. His rotten teeth immediately drew my attention.

'Oh yes. I like America. I like the women,' Joe replied tilting his head and nodding. He wore a faded tweed suit and kept pulling the sleeves of his jacket down but they didn't quite reach his wrists. The olive green t-shirt he wore underneath was every bit as drab as his own scruffy appearance. He stood there staring at me, which I found most unsettling.

'Hey Joe. How can you wear that hot suit in this weather?' I asked him quietly. His skinny white hands began carefully dusting off the material as his eyes meticulously roamed the fibres of his jacket for any frayed threads.

'Oh, I only have this one. No nothing, no carrots, no potatoes, no tooth-a-paste. Yes, yes impossible,' he gibbered unintelligibly and waved his hands as he spoke.

'You American Joe Hay?' asked Pang sarcastically. She was easily frustrated by him because he kept saying he was an American, but we all knew he wasn't.

'Yes I am American people. Santa Monica, California, Santa Barbara, oh yes. Thank you. I like the woman,' he responded. His fingers gently stroked the fine hair on his chin. I looked at him for quite a while, trying to figure out what was wrong with him.

Joe was so skinny and so dirty and smelt as if he hadn't bathed for years. The reason he didn't take a shower was simply because he hadn't any clothes to change into. He didn't brush his teeth because he didn't have a toothbrush or toothpaste. He didn't shave because he didn't have a razor, or comb his hair because he was without a comb. In fact, the more I observed, Joe seemed to have nothing at all. Not even a pair of shoes. How long had he endured like this? It was too horrible to imagine.

'He cannot remember anything I think. His mind is crazy,' said Anouhack. Joe sat on the small stump a few feet away from us until Pang told him to move.

'Joe Hay go away! You stink so bad!' she barked at him. I watched his face crumple with sadness as he stood on his bony legs and bowed in apology to Pang.

'I'm sorry,' was all he said, before moving away to continue his endless wandering around the prison. Joe never sat completely still. He was always moving in some way or another. Whether he was sitting alone under a tree kissing his hand and calling it Robyn, or whether he was walking back and forth crying to leave Asia, Joe was always restless.

Both Kerry and I felt sorry for him because no one else cared. We gave him soap, toothpaste, and even a set of clothes, and from then on, Joe took a bath every day. We got a comb from the Embassy so he could comb his hair and at least feel human. I convinced Joe to let Mr Joy cut it which I might add, was no easy feat.

'Joe don't be afraid. Mr Joy is my friend. He won't hurt you,' I said to him calmly. But Joe's eyes were fearful. He didn't trust Asians and made no secret of it.

'I don't like! I don't like!' he shouted and ran away. I watched the tall man wrap his arms around his own body and walk the perimeter of the prison. He always did that when he was stressed. I waited for him to complete a full circle.

'It's okay Joe. You take a hair cut or you get locked in the room and then I cannot see you,' I said to him. Joe stopped pacing and stood before me trying to come to a decision. It was as if I was looking into the eyes of a wounded animal. Joe had not trusted anyone in such a long time. I watched his expression flick between uncertainties.

'Joe. Sit here now and don't be silly. Otherwise I cannot be your friend anymore!' I spoke sternly. Joe responded and sat quietly in the chair as Mr Joy smiled and reassured him that he was not about to cut his throat with the razor.

His eyes never left my face the whole time. It didn't surprise me that Joe was afraid. We were all afraid but it was just that some showed it more than others did.

'Isn't any wonder,' I said to Mr Joy who was concentrating on removing Joe's fair beard. 'If they treat people like animals, don't be surprised if they act like animals.'

Mr Joy smiled and I watched as he began to relax. I knew Joe took comfort in the songs I sang to him. He loved music and would sit with his eyes half closed, his hand on his heart, and slowly move his head from side to side. Softly I began to sing to him, a song I knew was a particular favourite of his.

Every day we sang songs by Madonna, Michael Jackson and even a few Frank Sinatra melodies. Joe loved it when we sang New York, New York. Of course, everyone else thought we were crazy because we got right into our performances. He did a mean werewolf impersonation from Michael Jackson's song, Thriller. The prisoners locked in the cells thought we were good entertainment.

CHAPTER ELEVEN

African Torture

We sat eating our prison rations of pig fat water soup and sticky rice when a commotion sounded from outside the black door. The guard in the tower stood with his AK rifle pointed at the gate. A few minutes later, he casually slung it back over his right shoulder.

'Someone coming,' said Toom. We moved to the cell window to take a closer look. I was the last to the window because I had to dispose of my letter, thinking a raid was imminent.

'Black men,' whispered Toom.

I looked anxiously at Pang as a group of black men filed into the interrogation room. My heart pounded. Suddenly the girls in my cell became anxious as our eyes became transfixed on the interrogation room. Thirty minutes later, we watched as the police led them slowly towards our cell block, their black hands bound at the wrists. I was too frightened to go any closer to the window so I hid behind the steel door and observed through the bars. The police escort were strangers and looked more like Vietnamese soldiers. They pushed each African into a separate cell.

As dusk turned to night, Mon sang in Thai to take my mind off the Africans. I didn't want to know why they were here. I just wanted them to leave. I had a bad feeling about them being here.

A week passed and the Africans' interrogations began in earnest. Sam was the first they dragged off. We could tell by the look of confusion on his youthful face that he had no idea what was about to happen. Had we all looked like that, bewildered and wanting reassurance? In slow motion, he passed me by. His dark brown eyes searched mine but I lowered them to the ground. He would face his journey alone just as everyone else in Phonthong had at some time or another.

Sam entered the room quietly. I watched from metres away with the others, while the door slowly shut behind him. Everyone waited. An hour passed. The prison was quiet except for the occasional raised voice we heard coming from the interrogation room. No one moved. Not a word was spoken and then we heard it. The inevitable had begun. His blood-curdling scream broke the silence.

'Stop. Please don't hurt me,' young Sam cried. I could hear the fear in his voice, the shock; the disbelief that they could do whatever it was they were doing to him. He screamed again and again. For hours we stood in complete silence and listened. I wanted to close my ears but I couldn't. His cries filled my heart with anguish.

Hours later, Sam's bloodied body was half-dragged back to his cell. His skin took on an ashen tone. His eyes stared right through me. I hugged my body tightly and lowered my head, ashamed that I had stood and done nothing. I felt a chill despite the heat of the day as the police stalked him all the way back to his cell. After they shoved Sam into his cell, the police walked quietly along the veranda and back down the stairs. I found myself transfixed as they moved by.

'Kay. Come sit here,' Pang whispered. But I became frozen with fear. Their hollow, emotionless eyes stared at me.

'Madam?' His voice questioned. I lowered my eyes quickly and held my breath. Quietly I willed him away.

'Kay. Come here,' Pang called when the interrogators left the prison. I dragged my eyes towards my friend who sat under the tree with the Laotian, Oudai. 'Don't stand there when they come! You want to go in that room too?' she barked.

The next day they came again, but this time for Abrahim, a young man from Liberia. We heard he was married with a baby on the way. The prisoners said he came to Laos to get a three-month visa for Thailand, which was a common occurrence amongst foreign travellers.

Abrahim was a Muslim and prayed every day in the cell next to Sam. I knew he had faith in Allah, but would that be enough to help him to endure? I wasn't a Muslim but I prayed at the Holy Tree that Abrahim would not suffer too much.

Four hours later, after much the same treatment as Sam endured the day before, Abrahim was dragged back to his cell. When the interrogation police left Phonthong, I quietly passed painkillers through the bars. Abrahim wept and whispered in despair.

'Madam, they burnt my seed,' he said in shock as his eyes lowered from mine to his trousers.

'Sshh don't talk. Don't think too much,' I whispered but my eyes filled with tears.

I went off to beg the nurse for more painkillers. The codeine helped a little but it was useless against broken ribs, cracked jaws, and burnt genitals. We were certain that the torture was far from over and the very next day, they came again for Michael. The day after that, Mensuh, and finally on the Friday, young Abou.

★★★

By the end of the week, all five Africans were pissing blood. We had never seen so much evil inflicted on so many prisoners in such a short time. Kerry and a Thai prisoner tried to set Abou's broken wrist with a torn sheet and a wooden splint but they got in trouble. The police told Anouhack to explain to Kerry that it was against the regulations for him to communicate with another prisoner still under investigation. Kerry said he didn't care and told Anouhack to get the Commander of the prison.

Fifteen minutes later, the second in charge at the prison, the 2IC, sat at the bamboo hut metres from the black door with my husband who quietly demanded the fair treatment of prisoners in accordance with the UN Declaration of Human Rights. Silently the tears fell down my cheeks as I listened to him asking that Abou receive proper medical treatment.

Two days later, the 2IC returned with one of the interrogators and according to Anouhack's translation, aired his concerns about the treatment of the Africans. The special interrogator apologised to the Africans and told them to take care of their health. That Thursday we went to our Consular visit and Kerry informed the Jonathan about what had occurred. Jonathan was appalled and following the meeting, wrote a letter to the Australian government. A week later, the torture resumed.

'Lumpini coming,' I cried to Sam when I saw the same police come back. We called them Lumpini because it was the name of the famous Bangkok Boxing stadium in Thailand. It seemed a befitting title. At times, they didn't even bother to shut the doors or the windows. We watched them put Sam's legs into the wooden leg blocks as they made him sit on the dirty concrete floor. They cuffed his hands behind his back and shoved a dirty rag into his mouth. They beat him for what seemed like forever. When he still refused to sign a confession, they became more brutal, forced him to lie on his back while they held him down, and bashed him with a steel tyre brace. Every part of his body was hit repeatedly until he was close to unconsciousness. Then afterwards, they dragged him back to his cell and left him there without any medical treatment. For three days, Sam coughed blood. And then they came again the following day for Abrahim and the others, throughout the rest of the week.

We complained to the prison police that their screams were affecting our emotional wellbeing. We begged them to stop, or at least, to take them outside the prison and not force us to witness their torture. But instead, they put gaffer tape on the Africans' mouths to stifle their cries. They put cigarettes on their genitals and ash in their eyes. I watched each day in silence as the Africans endured the pain. Silently I prayed that somehow the United Nations would find out about the evil in Laos and the treatment they inflicted on helpless prisoners. But how could they do anything when no one but us could hear the screams?

When the police finished torturing the Africans, they left and never returned. But the fear of their return kept everyone on edge for weeks. Then another group of police came and this time they tortured the newly arrived Burmese and Chinese prisoners. Lek, a young Thai-Burmese girl, couldn't take it anymore and attempted suicide a couple of times. We told her to walk to the interrogation room without fear, but she wouldn't listen. She was too afraid.

Each time she returned her body was covered in bruises. I felt sorry for Lek because she was only a mere slip of a girl. They beat her husband too. His trousers were splattered with blood as he limped back to his cell. They'd broken his jaw and his left eye had closed over. I made a fist over my heart and mouthed the words, 'Be strong.' That afternoon, we did the rounds with the painkillers.

The police only came one more time for Lek and her husband. Their beatings were much worse than anything I had heard before though. We tried to ignore her childlike screams and wondered how much longer it would take. Hours later, Lek told us that she'd signed a false confession against her husband. Our words were of little comfort to her when she heard her husbands anguish, four metres away. She was responsible for his pain, or so she thought. We told her it wasn't her fault. They would have tortured him regardless.

Left: Where it all began—our security headquarters in Vientiane. We established ourselves as *the* reputable security company for foreign and local investors, and offered our staff expert training and superior working conditions.

Right and Below: Kerry (on my left) and I were extremely worried about our fate when we were eventually brought to court after months locked up in Phonthong Prison. The judges did not even look at the Book of Evidence that would have proved our innocence, so the trial was a foregone conclusion.

While I was imprisoned, my eyes were opened to another world of suffering the Laos Government doesn't want the world to know about. The extreme poverty in which much of the nation lives (**Below Left**) was nothing new, but the persecution of the ethnic Hmong minority (**Above and Below Right**), branded as rebels and treated disgracefully, means that the most bombed country in the history of the world remains a dangerous place.

Right: Both Kerry and I had birthdays approaching and were delighted to receive gifts from our children upon a Consular visit. It felt strange sitting with Ian Kemish, Director of Consular Operations, and speaking to my children on the phone, while still wearing the prison uniform.

© Australian Embassy Laos

© Author's Private Collection

Left: After ten months imprisoned in a Communist gulag, Kerry and I were finally released into the care of Ambassador Jonathan Thwaites, pending our Royal Pardon. Though only ten miles from Phonthong, it was a world away from the prison. We delighted in the luxuries of hot water and clean clothes, but were still anxious and could hardly wait for the day when we could go home to our children.

Right: Countless delays and setbacks kept us waiting anxiously, but the day finally arrived when we were granted our Royal Pardon. Ambassador Thwaites showed excellent diplomacy in dealing with the Laos delegation and ensuring our freedom.

© Australian Embassy Laos

Above: It was so good to be reunited with our children at last. From the left, Sahra, Nathan and Jess, were just as happy to see us.

Below: I felt it was my duty to tell the world what I had seen and experienced in Laos, and how the people suffer under the dictatorship. I testified at the US Congressional Forum on Laos in 2002, on behalf of those prisoners I left behind, and continue to speak out against the corruption of the regime in Laos to this day.

That night when the police locked the doors and we all slept, Toom saw Lek tie a piece of cord around her neck and the other end to the steel door. The cord wasn't strong enough to hold her weight and cut into her flesh. I awoke early the next morning and was first to take a shower. I became enraged when I saw the blood spills on our washroom floor.

'What you do Lek?' I leaned over her as the others in my cell woke suddenly in confusion. I ranted and raved at her and told Mon to translate everything I said. It would save me from repeating myself.

'Think of Mr Joy, or Oudai who suffer more than you do and they don't kill themselves!' I shouted and waited for Mon to translate.

Lek promised me she wouldn't hurt herself again. I don't know why I got so angry. I guess I was scared. Two months later, the police released her and her husband. Tan Sombut got his prisoners mixed up because the Chinese had similar names. The Chinaman who'd entered Laos on an incorrect visa was supposed to have been released, not Lek's husband. The prisoners said that the Laos authorities wouldn't care and that he would now stay forever despite their mistake.

***

We went to our twentieth Consular visit on 31 May 2001 and were allowed to sit in the same room again.

'Now, I want you to sign a letter of apology to the Lao Government,' began our Australian lawyer

'What the hell for?' Kerry started with annoyance.

'Look,' he leaned forward, 'It's something we have to do to show good faith but don't worry, it doesn't change anything.'

We signed the apology because we had no other choice. Our son's 8th birthday was approaching. We'd missed our daughter's 12th birthday, my father's birthday and Mother's Day. My son's letters broke my heart just as much as his voice did when we spoke on the phone.

'Mum, I sure hope you and Dad get home for my birthday !' he said.

The Australian Ambassador Jonathan Thwaites and the Special Envoy, John McCarthy met the Minister to the President's office, Soubanh Srithirath and emphasised their concern. Soubanh said he had discussed our case with the President of the Lao PDR and its Prime Minister, and would pass these latest messages to the President. He agreed that the Lao Prosecutor and Defence Counsel should meet to discuss their respective cases and evidence. He said that the Government had assigned the case to the Foreign Minister Lengsavad and appropriate justice authorities. He also said it was important to avoid embarrassing Laos.

McCarthy said that the lack of any resolution after four and a half months was putting the strong bilateral relationship that had lasted almost fifty years in jeopardy. Some Australians were questioning why their Government assisted Laos when Laos treated Australian citizens so inappropriately. McCarthy said that extensive counter evidence collected by our lawyers refuted the allegations against us. He gave a copy of a summarisation of our case to the Minister and made several offers for our lawyers to present the points directly to him. These offers were ignored.

That same afternoon, the police brought us to meet Mr McCarthy at the Lao Immigration office. There were fewer Lao officials than usual attending our meeting, which made me think they were putting on a show for the high-ranking Australian diplomat. McCarthy told us that his visit marked a further stage in the Australian Government's continuing efforts to secure our release. They were making progress, albeit slowly.

'Are you eating, Kay?' asked Louise. She worried about how much weight I'd lost.

'Yeah, I'm fine,' I responded.

It was true that I'd lost a lot of weight because there was nothing else to do but exercise. Better to run on the top of a stinking sewage tank for an hour than sit and watch the second hand tick over. The stifling humidity in the cells also played its part.

'Don't worry Kay, for the first time, we have an opportunity to sit down with the prosecution and address the allegations in detail,' my lawyer stated.

'Do you think they'll free us then?' I asked. I knew in my heart that Laos would never allow us to leave innocent. But our lawyer remained optimistic.

'I'm confident they are now concerned about how all of this is impacting on their relations with Australia,' Tzovaras said.

The following day, McCarthy, Jonathan Thwaites and our lawyers met with the Lao Justice Minister who confirmed that our trial was pending and would be handled fairly, in accordance with the Laos law. He requested the Australian Government respect that process. The Australian Government acknowledged that we were subject to Lao law but were perplexed as to how the Lao prosecution would present a case against us when they had never met with our defence team to receive detailed information and counter-evidence collected. The Lao minister wished to maintain good relations with Australia but refused to be drawn into further discussions of a political nature, other than to recommend further discussions between all the relevant parties.

Our lawyers tried to meet and discuss their respective information with the Lao Prosecutor's office but were told that there was nothing to discuss. Eventually Jonathan and McCarthy did meet with Lengsavad and listened carefully as the Foreign Minister made his point.

'The only reason why we don't take them to court before now is that your Government asked to delay the proceedings', Lengsavad concluded.

'Your Excellency … the reason we had sought to delay the court proceedings was that the Defence has been unable to put forth its case,' responded McCarthy. Lengsavad also insisted that the case be kept out of the public domain.

Discussions, while cordial, were frank on both sides. Lengsavad clearly believed we were guilty however; he was unwilling to divulge, if he indeed knew, what evidence they claimed to have against us. The Laos Government was being pressed to, at least, address the case again, and seemed to appreciate that the issues were grave ones from the Australian Government perspective. Jonathan would follow up with Lengsavad's office the following week to hear the outcome of his discussions with the Public Prosecutor. But what puzzled the Lao government most was why the Australian Government had attached such importance to our fate. Surely, what mattered more than anything were the wider national interests?

Our lawyer submitted comprehensive depositions with certified attached documentary evidence, from our clients, family and friends, while the Embassy sought meetings with the Ministry of Interior to confirm our next Consular visit. Everybody was given the run around by the General Police Department. Louise Waugh personally haunted the corridors of the Interior Ministry in order to secure our next visit. When she eventually got a meeting with the officials, she discussed the possibility of transferring us from the detention centre to the Immigration centre. The first official gave the impression that it might be possible, but after speaking to the Deputy Head of the General Police Department, in charge of detainees, it was apparent that if left up to him, we would remain where we were indefinitely.

'There can be no discrimination in favour of the Danes,' he said through a translator.

Louise continued to press the subject of our transfer with other members in the department but most said they were too busy to discuss our case.

Lengsavad met with the Prosecutor of Laos as promised and evidently discussed the possibility of granting our lawyer direct access to the prosecution's case or to submit defence evidence and arguments. The immediate response was negative. He did say, however, that we could, 'submit to the Prosecutor through a Lao lawyer because a foreigner cannot be heard in a Lao court'.

An optimistic interpretation of Lengsavad's instructions might be that it was impossible for the Lao Government or judicial authorities to withdraw without public international embarrassment. But they would have to do so in a way that did not undermine their integrity. Such matters would certainly take more time. Our continued detainment was beginning to take its toll. My state of mind had deteriorated over the past week. I'd also chipped my tooth on a stone in the sticky rice they fed us twice a day. There was no facility for treatment at the prison and we weren't allowed to leave to seek treatment. While the Australian Embassy submitted an application for me to go to the Military Hospital, I became anxious, thinking about the alternative. Though mine was only a small hole in the rear molar, I began to worry about toothache and decay. One of the Thai prisoners practiced a crude dentistry in Phonthong with a rusty nail.

***

There were many horrors in Phonthong. Prisoners were reduced to surviving on next to nothing. Some had already succumbed to eating giant river rats, poisonous snakes and warty toads. I was suffering terribly, but I was one of the luckier ones in this luckless place. I got permission to order in weekend food supplies, sent by our housekeeper Mr On, and passed on by a prison guard. Every Friday afternoon he would make a special delivery of 2kg of white rice, six carrots, 500g of beans, three onions, a cabbage, a bottle of oyster sauce and 2kg of beef. From this Kerry and I fed thirty prisoners steamed rice and stir-fry. It became routine that prisoners would bring me their polystyrene containers that I'd collected from our own daily food deliveries, to receive their only decent meal for that week. Many came with tears in their eyes as I filled their bowl. It was all I could do to help.

At our next Consular visit, we met with the Embassy Doctor, Ben Burford. He and Louise teamed up to fill my broken tooth with some cavet sent from my sister Karen in Australia. Their methods weren't as primitive as the so-called prison dentist. But the temporary filling didn't last long and since Jonathan Thwaites had requested it personally, the Lao authorities finally gave me permission to go to the Lao Military Hospital. It was an experience that almost turned bad. I found myself seated in a room that smelled strongly of disinfectant while a man, presumably the dentist, began inspecting my front tooth for extraction.

'Stop! Stop!' I said in alarm.

After carefully explaining his mistake, I pointed to my rear molar, saying, 'This is broken!' He apologised and began drilling. I smelt smoke after five minutes of drilling and so too did everyone else in the room. The Dentist packed my tooth with more cavet, then declared himself finished. I was charged 38,000 kip for the service (US$4) before they took me back to Phonthong.

It was quite funny actually, because on our return, the nurse kindly asked me if I wanted to stop for ice cream. I declined of course.

The next morning began like any other as the black door to the prison opened and we waited to see who was coming.

'Squeal! Squeal!'

A big fat pig protested as the police dragged it to the kitchen. By the time we got out of our cells they'd tied it up alive, but still squealing to be set free. Five police stood over it and I saw one of them give the head prisoner a long bladed knife. In the back of my mind, I wondered for a moment if we weren't all a little bit like that pig, afraid to die but helpless to do anything. So many things caused us to suffer, even survival. So we hardened our hearts and did whatever we could to make light of our situation. The pig scene looked very much like an interrogation.

'What is your name, pig?' I shouted to break the spell that had fallen on us. Phor was the first to laugh and laughed even louder when I repeated the question.

'What is your name, pig?' I demanded, and pointed my finger at my imaginary pig. Other prisoners turned their gaze from the kitchen to me. Phor sat on the wooden bench beside me. And so my game began. I copied everything the police were doing to the real pig at the far end of the prison. But I added my own version of the story because we couldn't hear what they were saying.

Each time I asked our imaginary pig to tell us its name, it squealed. I built the suspense and Phor joined in the fun. The prisoners still locked in their cells laughed. They looked at Phor and I and then to the police at the kitchen and then back to us. We knew it was only a matter of time before that blade sliced its way through the real pig's neck. They began washing the big old pig in preparation for the slaughter and Phor told everyone it was a form of water torture.

'Tell us your name pig,' Phor demanded.

He was so funny and got into the spirit of acting. Being a Thai police officer gave him a great deal of credibility and for a split second, I imagined him doing real interrogations. The imaginary pig refused to tell us its name and everyone roared with laughter. Moments later, they cut the real pig's throat.

'Die Lao pig!' I shouted. Phor laughed and slapped my back.

We sat on the skinny wooden bench and took our applause and for a while, prison life wasn't as bad as it usually was. We didn't think any more about the pig because we knew we'd see him again in the pig fat water soup they served us twice a day, every day. Quietly we sat as the hours passed.

The police dragged us out of the prison to meet the Embassy again on 7 June 2001. It was to be our twenty-first Consular visit.

Mr Khamkit greeted us warmly as we arrived and quietly motioned us to sit.

'I'm very confident ... extremely optimistic that you'll be released any day now,' said our lawyer. How many times had he said that? Was it sixteen or seventeen? How many times had he told our children those very same words? I couldn't bear thinking about it.

'The reports are saying that we're going to court. If that's the case, contact our clients who represent the World Bank, IMF and Asia Development Bank. They can witness the event and pressure the court to do the right thing,' Kerry said.

He spoke so quickly that I wondered if Louise was able to write any of it down. Our lawyer shook his head as he gripped Kerry's forearm, telling him it would never go that far because he'd arranged everything.

'Look, just make sure we don't go into that courtroom without support. Get the fucking UN there,' Kerry exploded.

We provided security for a number of United Nations projects in Laos and the managers of those projects had a great deal of respect for us. We had no doubt they'd come to the court if asked, and if nothing else, bear witness to our trial.

'Okay, okay ... I'll organise it. Just don't worry, everything's on track.' His tone was conciliatory. As I looked at my husband, I knew he was frustrated. He felt helpless to protect me. He worried about our children and was annoyed that no one seemed to be listening to him.

'It's like a battle strategy ... you can't leave anything to chance,' I heard him say. As we left the Immigration building under police escort, I noticed that the vehicle waiting to take us back to prison had parked on the other side of the street. The driver motioned us to cross. The Australian Embassy car was parked nearby with its Southern Cross and Union Jack beckoning me to safety. I looked at the police escorting my husband in front. They had not bothered to use the handcuffs on him this time so I figured it would be easy to slip into the Embassy car and lock the doors. I knew the Australian Ambassador was only a few feet behind me. I held my breath and waited, knowing I could not return to Phonthong.

We drew closer to the cars. I felt my heart pounding in my chest. Slowly we walked. Sweat glistened on my forehead and slid slowly down the side of my face. I could see my children calling me from inside the car.

'Mummy come home.'

'I'm coming,' I whispered. By now, I could actually see myself walking to the Embassy car and resting my hand on the door handle. Within seconds, I would be inside and free from the torment of my existence.

'Madam, this way!' the voice ordered. I felt the rough hand of the Lao police officer drag me back to reality.

For a moment, I gazed longingly at the Embassy car. The blue flags that once beckoned me, beckoned me still. If it hadn't been a dream, if I had run to the Embassy car, would they have dragged me from it?

'I'm so sorry,' I cried silently to myself. Thinking of my children and of how much I missed them caused my heart to break. I ignored the solitary tear that fell slowly down my face. It rested in the base of my throat where all the other tears had gone. I just wanted to go home.

CHAPTER TWELVE

Mystery Witness

On 7 June 2001, Ambassador Thwaites wrote a letter to the Chief Prosecutor of Laos stating that he understood the Lao Government was considering our release based on humanitarian grounds. He confirmed that his Embassy would use its best endeavours to ensure we remained at the Settha Palace Hotel, in the capital, and would take our Australian passports to prevent us from leaving the country. The Australian officials involved in the case were convinced that we hadn't a case to answer. Everyone assumed that since there was no evidence of wrongdoing, we would automatically be released. I silently prayed all week that it would happen.

I contemplated whether we would go to court or go home. At times, I thought it would be easier if I just didn't wake up one morning, but then that was selfish of me and I knew it. Nothing in life was certain and this was just another challenge. But in the back of my mind, I had to admit that leaving Phonthong would not be easy.

Anouhack devised a way to get our messages to the outside via his wife who lived in a neighbouring village. He was genuinely sympathetic to our plight and vowed to help us in every way he could. I often wondered why he did not receive the same level of support from his Embassy as we got from ours, and I asked as much.

'I'm half Asian,' he replied.

I felt sorry for the former project manager who had wound up in Phonthong all because of a decision his superiors made without truly considering the implications. Their subcontractors were engaged to complete a construction job for the United Nations. Anouhack's company had supplied them with a cash advance and all the earth moving equipment necessary to complete the task. When they failed to achieve the agreed deadline, Anouhack's superiors ordered him to confiscate the equipment. They would find someone else more competent. Only they did not count on the fact that the Lao Construction company bribed Lao police to hold Anouhack in lieu of his company awarding the subcontractors an appropriate amount of compensation for loss of profit. Effectively, Anouhack was a hostage too.

I began helping him draft a letter to the Canadian Ambassador in Thailand, asking him to take an interest in Anouhack's plight. With four years already behind him, Anouhack was doomed to remain in Phonthong indefinitely if no one helped him.

Anouhack paid the prison police to take his letters outside and his wife paid them a few extra dollars to deliver our messages to our lawyer.

At our next Consular visit, we learned from our Embassy that Anouhack's letter of appeal had been successful. The Canadian Embassy was sending its Consular Officer from Bangkok to Vientiane. It was the first time in four years that Anouhack would receive a visit from his own Embassy. He could barely contain his excitement. I was glad that our detainment had brought some good but I still could not help wishing it had been someone else behind bars and not me, not Kerry.

We called on the Embassy to request International representation for us at the trial we knew was pending.

'It won't even go to court,' our lawyer promised.

'Oh it will go alright,' Kerry threw back at him. 'The guards are laying bets that we'll get ten years each.'

'That'll never happen. It's all taken care of,' Tzovaras responded, leaning closer to Kerry to elaborate that one of his new found friends was closely linked to the President of Laos. He was trying to reassure us.

Of course, with a population of only 5 million people, it was easy to find many well connected Laotians. It did not however mean they could change anything. But just as we had to learn that lesson when we first arrived in Laos, so too would our lawyer.

***

Public exposure was the one thing that the Laos Government sought to avoid and much to their annoyance, my Dad continued to focus the world's attention on us. He called the regime a bunch of terrorists and I couldn't agree with him more. However, the Embassy warned that it wouldn't do us any good to antagonise the authorities. They said they would have no choice but to censor my letters to my father if I kept telling him to get the United Nations involved. A few weeks later, some of my father's letters came to me with sections cut out of the page.

Finally, the Lao Officials announced that they were lodging a case against us that centred on two principle allegations; the alleged loss of 3.5 kilograms of semi-finished stones and 265 items of jewellery. Neither were Kerry's responsibility. The second allegation involved the money I made from my contracts in Thailand. Those funds of course were subject to Thai tax and the KPMG audit report revealed no wrongdoing. The Lao authorities had no evidence whatsoever that we had done anything unlawful, but the taking of hostages was a serious matter indeed. Time was running out if they were to avoid a total disintegration of the long standing bilateral relationship between Laos and Australia.

***

My blue budgerigar had returned to the trees outside my cell. Mon's younger brother Anek stood in the middle of a group of prisoners with his arms stretched high towards the little blue bird, perched on a low tree branch.

'Oh please be careful,' I called to them. Bounchan, Oudai and Anouhack crowded around as the others edged closer and closer. Finally, Anek reached up and caught him in one swift motion. I was thrilled and leapt for joy. Anek came towards me smiling. He placed the little bird in my cupped hands. I kissed its soft feathery head and for that moment, I felt happy. I turned to show Kerry. He sat ten metres away, sweltering in his cell. The police had locked him inside for the weekend but he still managed a smile.

The former Thai congressman wanted the bird and kept pestering me for him.

'Be patient father,' I said.

I knew Phor wanted to set the bird free as was the practice in Thailand. They said it brought good luck to the person who released the bird but I wasn't worried about luck anymore. I had accepted that our journey through Phonthong was beyond our control. If it was our fate to die in this hell then no one could change that fact. Luck would have nothing to do with our survival or our demise.

Carefully I gave the little bird to Phor who smiled down at me as he carefully took it. He prayed to Buddha and as I stood beside him, I closed my eyes and prayed too. Then Phor straightened and bowed his head to his hands and ever so slowly released the little bird. A flash of blue took flight. My budgie was gone.

He flew high into the air and over the walls of Phonthong. I stared over the barbed wire fence to the sky above.

'No worry Mai Kue... the bird brings you a message,' Sue said later in the room. Exactly seven days later, the Lao Government announced that we were going to court. I silently prayed all week for the United Nations to intervene.

While we waited, and as the monsoon rains drenched Phonthong, they forced us to live like pigs in a quagmire. I sat on the narrow concrete veranda waiting for the day to pass. Those locked in the cell sat wishing they weren't. Endless hours of boredom set in and tortured their minds. Pang taught me to sew little flowers on a thin cotton scrap of material. It was something I'd seen other girls do in high school but never bothered to do myself. I much preferred to run laps of our school oval. Now I had all the time in the world to learn the things I'd never learned as a teenager.

Young Vittaya sat on the concrete steps and admired my handiwork.

'What if you don't go home Mai Kue?' he asked, his Hmong face filled with obvious concern.

'We will,' I said with an optimism I didn't feel.

Vittaya looked serious and paused a long time before speaking again. There were so many people walking back and forth that it made our conversation difficult.

'If you are lucky you will go home,' he remarked with brutal honesty.

I saw a terrible sadness in his eyes that he did well to disguise on other occasions. I knew he worried about us leaving.

'Don't worry Vittaya,' I said softly. 'I won't forget you and when I go home I will do everything I can for you.' He smiled but the worry remained in his eyes.

I felt sorry for Vittaya. Like many Hmong who had left Laos there was no Embassy to support them if they got into a problem. They were a people without a country, displaced. How terrible to imagine life like that. To be stuck in a country governed by a regime that didn't care if you lived or died.

Our situation was complex but at least we had hope. Our Embassy never stopped calling for justice and our lawyers tried every way they knew how to secure our release. But Vittaya could cry as much as he wanted and no one would care, not even the United Nations.

'Mai Kue ... if you leave this place, please don't forget us. If you can help send us a little food or money when you go, please do,' Vittaya's voice broke. His brown eyes welled with unshed tears.

'I promise you when I leave here, I will tell the world what I've seen and will try to make a difference to this hell,' I responded. Poor Vittaya couldn't even remember the faces of his children. He no longer cared about his freedom. All he wanted was a picture of his babies.

The following week we met our Embassy. Kerry told Jonathan that the Lao radio reported our pending trial and the news was not encouraging. The most senior official of Laos was already telling the world we were guilty. Our Lao lawyer, Phasith looked tired as he waited patiently for the Ambassador to update us on the latest developments of our case.

'I have so many headaches, Madam,' he said to me towards the end of our Consular meeting. Phasith's workload had increased tenfold because of us and he looked like he needed a break. Hopefully they would not send him to the mountain prisons of Sam Neua for simply acting as our attorney. He said not to worry. If we confessed and paid compensation to the Lao Government then everything would be resolved. The investigation team that returned to Phonthong the next day confirmed this. As we both sat together in a small office next to the interrogation room, they placed a tape recorder on the table and told us to desist in non-cooperative behaviour. It would serve no purpose. Then they requested we confess to our crimes and agree to pay compensation. We refused. A few weeks later, the Prosecutor returned with our Lao lawyer—Phasith. Everyone in the prison began whispering.

'What are they all whispering about, Anouhack?' I asked, as we sat under the tree near the sewage fishponds.

'They're talking about your lawyer, this is most unusual,' he responded.

'Why?' I questioned.

'It is because no-one's lawyer can come here. Only if they are with the one who try to put you in problem.' His voice was quiet. We watched Kerry being led to the room and within half an hour, he walked passed smiling.

'Just more of the same bullshit,' he said. 'They want a confession and even Phasith threatened he'd resign ... ha!' Kerry laughed and continued walking.

'No way?' my mouth gaped open in surprise.

'Don't worry my love ... we'll be fine,' he said with a wink. Phasith waved goodbye as he was leaving. I faked my biggest smile and called to him, wishing him very good luck. I laughed aloud. They wouldn't make me cry—not anymore.

A week later, they returned. The police told Kerry and I to go to the interrogation room.

'Kay go home?' whispered Mon as we walked past.

'I don't know,' was all I could say.

We sat side-by-side on a rickety wooden bench looking from Phasith to the Public Prosecutor. From under the bench seat, I linked my fingers with Kerry's. They shoved a sheet of paper towards us, written in Lao language.

'Sign!' said the Public Prosecutor and placed his pen on top of the document. Kerry and I just looked at our lawyer with puzzled expressions.

'This document is the record of charges against you,' Phasith explained carefully, not meeting our eyes.

'What?' Kerry asked.

'It says you have been found guilty of embezzlement of Government assets, destroying of assets and evidence, and a breach of taxation regulations.'

'And when was the court hearing?' asked Kerry. His tone strained.

'The court proceedings will be formalised next week,' Phasith concluded.

'Which means what exactly?' I asked, not at all certain I wanted to hear more.

'Which means that you will be taken to the court and it will become official,' Phasith explained. I swallowed and began to shake.

'It's alright babe. Just relax,' Kerry said quietly.

The reality of them finding us guilty in the absence of a crime was something neither of us had experienced before. How on earth could they get away with it?

'You must sign this document to say you have been informed and accept that the court will proceed,' counselled Phasith. His tone was official.

'But we can't even read what it says,' Kerry responded.

'Then you will sign your name to the bottom and write that you cannot read Lao language,' Phasith advised. The Prosecutor said he would attempt to get us transferred to better accommodation until the trial. He made hints that we would be released at the court but of course, he could have been lying for all we knew.

'Please just sign the document,' ordered Phasith.

I watched Kerry write a short statement that he was signing under duress and couldn't understand the document or the language it contained. He scrawled a signature underneath the statement and dated it. He had signed 'K. Duress' and not K. Danes. After I'd signed the same K. Duress, Phasith smiled awkwardly and told us to be patient, that it would all be over soon. Why did I have the feeling that by it being over, it meant that things had taken a turn for the worse? A feeling of dread washed over me.

The Public Prosecutor gathered his briefcase and returned his gold pen to his shirt pocket. We asked Phasith if we were going home but all he said was, 'Be patient'.

'Kay, Kerry what happen?' asked Anouhack who'd been eagerly watching as was every other prisoner who could get a view of the interrogation room.

'He said we've been found guilty and are going to court next week,' Kerry explained.

'Oh no!' cried Anouhack.

***

One afternoon, Anouhack brought good news.

'Kay, I just heard from another prisoner that Mr Downer has said that the Australian Government is determined to release you and Kerry. Your case has become a significant issue in the relationship with Laos. Your Government expects Laos to treat you properly.'

I listened the whole time without interrupting because I knew that soon someone would try to listen to our conversation and, most likely, report back to the police.

'Oh and one more thing,' he turned to look at me. 'Harold Christe?' he asked if I knew the name.

'Harold Christensen?' I asked puzzled. 'He's the Financial Manager for Gem Mining Lao.' He was also a good friend.

'He's coming to Laos,' Anouhack recited, very matter-of-factly.

'You're kidding me?' I gaped at him. The Public Prosecutor who made a five-minute visit to the prison later that day confirmed it.

'It's true alright,' said Kerry, walking from the interrogation room. 'Says he's coming to be the witness against us,' he laughed out loud.

'What?' I questioned in surprise.

'They reckon he's their star witness. Ain't that a trick?' Kerry stood beside us not caring that we weren't supposed to be so near each other. 'I sure hope he's got a good plan to get out of Laos afterwards!' Kerry threw over his shoulder and walked away. 'They just might keep him here!'

'Maybe they take him and let you go home Kay?' said Anouhack. For a moment, I allowed myself the luxury of thinking that might happen. But could I really leave my husband?

As I watched him walk to the steps leading up to the narrow concrete veranda that ran along the entire breadth of his cell block, I knew I couldn't. We were in this together and as much as I wanted to go home, I feared losing my husband more. I hadn't the right to betray him like that. When a week later they took us from the prison to the Department of Immigration, we did so under heavier than usual armed escort. I craned my neck to look beyond the driver's seat and window screen, hoping to catch a glimpse of Harold. As we neared the Immigration building, we spotted him standing out front with Jonathan Thwaites and Louise Waugh.

'There he is,' Kerry spoke quietly.

Harold turned simultaneously and towered over most of the Laotians. His beard was still as scruffy as it had always been and his curly hair tinged with grey, rested just above his shirt collar. For some reason I always thought Harold looked more like a rugged surfer than a high-powered finance manager. He had an air of casual calm about him but there was no mistaking his strong personality and no-nonsense approach. We met with Jonathan and Louise for our Consular visit first but afterwards they told us to wait while the so-called confrontation took place. Our Lao lawyer was the only outsider permitted to attend the meeting. When the Prosecutor stood before us with his questions, Kham-kue-ung from the Ministry of Foreign Affairs translated, since the Prosecutor still refused to speak English.

'Kerry, Harold says you steal the sapphires,' said Kham-kue-ung.

'That's not true,' Kerry responded.

'Harold, Kerry says you steal the sapphires,' Kham-kue-ung translated and Harold denied it.

'So, Kerry, you agree you steal the sapphires as Harold says you do?' Kham-kue-ung asked.

'What?' Kerry laughed at the question. We all looked at each other amused. Perhaps their English needed a bit of refining and so it went on like this for an hour. They never asked me a single question.

As we were about to leave I asked Phasith if he had a headache. He turned and smiled as he put his arm around the Prosecutor's shoulder. 'I have a headache, but I have paracetamol right here.' They both laughed and showed their close friendship. In the hallway moments later, we said our goodbyes to the Embassy and to Harold.

'Take care of yourself Kay', Harold said gently. He hugged me before turning to embrace Kerry. 'Probably see you tonight mate,' he joked.

'God I hope not,' Kerry replied. 'Thanks for coming Harold. I doubt there's anything that will prevent the court hearing next week but thanks all the same. It means a lot to both of us that you came.'

'No worries Kerry. I just wish you guys weren't caught up in all of this,' Harold replied.

The Ambassador walked us down the dark stairwell to the lobby filled with Lao police. I felt the anger burning in my subconscious, making me look around the foyer with hatred at the dozens of dark brown eyes that stared at me from behind their counters. I pushed my chin forward in defiance and wished with all my heart that I could just simply turn around and tell everyone to go to hell!

As we travelled back to Phonthong, I wondered if Harold *would* join us later that night. Oddly, the prison police allowed us to keep our letters and for a second I was happy. I walked through the black door with a smile on my face and my letters in my hand. This wasn't lost on the other prisoners who rushed forward to meet me.

'Let us see. You get any photo of your children?' one prisoner asked. I was glad to say that I had received photographs and there was just enough time to share these with my friends. I passed the photos of our children around and watched their faces light up.

'You are so lucky Madam,' cried Bounchan. 'We never see our children,' he stated simply.

In the quiet of the evening, I read my letters aloud for the girls in my cell to hear. My sister Karen said she didn't know what to write but thought she'd send us both some extracts from other emails my family received from a few of our loyal supporters. The warm messages of family, friends and strangers alike were so uplifting, and I felt truly grateful that so many people were thinking of us hidden away in this hell.

When sleep finally summoned me, I tucked my letters away and told myself that no matter what happened, I would not be forgotten. I had no idea how long I had been asleep when I suddenly awoke to a disturbance at the prison gate.

'A car!' Toom whispered to Pang. Something was wrong. In a place where routine controlled everything, it was easy to notice the unusual. I sat upright and watched Toom looking towards the black door. The guard in the tower was at the ready too with his AK assault rifle, also looking in that direction.

'A new prisoner coming!' Toom said.

'I think it is Harold,' I said absently.

'Harold? Who is Harold?'

'He was at the Embassy today,' I replied to Pang. But it wasn't Harold. It wasn't even a new prisoner. Whatever it was caused a great deal of commotion. For half an hour, we strained to hear what was impossible to hear. We watched as the guard in the tower looked down at whatever it was behind the big black door to freedom.

'Sound like two cars,' Toom whispered to Pang. 'They go,' she said and lit a cigarette. Pang looked at me, put her Vicks vapour stick to her nose, and inhaled. She always did that whenever she got nervous.

'Oh, I gotta get out of this hell,' Pang sighed as she lay back on her blanket. Her eyes held mine briefly before staring blankly at the ceiling above.

'Die Lao,' Sue Yang whispered beside her. Pang and Sue always slept side by side nearest the window. I often wondered how they'd coped these last four years. They were much stronger than I would have been. I closed my eyes silently praying for strength. God help me get through this, as I too began to stare at the ceiling above.

'Sleep Kay,' said the quiet voice of reason. 'Don't think too much,' Mon whispered to me and gently stroked my arm. If only I could go home! Mon fanned me with a thin plastic bottle Toom had beaten flat. With the artificial breeze caressing my hot skin, I willed myself to sleep and hoped my dreams would carry me somewhere safe.

In the morning, a police officer stood outside our cell and asked Pang for some shampoo. I watched as they talked quietly. Sue Yang was looking at me and fanning herself. Her back was to the officer but I knew she heard every word he spoke. Her eyes signalled to me that they were talking about me. When the officer left, Pang turned and told me to sit beside her. She whispered quickly and quietly. 'Mai Kue, he said last night Bounmaly come for you and Kerry.'

'What?' I whispered as my voice filled with shock.

'Sshh… quiet. Don't want the others to know because that officer is good… and risk a lot to tell us this,' she chastised me. 'He said the Major call the police to stand against the black door when they will not leave… they have guns… many guns… and briefcase,' she whispered quickly.

'What do you think was inside that briefcase?' I invited her response.

'I don't know,' she replied cautiously. I knew from past interrogations they carried guns in the briefcase. Some prisoners said they also carried mind-altering drugs. Joe Hay told me that they used these on him and after the interview, he was never the same.

'The police said to tell you not to worry… they cannot come anymore, in the night!'

'My God Pang! Who can stop them if they want to take us?' I cried. The other girls in my cell knew something was terribly wrong but they also saw how upset I was and refrained from asking any questions. Pang would tell them eventually. The whole prison would probably find out by the end of the day. That was just the way it was in Phonthong. There were never any secrets.

'Mai Kue, you must not tell anyone… you will get that officer in big trouble!' Pang cautioned.

What could I do? Whom could I tell? If I told Kerry, then he would surely tell the Embassy and then that officer would be taken away. The police would come in the night and take us too. The Embassy couldn't prevent that nor could they protect us. Bounmaly was right. We could just disappear as so many people did in Laos. I agonized the whole day wondering what to do and when midday passed, I dressed for our visit to Immigration. I picked up a small bottle of shampoo and made my way to the bottom of the stairs of our cell block. Kerry was standing on the veranda combing his hair with his fingers. He turned and saw me staring at him. His own eyes asked a question as he looked at me.

'Anouhack, give this to Kerry,' I called. The police officer lazily glanced in our direction but paid very little attention. He took the bait. He thought I was talking to Anouhack and telling him to give Kerry the shampoo. Just as well, the police could not speak English. 'They came last night to take us but the officer blocked their way… I'm so afraid,' I spoke evenly as if I was discussing the weather.

I walked away and went to sit under my favourite tree. Anouhack came over a few minutes later and set up his hammock between the two branches nearby. He began to fan himself and maintained a blank expression as I whispered across to him what Pang had told me. After about twenty minutes, he left. He didn't go straight to Kerry.

He went to his room at the back of the cell block and checked on the Chinese man who had taken ill the night before. Sometime later, I noticed Anouhack talking with Kerry. The police officer called, telling me it was time to go to Immigration.

I left it to Kerry to tell Jonathan about our visitors the night before. When we left the Immigration building to return to Phonthong, Jonathan hugged me and said not to worry. He told us that Harold Christensen had departed Laos safely, though not without drama. Harold wrote us a letter that was never delivered because it was too critical of the Lao Government. But the Embassy held it on file. Harold had had a few tense days, never knowing whether he was under suspicion or not, and constantly fearing that he might become a replacement scapegoat. He remained resolute however, even greeting Bounmaly by saying, 'Hello wanker, are you going to tell another pack of lies today?' before he found out that Bounmaly and everybody else in the interrogation room spoke enough English to understand the meaning of what he had said. He left feeling that our release was not far away, as he had clearly explained there was no crime to answer, but reflected on this in his last line: 'How silly of me.'

In supporting us, Harold placed his own freedom and his life at risk. Not one other person, apart from my own father, ever made such a sacrifice. But there continued to be friends rallying in our support and for that, we were grateful. Friends like Norma and Brigadier Bill Jamieson were amongst those who never gave up on us despite the fact that some questioned why they would even bother. They wrote letters regularly, not really knowing if I was getting them, as an Australian Special Forces veteran named Mick Malone also did. This was important to us. We needed to hear from friends. We needed to know that they didn't believe the lies told about us.

***

Despite the frustrating delays, and the laying of formal charges, the Australian Embassy remained cautiously optimistic that we would be released soon. They were of the impression that there was an 'in-principle' agreement among relevant Lao authorities to release us, although the precise manner and timing was uncertain.

On 15 June 2001, Jonathan Thwaites requested an appointment with Foreign Minister Lengsavad to discuss the status of our case. The Australian Prime Minister wrote another letter, demanding that we be kept safe at Phonthong. Soon after, the prison police called us the VIPs of Phonthong and took their responsibility for our safety more seriously.

On 18 June 2001, the Embassy lodged, under the Embassy cover letter, a full copy of the legal brief prepared by our lawyer for Lengsavad. Our lawyer was advised that a brief court appearance would take place prior to our release on either 19 or 20 June 2001. Tzovaras told the Embassy that there was an idea in place for a two-stage release. But then it changed. He then said that we would be taken straight from the courthouse to the airport, if there were an appropriate flight. If not, we would be detained overnight in a hotel and taken to the airport the next day.

We met the Embassy officials again on 21 June 2001. I asked them for sleeping tablets because I was finding it increasingly difficult to shut out the horrors that night brought. I'd lost over 15 kilograms of weight and it wasn't all fat either. I lost muscle tone from the prolonged stress. The Lumpini police had returned to torture the Africans. They were torturing young Michael and I saw them push his head deep into a bucket of sewage water just before the prison police dragged us away for our Consular visit. The Prisoners were called to revive him twice. I wondered if he had survived.

I felt my sanity slipping as the shock of their degrading treatment numbed me. How many times had I rocked back and forth on my haunches beside the Bodhee Tree? How many times had I wondered if we would ever be free of the horrors of Phonthong? I was so traumatised that I almost forgot we were still in a Consular meeting.

Kerry spoke to our children for the first time since his arrest and I was glad he did. We weren't sure when and if we'd see them again. Kerry told Jonathan that the guards upgraded the security at the prison. They were always armed whenever they took us to Immigration. When we walked down the stairwell I heard Kerry tell him that he worried about an ambush on the way to the court. I followed closely behind with Tan Phet at my side and Tzovaras reassured Kerry that we would be cleared. I honestly thought he was insane. But I had to admit that despite my feelings towards him, he had built an amazing legal case. The evidence in our defence, lodged with the President of the Court, was overwhelming. But would the Laos Government let us go home?

The Laos Ministry of Foreign Affairs sent a diplomatic note to the Australian Embassy. The hearing would take place at 8.30am on 28 June 2001. We just had to wait.

CHAPTER THIRTEEN

The Verdict

On the eve of our trial, Tzovaras convinced the Embassy that we would make a brief court appearance before leaving Laos at 1.25pm. The Australian Government would provide staff at 'transit posts' to assist appropriately during our return to Australia. They made flight bookings under the names of Mr Kevin Davies and Mrs Kathryn Davies on the VN841 Flight to Ho Chi Minh City via Phnom Penh.

It was 28 June 2001, two days before our son Nathan's 8th birthday, and the day the Laos Criminal Court would make a ruling on our case. We could walk free, or we could face up to seven years in jail. We just did not know. My cell mates wished me luck as I ran behind the steel door in our cell and stripped off my sweaty grey t-shirt. I couldn't believe they were taking us for trial. Did they really expect us to get ready as if it were just another ordinary day?

My blue shorts dropped down around my ankles. 'Here, your pants!' said Pang and threw me the dark green drill pants and white t-shirt I always wore to Embassy visits. They were the only clothes I had that the sewage hadn't eaten. Pang laughed as I stood in my underwear. Sue giggled from the doorway.

'I can't get my pants done up,' I wailed. My hands shook so badly.

'It's okay Mai Kue. Just wear your underwear to court,' Sue laughed.

'I'll do it,' Pang said softly. 'Be brave, it will be okay.'

I looked to my friend for reassurance and quietly pondered that today I would learn my fate. All this time, I had worried that this day would come. Sometimes I wished it would hurry while other times, I hoped our government might have found another way to secure our freedom. What would tomorrow bring? Where would I be? Where would my husband be? Would we be together? I began to fear the unknown as questions raced around my mind. I began to fear leaving my cell and those I'd been detained with now for seven long months. It seemed as if forever had passed and I'd barely noticed.

'Don't faint okay?' Pang smiled. She said it was inevitable that the court would find us guilty because there was no other way that we could leave Laos. She said they announced it on the local Lao radio already. The prison police said we should have just paid money and gone home. It was the Lao way. But I never understood why everyone around me thought that it was okay to sell your integrity in the hope of gaining your freedom. I had always thought that my integrity was worth any sacrifice. Obviously, I still had quite a lot to learn.

'I'll be praying for you Mai Kue,' Pang said as she finished tying my shoelaces, then quietly crossed the floorboards to retrieve her dark blue prison jacket hanging on the wall. Sue stopped joking around long enough to enter the room and hug me.

'Good luck, Mai Kue, don't worry!' she said seriously. 'If you lucky, you get a sentence and go home!'

'Here put this on!' Pang ordered, handing me the jacket. I slipped my arms into each sleeve as Pang stepped down onto the concrete floor. Her fingers brushed mine aside to do up each tiny button.

'It will be over quickly,' she said. I took one final look at my friends standing in front of me and sighed. I hugged them both as if it was good-bye.

'Good luck Mai Kue,' they said in unison. I turned to walk down the steps of our cell block and saw other prisoners standing nearby. Kerry was waiting at the foot of the steps with Anouhack. He wore the same dark blue prison jacket I did.

'You ready babe?' he smiled with all the confidence I wasn't feeling.

'I'm terrified,' I responded but forced myself to half smile.

'Good luck!' everyone called.

'Don't worry, we'll be here when you get back,' some joked.

Each of the prisoners in turn, and in their own way, said goodbye and wished us luck. Oudai, Chao, Phor, and Anouhack were all eager to give us their blessings. Even some of the more civilized police wished us good luck. Tan Sombut made sure we were both searched thoroughly before allowing us through the black door. I felt butterflies the size of elephants pounding away in the pit of my stomach as we left the prison.

'It's okay babe,' Kerry said encouragingly.

On shaky legs, I walked a few feet to where a white van was parked. As I feared, it hadn't any windows except for those in the front cab where the driver sat. Kerry climbed in first and moved to the rear of the van to sit on the vinyl covered bench seat that ran the full length of the inside wall. A police officer sat opposite him. I slid in beside him with another police officer on my left. The door slammed shut and locked from the outside. Within minutes, we began to move away.

It was dark inside the van except for where the light that filtered through a tiny perspex window at the rear. I watched the prison fade into the distance, hoping it would be the last time I saw it. My heart pounded as the van lunged forward and then sideways as we left the bumpy dirt road. The siren screaming overhead did nothing to drown out the rain that beat down like a hundred jackhammers. Disorientated, I clutched the arm of the young police officer beside me. I thought he would need pliers to detach my fingers from his arm but he didn't seem bothered. 'Do not worry,' he encouraged.

I'm sure by the time we arrived at the court I looked as white as a ghost. Stepping from the van, I felt physically sick. Why couldn't I breathe?

'You okay?' Kerry said noticing my white pallor.

'Sure.' I managed a response and told myself to maintain my dignity. That was the only thing they couldn't take from me.

I was allowed a few brief seconds to collect myself, before we climbed the dirty concrete steps to the court, ignoring the camera that flashed in front of us. We rounded a corner and the same Thai cameraman positioned himself again for what I supposed would make a great shot for the front page of the evening paper. As he was about to take our picture I raised my hand in front of the lens.

'Fuck off,' I whispered.

***

I stepped into the courtroom an unwilling participant. I saw the faces of a handful of strangers staring back at me. I turned slowly, just as Jonathan came striding towards me. He wore an expressionless mask but his blue eyes held genuine concern.

'Hi,' I whispered as we embraced.

'For God's sake where's the UN?' Kerry barked behind me. His voice carried across the quietness of the courtroom, breaking the uncomfortable silence that hung in the air.

'Now, Kerry, never mind that,' Tzovaras said, appearing from nowhere. 'Everything on track,' he whispered. 'When you go before the judge, just keep your answers short.'

As we moved towards the middle of the courtroom, I hoped that with any luck we'd get less than the twenty years that the Gem Mining directors got. I looked at Kerry for reassurance.

'We're fucked,' was all he said.

We sat on an old, brown church pew that leaned against a dirty, mouldy concrete wall of the dilapidated courthouse. There would be no jury and no cross-examination process. We would simply go before three judges to be sentenced.

It was unbearably hot where we sat. The ceiling fans overhead were off but I noticed those in the centre of the room were on. Did they turn ours off deliberately? The windows behind me were cracked but not enough to let in any breeze. I swiped at a small black mosquito circling my head wondering if it carried malaria like those inside the prison. The walls around me were stained and paint-chipped and the floor was covered in dust. It was a desolate place.

The Ambassador smiled at me reassuringly but I felt more alone than ever. Did Jonathan believe that we were going home? Louise sat beside him and next to her, the Embassy translator. Our former Operations Manager arrived. His eyes met mine briefly, as he sat in the row just behind the Embassy staff. To his right sat one of our interrogators from the secret police who had obviously positioned himself behind the Embassy for a reason.

Lengsavad's cohorts looked as excited as three monkeys: 'See no evil, hear no evil, and speak no evil.' Only in their case, they were evil.

Our Lao lawyer, Phasith, sought permission to sit between Kerry and I after we made a boisterous commotion that we couldn't hear the judge. When he was denied, Jonathan raised his own objections and the court was forced to concede. It was a small victory and probably our only one for the day. It didn't matter really, since the trial was just a face-saving exercise. But Kerry said it was important that they at least appear to follow correct procedure. According to the Universal Declaration of Human Rights and the

International Covenant on Civil and Political Rights to which Laos became a signatory on 7 December 2000, Kerry and I had the right to expect a fair trial. We had the right to a public hearing, the right to prepare a defence and to be assisted by a lawyer, and the right not to be tortured or ill treated in detention.

But every single one of our rights had thus far been violated, including those written in the Lao Law Concerning Criminal Case Proceedings (1989), which detailed the procedures to be followed in arrest, detention, and criminal prosecutions.

The reality of it was that very few cases ever made it to court. Those that did were denied access to lawyers and often remained in ignorance of the charges against them. Some were even known to receive an extra two years for asking for legal representation. The government said they should trust the court to decide their fate. I wondered how many extra years we'd get as a result of Kerry's outbursts.

'Just keep your eyes on me Kay and you'll get through this,' I recalled Jonathan saying, just before the trial began.

Three judges sat on the judicial bench, which was nothing more than three school desks slapped together, and a microphone centred in the middle of one. Their stage was set higher than the main body of the courtroom. A second microphone was positioned on the floor in front of the presiding judge from which the Defence and witnesses could address the court and answer questions. Mr Chan-than-kone was the President of the Criminal Court of the Vientiane Municipality. He looked like a shrivelled up prune in his pristine white shirt and greasy black hair. Mr Rasphone sat next to him and being younger had a particular arrogance about him. On his other side was the formidable looking Mrs Intha-phon who stared down her nose at us with skinny hawk-like eyes. Mr Sing-som-phou sat to the far right of the judges as the court adjudicator. The Public Prosecutor Mingboutha stood in the box on the left of the stage.

Tzovaras sat in the front row as a silent observer. I wondered if he knew that he was offending the judges as I watched his left leg cross over his right and swinging casually towards them. In Laos, the head is considered the highest part of the body, while the feet are considered the lowest, both literally and figuratively. Touching someone's head or pointing at people or things with the feet is considered extremely rude. What was natural to most foreigners was offensive to Laotians. I almost felt like berating our lawyer for his ignorance just as the police had done to me several times when I first went to Phonthong prison.

The Judge called on Prosecutor Mingboutha to take the stand while Phasith invited Kerry to walk with him to the centre microphone. Phasith translated for Kerry and told the court his name, age and occupation.

'You have been found guilty of embezzlement, destruction of evidence and violation of the State tax regulation. This is the reason for your detainment. Do you agree?' asked the Prosecutor. Phasith translated.

'I'm innocent,' Kerry responded.

'Were you the Manager of Lao Securicor?' asked the Prosecutor.

'Yes, I've been the manager there for two years,' Kerry replied.

'Did you have an agreement with Gem Mining Lao and what is the detail?'

'We had two agreements. One for their office and one for their private residence.'

'The regulation of your security company is supposed to provide security. Did you violate the regulation of the security company?' he pressed further.

'No.'

'When did you take control of Gem Mining Company?'

'I was instructed by our lawyer that I had been appointed as representative to Gem Mining two days after the Directors of Gem

Mining left Laos. But the appointment was never enforced because the Laos authorities rejected my appointment to that position.'

'Did you obtain permission from the Lao Authorities to look after the gems?'

'No I didn't. The Government hadn't yet seized control of Gem Mining. I merely put the processes in place to prevent any loss.'

'Did you know that Gem Mining had problems with the Lao Government?'

'I only heard the rumour but did not know the exact details,' replied Kerry.

'Did you know who was the owner of the stones, gems and everything?' he asked.

'I knew that Gem Mining was owned by Julie Bruns and Bjarne Jeppeson. I did not know anything about the ownership of the jewellery because it was not part of our company's responsibility.'

'You should have asked the lawyer,' the Prosecutor commented.

'I asked our lawyer if we should continue to provide security to Gem Mining in their absence and it was agreed that we should. Otherwise our company might have been liable for breaking our contract,' Kerry replied.

'How many items of jewellery you put somewhere?' the Prosecutor asked. 'Were there other people present at that time?'

'My secretary, Miss Ting, and Harold Christensen were present. Harold opened the safe and put the boxes inside that contained 156 pieces of jewellery. He then closed the safe,' Kerry said.

'So you put scotch tape over the safe corner yourself?' the Prosecutor asked.

'Yes. I put my signature across the tape too. It wasn't very good tape but it was all we had since there are no security devices available to us in Laos that we could have used instead. If anyone tampered with the safe then the tape would break across my signature,' said Kerry. 'We then took the inventory and put it inside the safe and made a copy for our lawyers.'

'Did you inform the Lao authorities?' the Prosecutor pressed on with his questions.

'I informed Mr Bounmaly Vilayvong, from the Lao Ad Hoc Committee,' said Kerry.

'Was he present when you put the jewellery in the safe?'

'No he wasn't. I went with our company lawyers to a meeting with the Ad Hoc committee the next day and informed them and Bounmaly what we had done.'

'Why didn't you cooperate with the authorities when they want to look inside the safe?' the Prosecutor asked.

'We were not responsible for the safe according to the Memorandum of Understanding,' Kerry explained.

'Did the Ad Hoc Committee sign this document?'

'Yes. As did the Chief of the Village, the lawyers for Gem Mining, Harold Christensen and myself on behalf of Lao Securicor. The court must have the document?'

The Prosecutor looked towards the judges and smiled. 'We have not seen this document. You should have submitted it to the Court!' he concluded.

He knew perfectly well that we had been prevented from accessing our paperwork at Lao Securicor. He also knew that our lawyer had submitted a 317-page book of evidence, which sat in front of the judge, unopened and in full view of the court.

'The key to the safe is where?' he asked.

'The keys are inside the safe. You open the safe with the combination, which I don't have, and then you see the two keys hanging in the door. These keys are only used to change the combination, not open the safe,' Kerry explained.

'Who looks after the key inside the safe?' the Prosecutor asked.

'No one. The key is inside the safe.'

The Judge smiled wickedly and revealed a box filled with hundreds of keys. They were from Gem Mining. We didn't know what they were for, but they looked like filing drawer and office desk keys. I remembered Kerry bundling them into a plastic shoebox the day we went to lock down Gem Mining. Kerry told our staff to secure the keys at our office, then he ordered our maintenance man to change all the main entry locks. He then locked our guard inside to secure the building. A new guard was changed every eight hours but always with the same instruction; let no one else in or out.

'Which one is the key to open the safe?' the judge asked.

'The safe only opens by combination,' Kerry replied simply.

'Do you know this letter that appoints you as the one responsible for the security of everything?' the Prosecutor asked, changing the subject. He held up a letter written on the Gem Mining letterhead.

'The Lao Government did not accept my appointment,' said Kerry in his defence.

The Judge read another letter aloud. It was a notice that no access would be granted to the Gem Mining Office as at 6 June 2000.

'Is it your signature on the bottom?' asked the Judge.

'I cannot see it,' Kerry responded. The judge called for Phasith to show Kerry the letter.

'It looks like a photo copy of my signature. And yes, it is our company stamp because your police took it from my office … among other things!' Kerry replied.

'So after you issued this notice no-one could enter Gem Mining office without your authority?' asked the Prosecutor.

'We were told by our client to secure their office,' Kerry responded.

'So one month after the Director of Gem Mining run away from Laos, you took strict control. So anything lost must be your responsibility,' he declared.

'No. We didn't have access straight away but no loss was ever reported and we handed back, to the government, everything that we were entrusted to secure,' Kerry replied.

Mingboutha became agitated. Kerry stood helplessly before the Lao court and government officials sitting in the back rows.

'Is it true that you did not co-operate with the Ad Hoc Committee?'

'It is not true,' Kerry responded. 'There was no order from the Lao Government to seize control of Gem Mining so my staff did the right thing in questioning them,' Kerry stated.

'It is the evidence that the Defendant did not co-operate,' the Prosecutor stated to the Judges.

'They didn't have the order to seize Gem Mining. My guards were simply doing their job,' said Kerry.

'You did not co-operate with the authorities regarding the safe!' the Prosecutor accused.

'But I did. When the authorities came and ordered the Gem Mining property to be handed to them, I immediately complied,' said Kerry.

'Why did you take the computer away?' the Prosecutor questioned, suddenly changing the subject.

'I was authorised to secure the computer at our head office. No data was erased.'

'Did you inform the Lao Authorities?' asked the Prosecutor.

'They weren't in charge of Gem Mining so we were not required to inform them.'

'But all the property was frozen. Your lawyer knew this so why did you take it?' the Prosecutor asked.

'If Gem Mining was subject to an order then our lawyer failed to mention it. In any case, she confirmed that it was appropriate for us to secure the property in the interest of all parties.'

'Who is the company DP Protection?' the Prosecutor asked suddenly.

'My wife traded as DP Protection to do security in Thailand,' Kerry responded.

'Did you pay tax on the money from your activities in Thailand?'

'My wife worked as a consultant in Thailand and paid tax according to Thai law. I was not involved in her work.'

'Did your wife participate in the removal of the computer from Gem Mining?' the Judge interjected.

'My wife made sure the computer was shut down properly before it was transferred to our head office for storage.'

'But you had the order from the Public Prosecutor to freeze the assets—so why remove the computer? Why didn't you ask permission from the Court or Public Prosecutors' office?'

'I did not know about any freezing order and was instructed by our contracted client to secure their assets,' Kerry repeated.

'Before accepting the responsibility, you should have checked why Julie Bruns gave you authority to do the illegal thing,' the Judge ordered. 'The computer contained information about sapphires and you took the computer and destroyed that evidence!'

'We were authorised by Julie through our lawyers to secure the computer at our head office. The information was still on the computer up until my detainment,' Kerry explained calmly.

'Why did you not hand over the sapphires to the Ad Hoc Committee? Why did you put it in the safe?' the Judge barked, clearly not at all happy with the Prosecutor's attempt to extract a false confession.

'I handed over 1.7 tonne of sapphires according to our Memorandum of Understanding. The safe was the responsibility of Gem Mining and not me, nor Lao Securicor,' Kerry responded, determined not to let them intimidate him.

I watched Tzovaras leave the courtroom. He said before the trial began that his intermediaries would advise him throughout the proceedings if there were any changes to our scheduled departure.

'Did you know why Julie appointed you as her representative?' the female judge asked.

'Probably because we were providing security services to Gem Mining and she trusted us,' Kerry replied.

'Did you know about the letter before they left that she would appoint you as the Gem Mining representative?'

'I never knew anything about the appointment or the letter until our lawyer sent her staff to our office with it,' Kerry responded truthfully. 'It was explained to me that the appointment was only temporary, until the Gem Mining Directors returned,' Kerry concluded.

'Do you remember exactly the contents and wording of the letter?' the female judge asked.

'No,' Kerry explained.

'If you don't remember the wording exactly then you don't know. How could you go in there to take control?' the female judge accused.

'My employer, Jardine Securicor, engaged foreign lawyers based in Laos and told me to follow their instructions for all legal matters and besides that, the Lao authorities also agreed that our company secure the office until the matter with Gem Mining was resolved,' said Kerry.

The interrogation continued for two hours until finally the judge called for a short recess. Jonathan argued with the police about taking us back to prison.

'If you don't bring them back here safely then you'll be in big trouble!' he declared.

★★★

We arrived back at Phonthong and everyone had been locked in their cells. Tan Suvvany said we could stay outside on the veranda so long as we behaved. He sat near the interrogation room, watching. The rain poured down in thick droplets. I was too nervous to eat and gave my lunch to Pi Chao who was anxious for good news.

The atmosphere in the prison became electric as the drama unfolded. An hour later, the police called us to the interrogation room for another body search. Then we were taken outside to the same white van that waited to return us to the courthouse.

'There's your mate,' said Kerry, when we were seated half an hour later. I followed Kerry's gaze. Bounmaly sat only a metre from me. He looked impressively evil with his sleek black hair combed away from his forehead.

'That's not a good sign,' Kerry whispered. I took my turn in front of the Lao judges and wondered if I would be treated any better than my husband. I was so nervous that my knees felt weak.

'It's okay, Madam,' soothed Prasith.

It was the first time in my life I had ever been in any sort of problem with the law. I had no experience of standing in front of a judge, let alone three; to answer for a crime I absolutely didn't commit. How does one prepare for that type of experience? I had no idea.

'Who told you to collect the jewellery?' asked the Prosecutor.

'I had nothing to do with that,' I stated honestly.

'Were you involved with your husband in controlling Gem Mining?'

'No,' I replied.

'Have you been to that premises?'

'Yes,' I said.

'Did you use the computer?'

'I switched off a computer which was already in a shut down mode. Then I told Kerry that it was safe to turn off and he unplugged it - this was done to prevent their staff from using or tampering with the computer.'

'How many times you went back to Gem Mining?'

'I don't know. In two years, I went there a few times,' I replied.

'You don't know how many times?'

'No.'

'Maybe one, maybe five?'

'I couldn't tell you exactly,' I responded.

'So the court will decide how many times you went there,' the Prosecutor concluded. 'Why do you not pay tax for DP Protection?'

'My work in Thailand has nothing to do with Laos. But in any case, the tax was paid in Thailand,' I said.

'How many branches you have in Lao?'

'None.'

'What about Lao Securicor?' he prompted.

'I am an employee of Lao Securicor and pay my tax in Laos. I asked our lawyer about my consulting as a security advisor in another country and she said it was perfectly legal.'

'But you didn't inform the Lao Government about this business in Thailand. It is a violation of Lao law,' the Prosecutor challenged.

'My lawyer said there was no violation of the law,' I countered.

'Did you tell the authorities that you were leaving Lao PDR on 23 December?'

'I told Bounmaly,' I said.

The Prosecutor called Bounmaly to the stand.

'What did you tell her on 23 December 2000?'

'I suspected they were about to leave the country so I told them stay and showed her the warrant for her arrest and her husband's arrest,' Bounmaly lied.

'Bullshit,' I whispered to Phasith. 'He lies.'

'Be patient Madam,' Phasith replied as he gently patted my arm. My interrogation lasted two hours and they twisted everything I said and even tried to get me to confirm Kerry's forged signature as legitimate.

'Don't worry Babe,' said Kerry as he watched me fall limply onto the bench seat.

The Prosecutor called the Lao Gem Mining manager to give evidence. Sommay had worked for GML since 1994. He testified that Kerry and I often went to their office and along with the testimony of other Gem Mining Lao employees—Mr Nokeo, Ms Latsamy and Mr Chanthavong, that I unplugged the connection and that caused the destruction of all the evidence in the computer.

It simply wasn't possible and besides, none of them were even there. We learned later that Nokeo, Latsamy and Chanthavong had been arrested a week after I was detained. Unlike me, they did have a large quantity of sapphires in their possession. It was in their interests to point the finger at Kerry and I. The Lao court accused me of conducting business in Laos without a licence but my company in Thailand had nothing to do with Laos.

At 4pm, the judges announced they would accept the final summary from the Prosecutor. Phasith asked if he could present a final summary but the judges questioned why he would even ask such a thing. To his credit, Phasith persisted and presented an impressive argument in his closing address. He spoke with quiet confidence though his hands trembled. I doubt there was one person that day who didn't want to stand beside him for moral support. His defence was impressive and by its conclusion not one person could have thought we were not innocent. But it didn't matter what he said. We were found guilty before the hearing even started.

Mingboutha had less trouble delivering his summary. He held up a pre-typed five-page statement from the judges, and proceeded to read it in a monotonous voice. He was impressive, as he stood high on the podium. His white shirt was pristine and pressed for the occasion. I got the impression today was as much his day as it was ours. His thick dark hair was parted slightly off-centre and combed from left to right across his brow. The yellow tie I'd seen before, but today it was radiant. He wore black trousers pressed to perfection. His gold ring flashed occasionally as he held the papers. There was no expression on his face. His voice seemed flat and different in some way. I'd heard his voice many times before, more animated, but today he seemed like a stranger. Was it guilt?

I hoped for at least regret. When he finished, the judges left the courtroom to deliberate for twenty-five minutes. They returned with a substantial typewritten verdict, which obviously had been prepared prior to the hearing. The court's verdict did not take into account the 317 page book of evidence presented by our defence to them on 28 June 2001. It lay unopened.

Kerry and I were sentenced to four years for embezzlement of state assets (moving Gem Mining equipment to our office), three years for the destruction of evidence (Gem Mining computer data that we allegedly destroyed but was still somehow used to convict its Directors) and tax evasion (because the Laos Government wasn't able to get any revenue from my Thai company in Thailand, which of course, it was not entitled to anyway). The court disregarded the Memorandum of Understanding signed by the Laos authorities which clearly stated that we had no responsibility whatsoever for the contents of the Gem Mining safe. It ruled us responsible for the loss of Julie's personal jewellery, 3.2 kg of polished sapphires and US$410 in cash allegedly taken from the Gem Mining safe.

Despite the fact that nowhere in the Lao law did it support any legality of their decision the court ordered me to pay US$66,847 as a fine on the charge of tax evasion for revenue my Thai company generated in Thailand. There was some good news. The Lao Court ordered the return of my money (US$98,000) that had previously been a cheque frozen in my account, and the payroll for my Thai Subcontractors (US$50,000) that the authority's seized at the Friendship Bridge when I was first detained. The proceedings were concluded. We were asked if we wanted to add anything. We declined. What could we say?

The three judges filed past and left the same way they'd entered. I lowered my head and gave them the traditional Lao `wai', a sign of respect, though I didn't respect them at all. I intended the gesture to be an insult to their integrity and felt it was the better way to make them lose face. I knew enough about Lao culture to know that shouting and screaming would only cause me to lose face and

I didn't want to give them that last satisfaction. As the Prosecutor came slowly down from his podium, he expelled his breath audibly. As he walked just a few steps in front of me, he lowered his head. I spoke softly and whispered 'Congratulations' as I gestured a *wai* to him too. There was no anger, just sympathy in my voice and sadness for what had just transpired. He met my gaze briefly. I saw that he knew it was all a lie. When the Prosecutor walked from the courtroom, I turned to Kerry but he was talking with Tzovaras, who had returned, and by the sounds of it, was venting his anger.

I walked slowly past them to speak with our former driver, Bounthong.

'I'm so sorry, Madam,' he said drawing near.

'It's okay Bounthong, you can't change anything,' I smiled and as I hugged him, I whispered in his ear: 'If you get the chance, get out of this God-forsaken country!' Our housekeeper, Mr On, was also at the court. He had tears in his eyes as he embraced me. 'Oh Madam, I'm so sorry,' he said.

'It's okay On. Are you alright?' I asked, trying to ignore the emotions pooling inside me.

'I am fine Madam. I just worry about you …' he cried quietly, 'in that place!'

Bounthong and Mr On had known us since the very beginning, when we first arrived in Laos.

'Don't worry Mr On. We're okay,' I comforted him.

I watched as Bounmaly and his Ad Hoc Committee slapped each other's backs as if they'd just won a football grand final. I caught Tan Nom's eye, the police officer from Phonthong. He was seated at the rear of the court with about ten other police officers. I signalled to him that he had lost his bet. He'd said we'd get ten years and we only got seven.

'Ten dollars,' I called to him.

I explained to Jonathan that Tan Nom had betted against us. He glared at the officers who were exchanging kip along the back row.

Understandably, he was outraged that they were publicly betting on our sentencing. Frankly, I didn't care since I won the bet.

'They can keep their money. Lao money's worth shit anyway!' I laughed.

Tan Sombut didn't fight with Kerry that day. He came to stand beside me and whispered 'Madam Kay, we go!' He was finally speaking English to me. Today of all days. Tan Sombut was embarrassed because his English was broken and he sounded more like a child than a high-ranking member of the communist party. The journalist from the Thai Manager Daily newspaper waited outside by the door of the police van. He raised his camera to us but didn't take the shot. Most likely because he was in shock at what I called out to him in Lao.

'Laos, Country of Corruption!'

The journalist lowered his camera. His mouth gaped open in surprise. I stuck my chin up in defiance before I climbed into the awaiting police van.

'Home, boys,' I ordered. The last person I saw before they shut the door behind us was the Embassy Consul Officer, Louise.

'Tell our children not to believe it,' I called to her. 'We won't be here that long.' Louise looked shocked. The van door slammed shut and locked from the outside.

'You all right babe?' Kerry asked quietly from the rear of the van.

'Sure,' I said despondently. All I wanted to do was get back to the prison alive.

Bounmaly stood at the back of the vehicle smoking his cheap Vietnamese cigarettes. I wished the van would just run him over. The Ad Hoc Committee stood beside him laughing. Slowly the police van started to reverse. We'd only gone a few feet when suddenly it halted.

'Ha!' laughed Kerry.

'What is it?' I asked.

'The fucking idiot's just run over a dog,' Kerry laughed again.

'Shit!' I replied, listening to the commotion outside. The van started to move forward away from the courthouse. We could see the dog crushed on the ground at Bounmaly's feet. I watched the cigarette fall from his lips.

As we travelled back to Phonthong, we wondered again if they weren't trying to kill us. The sirens screamed in our ears above the roar of the engine. I wondered why they made all the fuss but then Kerry shouted to me that they probably didn't want to risk us being kidnapped. I looked out the rear window and could just make out one of our company's white pick-up trucks following behind.

'I told Neil to make sure we made it back to the prison,' Kerry bellowed to me.

'They probably think he's going to kidnap us,' I laughed.

It would be so easy to overpower the guards and make our escape to Thailand, a mere ten minutes away. As we turned the final corner to the dirt road leading back to Phonthong Prison, we saw Neil's car halt. He was one of our closest colleagues, but he dared not risk coming any closer. The police van also came to a halt. Minutes later the door opened. The commander stood unsmiling outside his office as we were escorted from the van. I held the arm of Tan Nom as I walked towards the black door to the prison. Under normal circumstances, prisoners were not allowed to make physical contact with police but today was far from normal. When we stepped through to the other side, all the prisoners were locked in their cells. We walked unhurried along the dirt path. Kerry walked ahead and had already removed his dark blue prison jacket. Prisoners started to call out to us as we neared.

I saw prisoners press their faces to the dirty cell bars. Everyone was anxious for news.

'You tell 'em Kay,' Kerry said before he kissed me and quietly headed in the direction of his cell block. Raising five fingers on one hand and two on the other, I signified seven years. A sudden flurry of whispers sounded as I made my way to my cell. Everyone was quiet in the room.

'Someone die in here?' I asked as I removed my shoes and entered.

'You okay Mai Kue?' asked Pang, taking the dark blue jacket I held out to her.

'Sure. I don't care,' I responded dryly.

After I took a shower and changed into my white shorts and singlet top, I sat with my cell mates to eat and told them about the dead dog. Sue Yang said it was a sign that Bounmaly and his evildoers would suffer a similar fate. As the evening passed, the police patrolled hourly and some expressed sympathy. One gave me a can of ice-cold beer that I drank in the washroom and I almost cried at his thoughtfulness. But I wasn't going to cry any more and neither could I bear to think of the pain my children would be going through as they learned of our conviction. I started to sing to forget. I would think no more about the pain in my heart or that I longed to go home. I would just endure the minutes as each one ticked slowly into another.

CHAPTER FOURTEEN

Headlines

Our lawyer was forced to reconsider his advice since we were still trapped in the squalor of a communist gulag and not winging our way back home to our three children as he had promised. He told the Australian Embassy that no formal response should be given to the Laos Government over the following 24 hours. But Tzovaras had no control over the frenzied media when news headlines broke the next day.

Foreign Minister Lengsavad told Australian Foreign Minister Alexander Downer that with the judicial process fully concluded, the two countries could resolve the matter. Mr Downer however, was obviously not happy with the process that led to our conviction, reaffirming that we hadn't a case to answer. He promised to pursue further actions. He also warned that the result of the case would have a serious effect on Laos' international reputation.

I felt encouraged to hear one diplomat announce to the media, 'They are innocent. They have been caught up in power plays.'

Despite the fact that our Government stood firmly in support of our innocence, however, some media only ever reported that we were convicted gem thieves. It was after all, what sold papers. Did they honestly believe that it was possible to carry 160 kg of sapphires in my underwear?

Ambassador Thwaites informed Soubanh Srithirath, Minister to the Lao President's office, that Australia was bitterly disappointed with the conduct and outcome of our trial because the judgement had been prepared in advance. It did not take into account the day's proceedings or the evidence presented. Moreover, the Prosecutor briefed a Bangkok newspaper on the details of the judgement before it was even handed down. These concerns were treated with contempt and so the bilateral relationship became even more strained.

Finally, cutting through the double-speak and deception of the Lao government, Ambassador Thwaites made a statement: 'The Australian Government will not let this matter rest until we have what we want—the Danes' release.'

Aside from an initial half-hearted attempt to exempt himself from direct responsibility in the matter, and to suggest that an appeal would sort things out, Soubanh offered no real defence of the position of the Lao Government. He seemed quite subdued and sheepish, even saying he'd take the matter up with those of his colleagues more directly involved. It was apparent from his manner that he was fully aware of how serious things had become, and he didn't want to be too involved when the shit hit the fan. The Chief of the General Police was even told that the judgement in our case couldn't be justified. He issued an instruction to the President's office for my release, but not Kerry's. The Embassy assumed that further deliberation was required in Kerry's case. They weren't quite sure whether the judgment would be allowed to stand, with Kerry released on humanitarian grounds, or whether an appeal would be processed to clear him of the convictions. But in the history of Laos, no one had ever been acquitted once convicted. Our Lao Lawyer obviously thought an appeal was a complete waste of time and delivered his resignation to Tzovaras on 30 June 2001, urging a change in tactics: 'From now on, it belongs to His Excellency Australian Ambassador to fully play the role by meeting with the most decisive officials, such as the Prime Minister or another higher official, to settle this case in a fair and friendly manner.'

Tzovaras was cautious and appointed another Lao lawyer.

With our conviction handed down, the prison guards informed me that Kerry would be moved to a provincial jail, most likely Sam Neua in the far north, near Vietnam. I told Jonathan at our next Consular meeting. But what we didn't know was that my father had received similar information from a friend of ours, Stuart, who worked in China.

'Kerry will be moved 'up country' at 10am on Tuesday, 3 July 2001. Their appeal will fail,' Stuart stated. 'My sources reveal that Kerry will be treated roughly and that his death can not be ruled out.'

Acting on Stuart's information, the Australian Embassy advised that it might be better to delay the lodgement of our appeal until Tuesday, 3 July 2001, rather than Monday, 2 July 2001. They felt that a Monday lodgement would leave Lengsavad in a position to reject it on Tuesday and thus, make good on his threat to move Kerry. They directed a letter to the Lao Ministry of Foreign Affairs demanding it guarantee that both Kerry and I remain in Phonthong Prison.

By 12 July 2001, Kerry and I were thankful to be alive and together, albeit not physically, in Phonthong Prison. When we met with the Australian Embassy at the Department of Immigration, we were relieved to hear that the Lao Prime Minister had sent an encouraging letter to our Prime Minister. It contained an assurance that while we remained in detention we would be kept together in Vientiane. Unfortunately, he didn't mean 'together' as in, 'in the same cell' but we were happy with the news regardless.

Our new Lao Lawyer, Phivath Vorachak, was present for the last five minutes of our next Consular access visit. He met us as a matter of courtesy and because our Australian lawyer considered it important that Phivath be introduced formally. Phivath didn't speak English, nor did he attempt to engage us in any conversation through an interpreter.

According to Tzovaras, I was yet again about to be released from Phonthong. He told the Australian Government to take even greater care in the coming days, not to convey any suggestion of threat or sanction against Laos in retaliation for the unacceptable conduct of our case. He believed that the work he had done so far had been favourable and if there were no further unpredictable interruptions, I at least, and possibly Kerry too, would be released the next week.

The Australian Embassy pursued discussions with key senior Lao officials who recognised and valued the Australian connection as playing an important part in their work. All claimed they were baffled by the outcome of our case. They saw that the best line of approach was for our lawyers to lodge a Supreme Court appeal, despite the fact that no one had ever been acquitted once convicted. They predicted that the Embassy would find their difficulties resolved by the outcome of the appeal. The reality was that once the appeal failed, the best way forward would be through diplomatic resolution. It was apparent to the Embassy that Lengsavad had given his senior staff the understanding that our case would be a subject of a meeting in Hanoi in July. The reality of it was however, that there were no guarantees.

Seven months had already felt like a lifetime as I began calculating all the birthdays and other special occasions we'd miss. Our son would be 15 years old by the time we got home. But even then, if we didn't pay the compensation and fines to the Laos Government, we would never go home.

'You must not think like that Mai Kue,' said Pang when I told her my fears. 'Just don't think too much. You have your whole country fighting for you!'

The hardest thing for us to do was to stay positive and to keep hoping that we would not be abandoned. The Australian Government were advised that Wednesday, 11 July 2001, would be the best time to request a bilateral meeting in Hanoi between Somsavat Lengsavad and Alexander Downer. Letters were sent from the Australian Prime Minister and the Australian Foreign Minister, both expressing their strong desire for our release. The Laos Prime Minister and Laos Foreign Minister both made almost identical responses. They concluded that they were particularly keen to discuss our case in the hope of reaching an amicable solution that would see us reunited with our family. Ambassador Thwaites told us that he would go to Hanoi for the bilateral meeting. I felt better knowing he would be there. He knew better than anyone else that Lengsavad often said white and did black.

'I don't want you to worry while I'm away,' Jonathan said quietly. He walked me to the waiting police car signalling the end of our Consular visit. I felt safe with his arm around my shoulder. He said that Mr Downer was going to raise our case with the Chinese and Vietnamese Foreign Ministers; after all, the two super powers of Asia had significant influence over Laos. He said Downer would also follow up with the Thai Foreign Minister who had offered to take the matter up with Lengsavad.

***

Meanwhile back at the Prison, Anouhack and I sat under my favourite tree. The stench from the fishponds didn't bother me anymore.

'Hey, you two,' said Kerry. He sat down next to Anouhack. I immediately started looking around for the police, as Kerry looked at me and said, 'Fuck 'em.'
I looked searchingly at Anouhack who shrugged his shoulders and said, 'Fuck 'em.'

Kerry and I sat two metres apart for the first time since we'd been detained in Phonthong Prison. I was now able to tell him how I really felt.

Some of the other prisoners came to sit with us and they listened, but I was beyond caring. I told my husband that I worried about our children and he responded by saying, 'They're tough kids'. The police didn't bother with us at all. They may have seen that I had stopped fighting.

At the same time, unbeknownst to me, my daughter Sahra continued to write to our Prime Minister John Howard, asking for his help. He replied, promising my daughter that he and his government were doing, and would continue to do, everything they could to bring us home and back together again. Even when, for the briefest of moments, I stopped worrying and fighting for justice in our case, my family and friends did not.

CHAPTER FIFTEEN

The Four Point Deal

On 31 July 2001, Kerry and I met with our Embassy and Lao Lawyer at the Bureau of Immigration in Vientiane. The Australian Ambassador briefed us on the Hanoi meeting between Alexander Downer and Somsavat Lengsavad. Mr Downer's strong recommendation was for us to withdraw our appeal and allow the early negotiation of our release between the two governments.

'But if we withdraw they might use that against us and say that we accepted that we had no right to submit an appeal,' Kerry argued.

'The appeal won't succeed,' the Embassy advised.

'Well, that's most likely to be true,' Kerry responded. 'But shouldn't we pursue it?'

The Embassy could not advise. The Vice Foreign Minister of Laos suggested to the Australian Ambassador, prior to our Consular meeting, that he could give absolute assurances that if the four conditions set out in the Hanoi agreement were accepted, then we would be released.

'So what's the deal?' Kerry asked.

'You must withdraw your appeal and in doing so, accept the judgement of the court,' he said.

'No Jonathan!' Kerry responded without hesitation. 'But ... we'll accept that their court made a decision. But that doesn't mean we agree with it,' said Kerry.

Jonathan looked serious for a moment as the Consul Officer made notes of our conversation. A member of Lengsavad's office was also busy taking notes. Jonathan disclosed the second point. 'You will enter into an undertaking to pay the compensation and the Australian Embassy will certify reassurances to the Lao authorities that you will return to Laos if the compensation is not paid.'

'What?' Kerry responded instantly. 'They want us to pay the compensation too?' he bellowed angrily.

'Calm down Kerry,' said Jonathan.

The Lao officials looked from one to the other as Kerry took a deep breath.

'We don't have a million dollars Jonathan,' I argued.

'I know that Kay. The Australian Government knows that too and so does the Laos Government,' he replied.

'So they just want us to say we'll pay?' I asked, puzzled by the strange diplomatic language. 'I personally wouldn't give those bastards a million even if I did have it!'

Jonathan was patient as he explained the dialogue that Mr Downer had entered into with the Laos Government. We tried to come to grips with the deal they had done on our behalf. Was it the best they could do? Jonathan said the Australian Government would immediately send a task force of senior Foreign Affairs officers to negotiate our release.

'I have no intention of dropping the appeal,' Kerry decided.

'Well at this stage, I'd do a deal with the devil to get out of jail,' I said flippantly. 'But how does it affect our families and our employment prospects for the future? What about Kerry's military career? His superannuation? What happens when we go back home? If we withdraw the appeal and accept their decision then won't that give grounds to dishonourably discharge Kerry from the Army?' I asked.

'We're bloody innocent for Christ's sake!' Kerry exploded. 'Mud sticks Jonathan ... no one will believe us if we accept the false judgement of the court.'

'Look ... it's the best we've been able to do thus far,' Jonathan edged a word in.

'Since when did our government start doing the job of the interrogators? My God, are they behind me now saying sign, sign, sign?' I slammed my fist on the glass-top table in frustration and nearly broke it.

The Lao Government wanted a confession to justify its illegal takeover and nationalisation of Gem Mining. Our government expected us to give them one.

I really did not know what I had expected, but it certainly was not what I was hearing. I thought that since our government had accepted the fact that we were innocent, then they would fight for our integrity. I didn't understand their diplomacy or the need for it when truth was on our side.

'Lengsavad knows we'll never accept guilt for something we didn't do,' I replied with disappointment.

'That's right,' said Kerry, 'He'll be counting on that.'

I thought the SAS were coming to rescue us and that the United Nations would give a damn but I was wrong. I was so confused.

'You go tell them to shove their agreement up their arse!' I responded, clearly frustrated. Mr Khamkit's eyes widened. 'It's been a tough week,' said Kerry, immediately apologising for my outburst.

'I know it's not easy on either of you, but I have to advise you that if you don't accept this agreement, the Australian Government cannot guarantee your continued well being,' Jonathan responded.

'Can I talk to my kids please?' I asked Louise, who reached for her mobile phone.

'Sure Kay,' she said gently and dialled the number.

My head throbbed. Kerry wanted to give our lawyer another week but I didn't see the point to that. Tzovaras said he could free us from Laos without paying compensation but I doubted it. The odds were stacked against us.

***

Our next Consular visit was scheduled for 2 August 2001 but we weren't allowed to go because the Ministry of Interior said we'd already used up our visit on Monday, 30 July 2001. Thankfully, the Embassy persisted and we were granted Consular access on the Friday, 3 August 2001 at 9.30am. Our kids stayed home from school that day to take the call.

'When you hear my voice telling you we're free, that's when you can believe it,' I said quietly to our eldest daughter, Jess. 'Don't believe anyone who tells you otherwise.'

'Everyone gets their hopes up and then we're shattered. Poor Nathan gets upset the worst,' said Jess.

'I know mate. Just hang in there. I'm sure it won't be long now,' I comforted.

Towards the end of the meeting, I heard Kerry convey our appreciation to the Ambassador for all the attention his staff and the Department of Foreign Affairs were giving to our case. He added further:

'You know, I once had a Commanding Officer explain that the Army was like a game of football and we have to learn to juggle the ball in order to play the game.' They walked together down the narrow hallway of the Immigration building as he spoke. 'I told him that you've got to drop one of the bastards and sink the bloody boot into the other, if you want to score a goal,' Kerry laughed.

Jonathan laughed too but he understood clearly that Kerry was having difficulty coming to terms with the fact that his unit, the

SAS, weren't going to rescue us. Imagine spending the last twenty years training with the Special Forces unit in hostage rescue. How ironic would that be to become a hostage only to discover that your Government wouldn't risk a fifty year friendship with the communists to bring you home. It must have churned Kerry's guts more than any beating they gave him during interrogation.

At the end of the Consular meeting, they dragged us back to the prison where I sat with Anouhack and updated him on the latest developments of our case.

'Our lawyer made us sign an apology and request clemency to the Lao President,' I said.

'Did you sign?' asked Anouhack.

'Well, I don't know what we signed exactly,' I responded. 'I don't know about anything anymore,' I said shaking my head.

The stress had taken its toll on emotions I fought to control. Anouhack looked at me intently. He sensed my distress and smiled.

'Don't worry Kay, I'm sure you will soon go home,' he said.

'Thanks Anouhack,' I smiled back. It didn't quite reach my eyes but I was grateful in any case, for his kindness.

'Kay, come play,' called Bounchan.

Badminton had taken hold of the prison population with a vengeance now that we had convinced other prisoners to defy the guard's rules about having fun. I ran to my cell to change from my baggy, sewage-eaten t-shirt to a white cotton singlet. Lao women weren't supposed to show so much flesh. In fact, the Government only allowed them to wear jeans on the weekend since 1998. But as I kept telling the police—I'm not Lao! If they expected us to stay for seven years for something we absolutely didn't do, then I was going to join my husband and start stirring the pot.

Everyone sensed that we'd be going home soon but no one was sure. We simply lived on hope. But if we did leave this hell, who would take care of my Hmong friends who had become dependant on me? Certainly, the United Nations and the Red Cross had been powerless to stop the persecution of their race. It was a problem I hadn't any answers for. However, naively, I believed that I could change all that in time.

***

On 16 August 2001, the Lao authorities said that we would not be given Consular access because their vehicle was undergoing repairs. The Australian Embassy offered to send a car to the prison to collect us, but the authorities rejected the offer. Instead, they organised a private car that belonged to the Deputy Head of the Bureau of Immigration.

'Nice car,' I said sitting in the back with Kerry. Tan Peng also admired the fancy four-wheel drive. He smiled as he touched the leather upholstery.

'Very beautiful,' he commented in Lao.

At the Consular meeting, we received letters from home and a small bag of toiletries. I spoke with our children briefly and did my best to reassure them that we were okay. My mother said that my father was trying to get a visa to come to Laos with a TV producer from the popular news program, *60 minutes*. She said they were in the process of getting permission to film inside the prison. Immediately, I began to wonder what the repercussions of that would be for the 58 political prisoners secretly detained in Phonthong. There was no way the Government would allow a film crew inside and risk exposing political prisoners whose existence had been denied for decades.

It could only mean one thing and that one thing would be that my friends, Mr Joy, Oudai and the others, would certainly face transfer to a domestic jail, far worse than Phonthong.

'I don't want them coming Mum,' I explained as best I could. I couldn't just blurt out the real reasons why I didn't want the film crew coming to Phonthong. But I hoped that my Mum was able to pick up on the urgency in my response. Dad obviously felt frustrated at having to sit and wait. But Dad didn't know the reality of our situation and that it would have been selfish of us to sacrifice the safety of others merely to suit our own cause.

A US media company wanted to interview my father and were willing to pay large sums of money for an exclusive. But I was forced to tell my father to remain silent. I didn't know if it was the best decision I could have made but at the time, it seemed to be the right one. It must have been very difficult for my Mum to be caught in the middle. I had no idea she was suffering high blood pressure, or that she had aged ten years since that last telephone call I'd made when I wished her Happy Birthday on Christmas Day. That seemed such a long time ago!

Jonathan said that the Head of Consular Affairs was coming to Laos. Ian Kemish would fill in for Jonathan, who was being recalled to Australia for consultations and some well-earned leave. Jonathan reassured me of Ian Kemish's credentials.

'Ian Kemish has been closely involved in the management of your case. He's in direct contact with Mr Downer, and has visited and kept in direct contact with your family Kay.'

'You're coming back aren't you?' I asked.

'Of course I am,' Jonathan smiled. 'Ian will hold the full head of mission responsibilities while I'm away. He'll play exactly the same role ... don't worry,' he said.

As we made our way to the fancy four-wheel drive, Jonathan continued to assure us that his departure would not affect our situation. And when we climbed into the car, the police officer allowed us to wind down the window.

'I have something to show you,' Kerry smiled as he invited Jonathan to lean closer. Reaching into the pocket behind the driver's seat, Kerry slowly pulled out a long bladed hunting knife he had managed to smuggle out of the prison and into the car. Jonathan's eyes widened. Kerry carefully lowered the knife back into the pocket of the seat and smiled. He was formulating a plan to get us out of our own accord if the diplomatic efforts failed. The driver of the car began to reverse.

'See you when you get back,' I called to the Ambassador who was still standing in shocked silence on the pavement.

For some reason, the police decided to lock Kerry in his cell for the weekend. It seemed as if the small privileges he gained were taken away. Or perhaps it was just more mind games because they knew he wouldn't crack. I overheard Kerry talking with Anouhack standing with the male nurse 'Tan Maw' outside his cell.

'You wear your gun like that is no good. You shoot your foot,' Kerry said, speaking slowly in a mixture of broken English and Thai language. Anouhack translated. The officer had tied his pistol to a four-inch toggle rope that hung from his trouser belt. The safety was off which meant the gun could discharge at any time.

'I'll show you. Here let me see your gun,' Kerry asked through the bars. The officer showed him proudly.

'Oh not good. Not clean. You must clean,' said Kerry. 'Put in your trouser, see, put down there.' Kerry showed him how to tuck the pistol into his underwear for better safety. 'Good. Now tuck into your shirt. Good,' he explained.

The next week when we went to our Consular visit, I saw that all of the prison police wore their guns tucked into their trousers. I smiled when I figured out that Kerry was plotting against them. Obviously if their guns were inaccessible, it would give Kerry a few extra seconds to overpower them if we decided to go ahead with our plan of escape.

The Head of Consular Affairs, Ian Kemish, arrived in Laos on 23 August 2001. He was tall and impressively articulate and had an air of command about him and a look that said, in no uncertain terms, that he was here on behalf of the Australian Foreign Affairs Department and Australian people. The visit provided us an opportunity to discuss the true status of our case and potential need for a more official approach to negotiations. Ian confirmed that the Australian Government was ready to take over the official negotiations from our lawyer whom he'd already met, and confirmed their discomfort with his approach.

The Australian Government had been constrained from a more direct involvement in the negotiations by the repeated assurances from our lawyer that a release was in the offing. There had been so many false dawns, and in the absence of a breakthrough, we were about ready to cut our lawyer free. I left most of the talking to Kerry who must have used the word 'hostage' six times in three sentences. Ian Kemish got the message and agreed unofficially that we were hostages of the state.

'You don't hear me arguing,' he said.

But we did argue a few points in the Hanoi Agreement. Kemish gave no false hopes and explained the realities of our situation. Our incarceration was threatening the stability of the bilateral relationship that existed between two countries. Ian said that he was in Laos to negotiate 'the words' and would do his best to protect our interests. If, at the end of the negotiations, the current wording remained then we would have to reconsider our priorities. There were no guarantees and if we insisted, we might even face remaining in Phonthong for the duration of our sentence. If that happened, our personal safety would become a very real issue and although the Australian Government would continue to support us, they would be limited in guaranteeing our protection. Kerry asked Ian to relay to the Australian Government and Mr Downer, our warm thanks for all that was being done for us. We both felt an enormous sense of security knowing our government was on the case.

As we walked with the Embassy staff to the awaiting vehicle that would return us to Phonthong, I pleaded with Kemish to find the right words to secure our release.

'Please hurry!' my voice broke with restrained emotion. Kerry sat in the car behind the driver. 'Hey, Ian have you seen my knife?' he asked through the open window.

'No I haven't but Jonathan's told me all about it!' he said with an amused grin. Just as he had done for Jonathan, Kerry pulled the hunting knife from the pocket of the driver's seat and just as slowly returned it. Kemish's eyes widened.

'I'll see you next week then?' he smiled.

We drove away from the Immigration building hoping that our message was loud and clear. We would try to escape if we were not released. But was freedom worth risking our lives? We hadn't yet decided. Tzovaras promised that we'd be free within eight days but then conceded that if we were still in Laos by the deadline we'd given him, he'd step back so long as he remained part of the team. Our employers, Jardine Securicor, were also eager to know how long the case would continue, as they were now paying the legal fees.

CHAPTER SIXTEEN

Task Force Intervention

Pang didn't trust the beef we had one Friday, and grimaced in disgust as she watched me pick a sliver from the plate and toss it into my mouth.

'You worry too much. I'm not gonna die from this. Only die if Tan Bounmaly come back and shoot my head,' I laughed and took the dish away.

The next day I had to admit to Pang that it had been a mistake to eat the beef. I felt terrible.

'Mai Kue you don't come outside?' called Pang. 'What's wrong with you?'

'I'm not well,' I groaned, curled up in the foetal position. For the entire weekend, I agonised in the room and felt I was close to death. By the time Monday arrived, I wasn't any better.

'I think I got food poisoning,' I groaned, clutching my stomach.

'Here take this Mai Kue,' Sue Yang whispered. She was a Hmong Shaman and often mixed up strange concoctions to ease the suffering of others. The last thing I felt like was drinking one of her strange potions. But I did it anyway because the pain in my lower abdomen was excruciating.

'It tastes bitter,' I moaned as I took a sip and allowed my head to fall back to the hard wooden door.

'I think you need a doctor Mai Kue,' Pang replied, concerned. I was running a fever and had a severe headache. I felt lethargic and wondered if I wasn't just going to melt into the floorboards. One of the prisoners must have alerted Kerry because I could hear him yelling in the distance for them to get a doctor. I felt certain I had salmonella but hoped it wasn't botulism, which could result in death. Pang got Tan Maw the doctor to come to our cell but all he did was take my temperature, feel my stomach, and say 'be patient'. And so, after about five days of feeling absolutely lousy and drinking Sue Yang's bitter herbs, I began to return to the land of the living. I sat in the middle of the room as Mon and Toom sat either side of me.

'But I feel fine now Pi Sue,' I said as she prepared the needle.

'We must be sure what your illness is from,' she spoke quietly. Sue gently patted my head with a damp cloth, then as the water ran from the top of my head to my shoulders and down my arms, she followed its path with her healing hands. She tied a piece of cotton around my middle finger on my left hand. I could feel it throb as the blood rushed into my fingertip. A short, sharp jab pricked my finger.

The blood spurted into a bowl of water Sue placed under my hand. She gazed thoughtfully into the bowl as the blood sank to the bottom and a brown discoloration rose to the surface. Satisfied, she announced that the beef I'd eaten last Friday evening had poisoned me.

'I told you not to eat it Mai Kue,' said Pang laughing. 'Next time you better listen to me!' I started to move away.

'But wait, we must do the other side too,' Sue exclaimed, in a matter-of-fact tone.

'But it hurts,' I cried, as she moved to the other-side of me.

'Oh don't be a baby. You don't want to go around unbalanced do you?' Pang chuckled.

***

In Phonthong, we weren't given any real medical attention so when someone became ill, we did our best to help each other. Mr Vanchop, a Thai man in Kerry's cell, got sick. The police allowed me to go near his cell to see what was wrong with him. Kerry had described the infection, but I almost threw up when I saw for myself. Vanchop was in severe pain. His shaved scalp was badly infected and was a mixture of colours: red and purple. Kerry told me to order an antibiotic. Mr Vanchop looked at me with his brown eyes pleading and filled with tears, as he begged, 'Please help me, Madam!'

I got permission from the police to write to our housekeeper Mr On, for the medicine.

'And tell Mr Joy to stop cutting hair with those bloody clippers, they're spreading the infection,' Kerry called.

The medicine came two agonising days later and Mr Vanchop cried unashamedly. His infection began to clear up over the coming weeks. He called out to me, 'I love you, Madam,' and to Kerry he bowed, thanking him profusely.

Mr Vanchop had survived in the dark room at Savannakhet for two years and had been a prisoner of Phonthong for three. He had once tried to escape so they kept him locked in the room indefinitely. He only ever came outside for a haircut, once every three months. Though he was Thai, he never got to go to the Embassy. The Lao transport budget was depleted affording our transportation costs so in the end they agreed that our Embassy could provide a vehicle to collect us each week.

***

On 30 August 2001, Mr Thong collected us from the prison and under escort, drove us to the Immigration building for our meeting.

'How's everything Mr Thong?' Kerry asked as he sat in the back seat with Tan Peng.

'Oh slow but I think your government can work it out,' Mr Thong encouraged. We arrived at the Immigration office in good time. Ian Kemish stood smiling to greet us, with the ever-present Louise beside him, just as Jonathan always did.

Most of the visit was spent discussing our request for the Australian Government to take control of the negotiations to secure our release.

'Yeah, I'm sick of the promises of going home and then we don't. Imagine how our kids must feel,' I stated in disgust.

Ian said he would inform the Australian Government to proceed with their plan in sending the negotiating team to Laos.

'We'll let your lawyer stay involved in the event we need him to provide legal advice, but you'll have to make sure he understands that you want us to take over,' Ian said and handed Kerry the cell phone. Kerry told our lawyer that we had handed full control of our case to the Australian Government.

'Please hurry Ian. I can't do this for much longer,' I cried quietly into his shoulder at the end of the meeting. 'If we're not out soon then I think we'll have to make our own plan.'

My voice was filled with despair as I told Ian that we had found a way out of Phonthong.

'Don't do anything Kay.' Ian's voice was serious. 'You'll end up with a bigger sentence!'

'No Ian, we'll end up worse than that,' I whispered with eyes that expressed my desperation.

I couldn't tell him that Kerry had been contemplating our escape for the last couple of weeks.

'Just hang in there Kay,' he smiled in reassurance. 'We'll move as quickly as we can.'

Louise smiled and hugged me goodbye. I didn't know how much longer I could endure leaving those who were my only link to the outside world. Kerry and I agreed that there was no way we would stay seven years in Phonthong. If the Australian Government failed to secure our release within the next month then we would reconsider our alternatives. Apprehension consumed me. Suddenly the car halted in reverse. We heard the first secretary of the Embassy babbling in Lao language.

'I'll get a lift with you back to the Embassy,' he said in Lao for the benefit of the police. For the journey back to Phonthong, we sat in the back of the Embassy four wheel drive with Robin Hamilton-Coates, who gave me his cell phone so that I could speak to the kids, for the second time that day.

'Robin just jumped in the Embassy car and said he was coming with us!' I told my daughter down the other end of the line. She was obviously surprised to hear from me again so soon.

For twenty minutes, I talked to my children. Mr Thong took the long way back to the prison, which gave Kerry an opportunity to press Robin for more details about our case.

Yet another week went by and Anouhack received the good news that he was going to be released. He waited all weekend for the black door to open on Monday morning. We joked that he would be making love to his wife by Monday evening. Anouhack blushed. But when Monday morning came and went, he became anxious. In the afternoon, we stood in the line waiting to be told the regulations. Anouhack kept looking back to the black door. But it didn't open.

'Don't worry Anouhack,' I said, trying to comfort him. 'Maybe they take you out when we are locked inside.'

'Yeah, maybe,' he said despondently. But in the morning, he was still in Phonthong, and in the following days, he became more depressed than anyone had ever seen him.

'Just hang in there Anouhack,' I whispered to him during the morning line up. His face remained blank. I knew he was struggling to maintain control. We all were! How stupid was it to tell someone to be patient when they had already overstayed their sentence by a year and a half?

The Australian Embassy wasted no time contacting the Lao President's office on our behalf, seeking a response to the Ambassador's letter regarding the negotiations of the Hanoi Agreement. The Secretary agreed that he would follow up on it. Meanwhile our lawyer told the Embassy that a meeting had occurred on 1 September 2001 and involved the Lao President, the Minister of Justice, the Ministry of Interior, and the Foreign Minister Lengsavad. The Lao authorities were looking for a face-saving solution to our case, which would enable them to release us on humanitarian grounds. But all senior leaders needed to agree.

By 6 September 2001, we were taken from Phonthong to Immigration in the Embassy's four wheel drive. Anouhack accompanied us to meet with this own Embassy official. Ambassador Thwaites had returned to Laos. I was so happy to see him.

'It's so good to have you back,' I beamed as he hugged me.

During the meeting, Jonathan outlined that unless he was called in by the Foreign Ministry to discuss our case further by the end of the week, he would be requesting a meeting with Foreign Minister Lengsavad on Monday, 10 September 2001. Subject to the outcome of that request, the negotiating team would be in Vientiane as early as Wednesday, 12 September 2001.

My family were finding it tough to deal with the continual set backs. My Dad in particular was frustrated beyond belief and said as much to Ian Kemish when he called on them following his departure from Laos.

'I'm fed up with all the false promises. The kids can't handle any more of it. They're just kids Ian!' he broke down crying. It became obvious to the Australian Department of Foreign Affairs that they would need to handle my family with even greater sensitivity. The pressures were beginning to take their toll on everyone.

The Australian Embassy continued to push for an early meeting with Lengsavad, before he left for meetings in New York. The Australian Government was ready to send a high-level team to Vientiane overnight as soon as the meeting was in prospect. Ambassador Thwaites asked the Lao Ministry of Foreign Affairs to back up the Embassy's approaches to Lengsavad's office by making it quite clear a meeting was of major importance. The Embassy didn't have to wait long for a response, although it wasn't from Lengsavad's office.

Unbeknown to us, our Lao lawyer, Phivath Vorachak, prepared, in close consultation with Tzovaras, a formal request to withdraw our Supreme Court appeal. Of course, the Australian Government remained cautious of the interpretation that the Lao Government was ready for the first time to contemplate the withdrawal of our appeal as a means of securing our release.

Jonathan met with Lengsavad on 13 September 2001. Lengsavad asked whether he had received a copy of the ruling of the Supreme Court to which the Ambassador confirmed he had. The Supreme Court ruled that our appeal had no basis for application. Since the legal proceedings were evidently completed, there was no reason why they couldn't move to the agreement reached in Hanoi. Lengsavad welcomed the invitation and said that he had no wish to lengthen the process; it was the 'offenders' decision to not withdraw their appeal that had delayed matters. Jonathan confirmed that with the legal process concluded, we did not object to the Government-to-Government negotiations.

The Australian Government wished to begin immediately and stood ready to bring senior negotiators to Vientiane at very short notice. Lengsavad said that all aspects of the legal case, including the civil aspects, would have to be cleared up soon. He urged the quickest way of doing this would be for us to withdraw our appeal officially and agree to pay the fine and compensation. After much to-ing and fro-ing it was finally made clear that we could not possibly pay the compensation asked of us and that it would be pointless to insist on it. It was also made clear that we would have to write an official statement removing our appeal, to 'go through the proper channels'. Only then could the two governments meet to come to a satisfactory conclusion. We were left on the sidelines of an exercise in diplomacy.

Our government was eager to bring this to a resolution but it seemed the Laos government was determined to frustrate proceedings with delay tactics. In the end, after many negotiations, a document was placed in front of Kerry and I. As we read the words on the page before us, we remained silently thoughtful:

'I accept and realise that according to the binding decisions of the People's Supreme Court and the People's Court of Vientiane Prefecture, I have broken the law in Lao PDR. I sincerely regret that we are unable to pay the compensation and the fine, as we simply do not have the means to do so. I also regret that the Australian Government cannot under Australian law pay the compensation and fine on our behalf'.

Jonathan quietly explained that the diplomatic language should not concern us.

'We oppose to signing anything that could be construed as an admission of guilt,' Kerry said adamantly.

'I know Kerry,' Jonathan replied quietly. 'But the wording of the passages does not amount to a confession of guilt,' he explained. 'I've spoken at length to Lengsavad and he's adamant that if you don't take this deal then we can't go any further.'

'What aren't you saying?' I asked.

'He basically told us that if you won't agree then we would have to just leave you where you are. And in that event, the Australian Government would not be able to guarantee your continued well being.'

'So if we don't sign we stay? What sort of choice is that?' I begged. 'The Australian Government wants us to agree to this?'

'Kay, we can't make the decision for you and just as I told Lengsavad, we can't force you to do anything.' Jonathan leaned closer to explain. 'It's your decision.'

'My God!' I said as the shock hit me.

'Listen, it's an interpretation, not an admission of guilt,' said Jonathan.

'And it's the only way?' Kerry asked.

'According to the Foreign Minister there appears to be no other way,' Jonathan replied.

Reluctantly, Kerry and I signed the letters accepting the Supreme Court verdict.

***

We learned from Jonathan that Ian Kemish and the Ambassador to Vietnam, Michael Mann, were returning to Laos to further negotiations with the Lao authorities on 24 September 2001. When we met with them the following week, Ian told us to be patient and reassured us that they weren't wasting any time to get us home. Acting Foreign Minister Phongsavath confirmed that the Lao Government and the Australian Government would finalise the 'words' addressing compensation. Perhaps Ian Kemish should have come sooner, as things seemed to be moving faster than before.

But I doubt our Australian lawyer Tzovaras would have agreed to it. He continued to be at odds with the Australian Government and expressed his anxiety that their involvement would either derail or delay arrangements in place. Kemish emphasised to our lawyer that the Australian Government would press ahead in their discussions with the Lao authorities. Our lawyer was rightly sceptical that the Lao authorities, Lengsavad in particular, would keep their end of the bargain. I was tired of being strong and I just wanted to go home. I found myself becoming unusually irritable.

***

This had made life even harder for me in Phonthong. I had fallen out with Mon, making our living arrangements even less tolerable. There wasn't really any reason for our falling out, it was just our time. Living in a 3 X 3 metre cell with five other women is difficult, and though we did support each other tremendously, it wasn't harmonious all of the time. Little things were exaggerated and became huge problems. An argument can start if you move someone's coffee cup. Mon had fallen out with the two Hmong women in the cell and expected me, as her 'sister', to side with her. I couldn't, so Mon turned to the Thai woman Toom and pretty soon they began whispering and acting secretive, only talking in Thai. The Hmong soon felt that Mon hated them for being an ethnic minority and refused to eat their food. This was a huge insult. Things became really tense in the room. Mon became distant from me. She hated that I had taken a Hmong name, Mai Kue. After that, Mon would no longer eat my food either, so I stopped drinking her coffee.

Mon began spending time with Noi and Pon-Phit instead of me, even though I knew she didn't like them, and so I kept a distance. I missed her terribly but we were both very stubborn and the close confinement of our cell did not help. In hindsight, I think we both could have made things better, but we were protecting ourselves from being hurt. We knew our friendship could not last, and this was the easiest way to create some distance.

I'd lost so much weight that people said I looked like a skeleton, but since there weren't any mirrors in the prison or at Immigration, I really had no idea what I looked like. I knew my pants were tied up with string to keep them from falling down and that my shirt had holes in it from where the sewage water had eaten through. I also knew that my life had changed in more ways than one when the Embassy doctor, Ben Burford put me on anti-depressants because I'd said to Kerry that I felt as if I was constantly living under a black cloud. Kerry too was beginning to doubt the prospects for a negotiated settlement and for the first time, he mentioned that he too would 'do a deal with the devil' to get me out. It was a worrying change in Kerry, suggesting that my indefinite detention and my obvious deteriorating stability were finally having an impact on his spirit. Though we were both in reasonable condition in the circumstances, the doctor concluded that we were both showing signs of stress. He also prescribed us with anti-fungal medicines because the conditions inside Phonthong were appalling, and like everyone else, our toes bled daily because we were unable to keep them dry. Towards the end of our Consular meeting, I overheard Kerry complain to Kemish that he was frustrated beyond reason that they were still holding me.

Clearly, he was tormented more than anything by that fact and was adamant that if we weren't out by the end of October, we'd find our own way home. I didn't really think much about the consequences because I was too desperate to care what happened if we got caught. Part of me could feel that I was losing control of myself as my reality began to merge with fantasies of freedom. My mind became consumed with thoughts of escape and rejected the risks that common sense should have over-ridden. Even the idea of others failing in their attempts did not dissuade me. I convinced myself that I wouldn't be clubbed near to death if captured, as they had been. I would not be thrown in the dark room or beaten every week, or left to sit in my own waste.

My idea was that Kerry and I would commandeer the car that took us from Phonthong to the Bureau of Immigration. We'd drive as fast as we could for the ten minutes it would take to reach the banks of the Mekong River. We would meet a former CIA contact who would be waiting with a fast boat to take us the remaining distance to Thailand, then on to the Temple of Nong Khai where he would have secured sanctuary for us, until my Thai colleague came to evacuate us to a safe house in Bangkok.

Back inside the hell of Phonthong, I kept my fears and doubts locked deep inside my subconscious as I gazed out across the prison grounds, beyond the high wall with its three-strand barbed wire and to the distance where the palm trees dotted the horizon. One day, I would go beyond that far away tree. One day, I would be free.

***

On 26 September 2001, we met again with the Embassy at the Bureau of Immigration. Kemish outlined their proposal to the Acting Foreign Affairs Minister Phongsavath Boupha. They wanted us to agree to pay compensation by instalments and forfeit the US$150,000 that had been returned to us by the Lao court.

'Naturally it is an important decision that should not be taken lightly', said Ian as he looked directly to Kerry. 'Your lawyer is of the view that you should first wait for a letter that he is expecting to receive within a few days.'

Kerry reiterated over the phone to Tzovaras that the Australian Government was in charge of the case. I blocked out the heated exchange that followed as the Embassy told me that my assets would be forfeited as an initial payment towards the compensation and fine.

'I knew when I was detained I'd never see that money again!' I responded. 'Besides, they've probably spent it all anyway.'

Ian sighed. There was nothing he could say in response. We all knew that my suspicions were most likely correct. To ensure there were no future misunderstandings between our lawyer and the Australian Government, we gave written consent authorising the Australian Government to proceed immediately, to advance discussions with the Lao authorities on the matter of compensation. It was noted that we understood it would involve forfeiting our assets in Laos. We would be expected to provide an undertaking to pay the remainder of the compensation following our release and departure from the country.

As Louise shuffled the papers we'd just signed, Ian asked her if there were any other issues that needed to be discussed.

'Yes, there is something you should know Kerry,' she said, putting the documents into a small briefcase she carried. 'We received a fax from Lao Securicor yesterday advising that the company will cease all business operations and will close down completely at 7am today,' she concluded.

'What?' Kerry asked.

'I know. We were as shocked as you to hear the news. More so because it was so sudden. Of course, the Embassy has had to make arrangements with an alternative security company to commence guarding services immediately,' she concluded.

'You don't mean Lao Security Services?' I asked.

'I'm afraid so,' Louise replied.

Securicor's joint venture partners, the Ministry of Interior, operated the opposing company. Lao Security Services was supposed to have been shut down when the Laos Government invited Securicor into the country, but they didn't.

'Ha!' Kerry laughed. 'Looks like we've come full circle,' he said dryly.

'So what happened?' I asked Louise.

'From what we understand the shareholders have reached the end of their tolerance. As you know, many of the expatriates employed by the company have fallen foul of the authorities.'

'Yeah don't we know it,' I interrupted. Louise smiled.

'And the acting manager has had to try to operate the company from Thailand in recent weeks,' she said.

'You mean he's gone?' Kerry asked.

Louise shifted slightly in her chair and looked slightly uncomfortable. Her body language indicated something was wrong.

'Well, we can discuss that at another time perhaps,' she responded.

'So what happens now? Are they going to dump us?' I asked.

'No actually we've been told that they will continue to maintain their commitment for the time being,' said Louise.

'Yeah right!' Kerry drawled sarcastically but let the matter rest.

There was never enough time to get all the information we needed to make decisions or relay our frustrations at having tried to make decisions in haste. We worried constantly that we would never be released and would be forced to spend the rest of our lives in detention. We worried that the mosquitos at night would carry malaria through our veins and that the secret police would take either of us, or both of us, away in the night like they had once promised. On top of that, I worried constantly about my company in Thailand.

'Please hurry,' I begged Ian as he walked us to the car waiting outside.

I waved to them as we departed and did my best to ignore the despair I felt. Ian said he was scheduled to meet with our lawyer following the Consular meeting to begin discussions on the approach they'd take to secure our release via diplomatic negotiations. Together they drafted a submission to the Prosecutor who expressed his own view that the content of the draft paper would be acceptable. He further indicated that on receipt of a formal version of the document, signed by the Embassy and us, the Lao authorities would move as quickly as possible to resolve the issue. No time frames or guarantees were given, but there was always hope.

'I'm so tired of this,' I said to Kerry when we walked back through the prison gate.

'The Australian Government is on the ball now. It won't be long,' he replied.

***

The Embassy issued a request to the Lao authorities that we be moved to more comfortable accommodation pending the finalisation of the matter. They emphasised it as a request, not a condition. The compensation payment issue seemed to go on and on and due to several delaying tactics, Ian delayed his departure from Laos, having decided to stay until the very end of the week.

On 28 September 2001, Jonathan, Ian, Louise, and much to our surprise, Tzovaras, were all waiting at the Bureau of Immigration for us to arrive. It was 10.30am when we entered the office of Mr Khamkit and we were overwhelmed by the amount of people there. I looked to Jonathan who was smiling broadly and as he hugged me tightly, he whispered that they were close to finalising their negotiations.

'Just hang in there a bit longer Kay,' Jonathan spoke quietly into my ear.

I shut my eyes briefly and hoped that I would be leaving this room a free woman. Ian invited us to sit down and as we did, Tzovaras began reciting a long, drawn out synopsis of what was to come. We didn't know how much time we would be given but we knew one thing, we weren't in the mood for this.

I laughed for the first time in a long time. Ian took the opportunity to take control of the meeting and in more diplomatic language he silenced everyone. A Lao official was armed with the original of the agreement signed by Jonathan as Ambassador, which had been sent to the Lao Ministry of Foreign Affairs the previous day.

After a brief consultation, Jonathan read the agreement aloud and we duly signed and handed it back to Ian, who in turn handed it to the Lao official again. The Australian Embassy tried to find out what would happen next from him but he was unable to respond precisely, saying the court would now need to 'consider' the signed agreement. He had earlier told the Australian Embassy that he did not see a problem given that the Governments had agreed to the wording. We said our farewells and once again headed back to the prison. Almost immediately after our meeting, Jonathan, Ian and Louise called for a third time during Ian's visit to Laos, on the acting Foreign Minister Phongsavath Boupha. This appointment was arranged on 15 minutes notice.

Ian thanked the Minister for the cooperation and progress that had been achieved during the week, and re-emphasised the Australian Government's earnest wish that any remaining procedural steps to be taken should be done with the utmost expediency.

'What would be the Australian Government's preference for the Danes removal from Laos? Expulsion or Presidential Pardon?' the Minister asked. 'Normally a Pardon from the President would mean that you must wait until National Day on 2 December, but in the present case, it would be possible to expedite the procedure,' he concluded to the surprise of the Australian delegation.

Jonathan responded that the Australian Government's primary concern was that we were released as soon as possible. However, if it were just as fast, then a Pardon would be preferable to expulsion.

'Expulsion is faster,' replied Phongsavath.

The Australian Delegation sought clarification that if our departure from Laos were to be by expulsion that we be taken directly from the Detention Centre to the airport. The Embassy requested that sufficient time be given to the Embassy in advance of any decision so that they could make the appropriate flight reservations. Phongsavath agreed. At 2pm, the Australian delegation received confirmation from the President of the Vientiane People's court that the Justice Ministry had received the Agreement countersigned by us. He was now required to prepare a report for the Minister of Justice on the method of payment of compensation. He hoped to have prepared it by the following week.

Overall, the behaviour of all Lao officials suggested firmly to the Australian delegation that they had moved into a new phase. Given that the discussions were now out in the open it would be more difficult for the Lao side to renege on the agreement.

It was now 4 October 2001 and we had been in Phonthong for ten months. We were driven to the Bureau of Immigration for another meeting with our Ambassador. Jonathan never gave any promises, he just continued to encourage us to be patient.

'You need to sign these originals of the Agreement,' he said seriously as he placed the documents in front of us. 'There are four identical copies that we'll hand to the Lao authorities after this meeting.'

'Then what?' Kerry asked, almost impatiently.

'We're very close,' Jonathan said as he witnessed our signatures. 'We have just got to play out the last steps,' he added honestly.

CHAPTER SEVENTEEN

The Tide Will Turn

On 5 October 2001, the Ministry of Foreign Affairs announced that it had decided against expulsion and opted instead for a Presidential Pardon to enable our release. We would be placed in the care of the Australian Ambassador pending our application for clemency. As we travelled to the Bureau of Immigration, we hoped to be heading towards freedom and not another disappointment. Mid-way on our journey, Mr Thong handed me his cell phone and said Louise was waiting to talk to me.

'What's going on, Louise?' My voice was filled with anticipation.

'Just listen to me and don't say anything. There's a delegation of Lao officials here at Immigration. The Ambassador and I will meet you downstairs when you arrive. I want you both to remain calm and do not talk unless addressed,' Louise cautioned. Her usually friendly tone was replaced by a more official, serious one.

'Okay. Is it over Louise? Are we going home?'

'I'll explain it all to you when you arrive. Just stay calm and work with us on this.' And with that, Louise ended the conversation.

'What'd she say?' Kerry asked as soon as I hung up.

'Well, her voice was really serious and she said we have to stay calm. There's a delegation of officials waiting for us,' I said, handing the phone back to Mr Thong.

'Is it over?' Kerry asked.

'She just said we have to work with them. I guess we'll find out soon enough hey?' I responded.

'You go home, Madam?' asked the prison officer sitting beside me. All I could say was that I didn't know.

Tan Peng was one of the nicer officers at the prison. He used to bring his baby son to our cell and we'd feed him biscuits from the Embassy. It was strange to be able to form such bonds with our captors, but then most Laotians were just as imprisoned as we were, and the police and military officers even more so. Their official capacity meant they were never allowed to leave the country, unless sponsored by the Communist Party. Their prison borders were unseen. I knew that if an opportunity were present, just about every prison officer in Phonthong would have gladly left Laos.

We passed through the round-a-bout where Vientiane's Arc de Triomphe, Anousavaree, renamed 'Patuxai' when the communist seized control of Laos, stood in all its prominence. It was a large concrete structure built in 1969 to commemorate the fallen Lao soldiers of various wars. A stairway led right to the top and provided panoramic views of the city. When they were building Anousavaree, they ran out of cement so the Government diverted tons of cement donated by a US aid program for the reconstruction of the Wattay airport, to the site to finish the monument instead. Some locals jokingly referred to it as the 'Vertical Runway.'

The traffic was light as we travelled down Lane Xang Avenue where the Royal Dok-mai-deng Hotel quietly waited for someone to restore it to its original beauty. As we travelled further down the road, I knew that Talat Sao, the Morning Markets, would soon be upon us. There you could shop from 6am to 6pm and buy all kinds of goods, especially silk and cotton weavings. I used to spend my lunch times at Talat Sao discovering a world within a world. The road just before Talat Sao veered left. As we passed by, I remembered all the times we travelled it to our home in the village of Thong Khan. We had moved to that village from Sap-han-thong to be closer to our office. I felt incredibly sad for a moment as my mind flashed with memories of our life before Phonthong. It seemed a dream of long ago and I wondered if any of it was real: the carefree existence I had once enjoyed beneath the oppressiveness of the communist state that had become my home.

Within minutes, we turned into Hatsady Road where our journey had first begun. It was in Hatsady where I first began working for Lao Securicor. The street was so familiar that I wondered if time had simply stood still. The car slowed and then came to a halt just outside the noodle shop across from our old office where I often ate lunch with our employees. They taught me to ignore the ants floating in my soup. I laughed and waved to our security guard who stood by the bank entrance. I got out of the Embassy car. He smiled back and I wondered momentarily what our guards thought had happened to us. Whether or not they knew what had really occurred or whether they believed the lies told to the people in order to defame us. I comforted myself by believing they knew the truth and that if it were otherwise, their faces wouldn't light up as they did whenever they saw us. Kerry walked ahead of me to greet Jonathan and Louise as they waited just outside the doorway to the Immigration Building.

'It's looking good,' Ambassador Thwaites said calmly, shaking Kerry's outstretched hand.

'Hi Jonathan,' I smiled as I hugged him. Louise was smiling when I turned to hug her too.

'We're nearly there Kay,' she whispered in my ear.

'Thank God!' I responded.

With our police escort following close behind, we made our way into the building and kept walking towards the rear of the office and to the stairway that would take us up to Mr Khamkit's office.

'Remember the first time we climbed these stairs?' I asked putting one foot slowly after the other.

'Yeah, let's hope we only have to do it one more time,' Louise answered.

Mr Khamkit's office was crowded with police, Ministry of Interior officials, Lao Foreign Affairs Officials, Immigration police, and half a dozen others. We could barely fit our own police escorts inside. As we sat down our Australian lawyer leaned over to Kerry and said: 'Everything's on track, guaranteed'. Kerry sat close-by on my right, which brought a smile from Tan Peng who noticed the seating arrangements and said nothing. We couldn't have our conjugal visit but we were getting there. A representative of the Lao Foreign Ministry made a long-winded speech in Lao language. We did not understand a word of it but respectfully kept silent. Everyone in the room looked serious but Kerry and I kept our expressions blank. I looked at the floor and concentrated on remaining as calm as I knew how. Inside however, I was trembling as our fate was, again, being decided. The Australian Embassy translator said a few brief words to the Australian Ambassador who looked at the Minister and smiled. Moments later the Minister handed a pile of documents to the Australian Embassy translator who in turn placed them on a table before the Australian Ambassador.

'You're about to be adopted,' Jonathan smiled at us and took his silver pen from his breast pocket. The Embassy translator showed him where to sign.

The Australian Embassy seal was affixed to each signature, making everything official. The papers were collected and passed back to the Lao Minister who also signed the documents and affixed their own ministerial seal. The Australian Embassy translator began translating the Minister's final remarks.

'We are happy that both Governments have been able to resolve this situation in the best interests of the long standing relationship our countries share.'

After a few moments, the translator explained to us that the Australian Ambassador had just accepted responsibility for us and that we would be transferred from the prison in due course. They didn't say when. Jonathan just cautioned us to be patient. The Lao Government asked Kerry and I if we had anything to say in conclusion to the meeting. Kerry declined to say anything. He despised them and did not really care that they knew it. I on the other hand feared they might change their mind if they sensed any arrogance. So I raised my hands together in the traditional prayer-like gesture and said with all sincerity that I was very happy, and thanked them in Lao. Every Laotian in the room smiled broadly and one Minister proudly announced that I spoke Lao language very well indeed. No doubt, they thought their system had re-educated me into a good communist and they probably had for all I knew. I learned to hide my feelings and my fears behind a smile. I learned to beg like a dog in the hope that I might be treated as a human. I learned that Laos was shrouded in secrets and that few people ever saw the horrors I saw. I learned that human life and freedom were not as precious to some as they were to others.

Kerry was annoyed that I had become so Lao. When we were escorted by the police back to the car, he vented his displeasure.

'Fuck them Kay ... they don't deserve to be spat on!' he said angrily, not wanting me to speak their language.

'I just wanta go home Kerry. I don't care if I have to be humble,' I responded in defiance.

Kerry was always angry and I suppose he had every right to be. They had locked him in a cell for five months, beat him repeatedly, and took away his dignity. The one thing that hurt Kerry the most, it was having a shadow cast across his integrity. We said our goodbyes to Jonathan and Louise and climbed back into the Embassy car that would take us back to hell, for what we hoped, was the very last time. As we drove back to the prison, we held hands. Tan Peng didn't care.

We walked back through the black prison door together, just in time for roll call. When they called my name in the line-up, I responded.

'Here, but not for long.' Everyone laughed.

***

I could barely contain my excitement but I knew that it was pointless to get my hopes up. One of the younger police officers who always helped us order supplies from the outside market came to my cell as Pang and I were making coffee.

'Nang Kay,' he whispered to me from the doorway and signalled for me to come closer. He obviously had something to tell me. He was nervous because he kept looking around behind him.

'What?' I asked.

He said we were going home on Monday. 'Cannot today,' he said apologetically.

'Why not?' I asked but he looked puzzled. 'Pang… come back here', I called to Pang who had walked outside.

'What is it Mai Kue?' she asked quietly.

'Ask him quickly. He says we go home on Monday,' I whispered. Pang and the young officer talked for a few minutes before he stood looking at me, waiting for her to translate. She told me that it was true, we were going to be released on Monday, and he was sorry that it could not be today as they expected it would be.

'Yippee,' I squealed with delight and kissed the young officer on the cheek.

'Oye Madam,' he said shocked, and even blushed. Pang told me that it was still a secret and we had to keep it quiet. She also told me that they wanted a donation before I left the prison. It seemed that the US$600 held in my prison account had disappeared.

'You explain to him when he comes back that I cannot give them all that money,' I said, shocked that they wanted more.

They were always asking the foreigners for money and threatening to lock them in the room indefinitely if they didn't pay up. I didn't care if they wanted it kept quiet, I was telling Kerry and in turn he must have told Anouhack and before too long, everyone in Phonthong was whispering.

'At least they're keeping it quiet,' I said to Anouhack, who was grinning and laughing. Anyone would have thought it was him going home.

I met Pi Chao and our other Hmong friends in the workshop, a forbidden place for females, but it didn't seem to matter now. I gave them the news and they were happy for us, but sad that we'd be leaving. I agonised for the next two days worrying about them and the others we had taken care of. There was no way to explain to my old friend, Gin-Gin, what was going to happen. I wish I could have spoken her language if only to tell her that I would always think of her. I felt particularly distraught to be leaving Gin-Gin because I doubted anyone would take care of her the way I did. Her life would be difficult again, and lonely. The little happiness we'd brought to her life would disappear. How appalling for a woman her age to be doomed to such an existence.

On Sunday, Gin-Gin gave me her favourite green beret. I'd been trying to get it off her for the last ten months but she always said no. I said thanks, in my limited Mandarin dialect. Gin-Gin smiled as I proudly paraded in front of her cell with my newly-acquired hat firmly on my head. She muttered clearly in Chinese some words that I knew meant beautiful.

There was an air of excitement and many people begged us not to forget them. Kerry and I had coffee together on the veranda with Gin-Gin, while other prisoners came to us, wishing us good luck. By the time Monday came around, I was packed and ready to go. I'd said my goodbyes to Pang and Sue and told my Hmong friends and my Lao friend Oudai that I would worry about them, but would never give up trying to change the brutal system that kept them imprisoned at the whim of the government. I gave my blankets to Pi Chao. To Joe Hay I gave shampoo, soap, two tins of milk, and some beef noodles. He promised he would hide them well so the other prisoners wouldn't take them. Poor Joe. How would he survive?

The moment finally came when the police called for me to go outside. This was it, the moment I thought would never come. I breathed a deep sigh of relief and looked around to the faces looking back at me. My heart beat heavily in my chest. How could I say goodbye? I walked slowly down the concrete steps.

'Don't worry Mai Kue. You just go outside and then come back to get your bag,' Pang spoke quietly and continued to sniff her Vicks inhaler.

'Are you sure?' I asked. My eyes flashed suddenly to hers for reassurance.

'I'm sure,' she nodded, her dark eyes serious.

Kerry stood just outside his cell and gave me the thumbs up. I watched Anouhack walk away from him and slowly come towards me. In his dark Laotian face, I saw the same reassuring smile I had seen many times before.

'It's okay. You just go out and then come back. I confirmed with the police already,' he said quietly.

'What if they don't let me back inside? I cannot leave Kerry,' I whispered.

'No, no Kay. They will let you. Don't be afraid,' he said with quiet confidence.

Looking once more over my shoulder, I turned slowly as I neared the black door and glimpsed my husband who stood motionless, one hundred metres away. All I had to do was step through that small pedestrian gate. Why did it seem such a difficult thing to do when so many times I had imagined myself crossing to the other side? Kerry waved me away and with my head and heart filled with uncertainty, I breathed in deeply and held my breath as I walked through the black door. On the other side, a guard grabbed my arm and escorted me along the narrow dirt track that dipped into a small creek. The familiar greenish-black water still did not glisten in the sunlight as we stepped on a log to cross. Part of me felt like I was watching a movie in reverse. The scene was just as it was the day I had arrived at Phonthong. Only now, I was different. My eyes saw the world in a new way. Tan Kanya sat at the table they used to sort deliveries from the relatives to the prisoners.

He opened a book and I sat quietly waiting for him to scrawl several notations of Lao text. After several minutes, he took me to the Commander's office where Tan Su-li-ya counted my money and placed my personal effects on the table before me. Surprisingly my sapphire engagement and wedding rings, bracelets and earrings were amongst my belongings. They were worth a lot of money. I never thought I would see them again. How odd that they would accuse us of sapphire theft and yet now return all my sapphire jewellery. In my mind, it simply reinforced the fact that no one ever really believed those ridiculous charges brought against us.

Major Suvvany sat down quietly across from me and smiled. He too seemed a little confused that my sapphires were returned but said nothing. He once told me to not be too worried about things of a serious nature and that life in Laos can change very quickly from good to bad and bad to good. Fifteen minutes later, the Australian Embassy vehicle arrived with Louise and Mr Thong.

'I want US$100 from my account to go to Oudai,' I spoke quietly to Tan Su-li-ya. His English wasn't the best but I managed to get my demands across with broken Lao language. 'And US$100 for Pi Chao and another US$100 for Tanaphan.'

Louise and Mr Thong stood quietly to the side and observed. The Commander of the prison sat at the far end of the long wooden table and said little. His eyes never left my face. His own face was serious. A pile of Thai baht coins sat in a plastic container in front of me. I pushed it towards Major Suvvany.

'Please go to the temple, to Sap-han-thong where I used to live and make merit for me,' I asked quietly, repeating my instructions in Lao. Tan Suvvany nodded. A smile crept into his face. Mr Thong addressed the Commander and thanked him on behalf of the Australian Embassy. I noticed that Anouhack was standing with Louise, talking quietly. How he managed to get out of Phonthong was anyone's guess. But knowing Anouhack, he had probably bribed one of the guards. After all, he was the famous Mr CNN. Evidently, Louise informed him that the Canadian Ambassador himself was coming to Laos. It was fantastic news for my friend who had never given up hope that he too would one day leave Laos. A half an hour had passed before they escorted Anouhack and I back inside the prison.

'Hurry Kerry. We're going,' I called to my husband and wasted no time watching Anouhack rush over to him with the news. I went to my room quickly and hugged Pang goodbye. Mon stayed in the washroom for a very long time. This was the moment we'd waited for but for some reason, the reality of leaving was almost too overwhelming. Tears welled in Pang's eyes but she bravely kept them in check.

I could tell that she was distraught. 'Quickly Mai Kue,' she whispered. It took me no time at all to get my things together since we had packed and repacked the night before. When Pang and I left our cell, many prisoners stood by the door waiting.

'Good bye Madam,' they chanted. My Thai friend, Tanaphan, gave me the traditional Thai *wai* in respect. '*Chok dee*,' he whispered, 'good luck', and bowed to me as if I were a queen. I choked back my tears and tried to tell Tanaphan that I would never forget him. His warm brown eyes brimmed with sadness and happiness at the same time.

'*Chok dee* my friend', I whispered in return.

The Frenchman, Joe Hay, stood quietly watching. I had to crane my neck up to look into his soft blue eyes. His pale white hand rose and extended in goodbye. I shook his hand and did my best to ignore the fact that it was the first gentle human contact Joe had felt in seven long years.

'*Au revoir soeur*,' he said. He put his hand to his heart.

'*Au revoir*, Joe. Be patient. I will tell your Embassy to come for you. But you must not forget everything we talked about okay?' I spoke slowly to him in the only French words I could remember. I looked deep into his pale blue eyes and saw the tears welling.

'Don't cry, Joe,' I smiled, shaking my head as I gently touched his arm. Joe's tall skinny frame almost buckled over from emotion.

'Yes, I promise my sister,' he said, and collected himself to stand a little taller. 'Please don't forget me,' he whispered.

'I won't Joe. I promise I won't,' I quietly assured him.

My African friend Sam shook my hand through the bars of his cell and told me he would take care of Joe. I gave Sam my old green bush hat that I had worn every day in Phonthong.

'Hey Sam. Be careful they don't see this.' I turned the bush hat inside out and showed him where I'd desecrated the tiny Lao flag. Sam smiled. 'I think I'll cut it out completely just in case,' he laughed.

'Good idea,' I responded.

'Don't forget us here, Kay,' he said seriously, as his dark brown eyes became as large as saucers.

'I won't Sam. You take care. I will get in touch with your brother. Don't worry.'

'Keep Joe speaking French won't you. I'll be in contact with the French Embassy when I get out of here.'

'I will Kay,' he promised. Sam was fluent in both English and French and was the one who had first got Joe to stop pretending he was American and speak French.

I promised Sam I would get in touch with his brother waiting in Bangkok. Sue Yang 'Mama' and I stood embracing at the front of the steps. She sobbed so much her small body heaved against mine. There was nothing I could say to comfort her.

'Don't cry, Mama,' I said gently, as I stroked her hair and held her close.

'I'll miss you Mai Kue,' she whispered back. I knew she was afraid, we'd talked about this day but she and Pang still had another two years to endure.

'I won't forget you Pi Sue. You take care with your health and we'll be together on the outside, where I'll be waiting for you and Pang,' I said quietly, fighting back the tears.

We stood that way for what seemed an eternity before we walked together to the interrogation room where they were ready to inspect my bag. Kerry was in the room when I arrived, surrounded by other prisoners. Pang never said a word to me as I entered the room. She just looked sad. The time had finally come for us to part and for the last ten months, we had depended on each other literally, for our lives. Sue stood crying unashamedly in front of Major Suvvany. It was a very emotional goodbye and one I could never describe, except to say it was the worst kind of grief I'd felt in all my life. I stood near the brown shuttered window looking out of the interrogation room for the last time. I had known horror in this place filled with ghosts and every form of despair there was. But I had also stood here amongst friends who kept me alive for those last ten months of hell. I would take their hopes with me, to a better place. Bounchan stood at my right, smiling but sad nonetheless.

Chanlee stood in front of me and whispered, 'Good luck, Madam,' as Kerry stood behind me talking with Tanaphan. We had seen only a few people leave Phonthong and today it was to be our turn. I didn't want the moment to end; I wanted to stay a little longer as I knew it would be our last goodbye. At the last Consular meeting, my sister Karen had sent me a tiger's eye bracelet that I wore for luck. I reached over to Homparn, and transferred my sister's gift to his left wrist as I spoke to him softly, 'for your daughter'. He didn't say anything but I knew from the tears in his eyes that he would not forget me. Reluctantly, I walked out of the interrogation room for the very last time with my good friend Anouhack at my side. It was appropriate that he should be walking beside me as I left the prison, just as he had walked beside me when I was first brought in. I shook his hand with my two hands and thanked him for everything he had done for us.

'I can't tell you what your friendship has meant to us both Anouhack,' I said.

Anouhack had been a true friend. He did everything he could to keep our spirits and hopes alive. He had now been in prison four years and nine months, which was a far cry from his actual sentence of three years and three months. Kerry and I owed our lives to Anouhack. We would never forget his generous spirit. We faced suffering of immense proportions, which formed a bond like no other. I was so happy to be going home, but I was more consumed by sadness to think of my life and what lay ahead. All I could think about were the dearest friends I was about to leave behind to an unknown fate.

I took one last look around at all those who had become so dear to me. I tried to capture their faces and permanently imprint them in my mind for years to come. Pi Chao and my Hmong friends were all standing together under the shady tree where we often stood. They now stood waving goodbye. I knew Pi Chao's vision would be blurred from the tears in his eyes. Mr Vanchop yelled goodbye from his cell.

'Goodbye, Chucky!' I yelled, as I waved my hands vigorously above my head.

Siv-il-eye was only one year older than I was. He merely smiled at me with a look in his eyes that spoke volumes. He seemed to will me to remember him and I did. I remembered all the journeys he'd taken me on as he travelled through memories of his life as a political prisoner transferred through thirteen Lao jails. I remembered the darkest hours in his cell, the many months he had spent alone as he lay beaten and broken on a dirty concrete floor, strapped into wooden leg blocks in the dark room, which for six months had been his home. He was unable to move or to clean himself whenever his bowels moved or he felt his urine wet the filthy rags that barely covered his body. Every moment he shared with me about those times I could not come close to imagining the terror he must have endured.

Mr Joy waved and smiled his toothy grin as he thought about the future. His hopes were great and he believed we would start a chain of events to raise awareness of their suffering. I prayed silently that Mr Joy would survive long enough to see some change, if not his freedom. I looked for my Thai friend Mon but I couldn't find her and the police were telling us to go quickly through the black door.

My final impression of Phonthong prison was one that would haunt me for months following our release. Saying goodbye to my dear Laotian friend Oudai was the hardest challenge of all. How miserable I was as I thought of how many friends he must have said farewell to over the last eighteen years. He didn't say anything and looking at him I cried so hard I thought I wouldn't stop long enough to say something in parting. We stood there staring through the tears and I said to him that I couldn't leave him there.

'I can't,' I tried to speak, but the words wouldn't come out. Oudai couldn't speak either. I imagine he was doing his best to be brave for both of us. We had become the closest friends, like family. Oudai pointed to the black door and said 'Go home'. I saw he was having just as much trouble keeping his emotions in check as his eyes watered. Twice he had to say it. I looked over his shoulder still trying to find Mon but she wasn't anywhere in sight. She had stayed away from me all morning, and wouldn't even look at me. I wanted so much to tell her I was sorry that we quarrelled but Tan Suvvany was telling me to go. He took my arm and gently led me out through the black door to freedom.

Looking back, I think Mon knew that I would some day be leaving this place, and that our argument had been a subconscious way of trying to shield ourselves from the hurt of leaving each other. I should have made peace with her, but she didn't try to say goodbye either, and to be honest, the sheer exhilaration of leaving was very distracting. I was pulled this way and that. It hurt too much to say goodbye, so I didn't. I would hear from Mon again, and it gave me great comfort to learn that she wanted to 'let bygones be bygones', and that she had moved into a cell with Gin-Gin for some time. I knew they would keep each other safe and well. Right now though, I was torn and deeply hurt, but I had to go.

'Come!' said Tan Suvvany quietly.

'Goodbye, Oudai,' I said, my hand outstretched as I stepped through the black door for the last time. Sadness was etched deeply into every line of my face. My grief was overwhelming as the tears fell like rain down my cheeks. There was no going back!

Many of the sixty barrack police came out to watch us say our final farewells to the prison police. Among my personal effects was a thin mattress that the Embassy had fought tooth and nail to get inside the prison. The commander said that I had to take it with me because it was against the regulations for prisoners to have a mattress and my case was an exception. Tan Peng stood nearby and since he had always been kind to me, I asked him to take the mattress for his baby son. He didn't say much in response except to bow his head slightly and whisper 'Thank you', but I knew my gesture was not lost on those observing. Despite everything that had happened and all that they had taken from me, I still had the ability to give. I still had my dignity and I still wanted them to know more than ever that I was never the 'Mafia mama' they once thought I was.

By 11am, we were transferred from Phonthong Prison to the Ambassador's residence next to the Australian Embassy. There we would remain under house arrest for an indefinite period. It didn't matter that nobody knew when we were going home. It might have been six hours, six days or six years. We were just happy to be free. I held my husband's hand for the entire journey as we travelled along the dusty roads of Vientiane. My eyes scoured the familiar sights around me as my heart ached from all we had endured.

The white wrought iron gates of the Ambassador's residence opened as we approached. Slowly, Mr Thong drove through them and onto Australian sovereign soil. There standing at the entrance of the residence was the familiar presence, the man who had made it all possible, His Excellency Jonathan Thwaites.

Though taking nothing away from Alexander Downer and his Foreign Affairs Department, our champion had always been Jonathan. He had pushed the Lao Government hard to secure weekly Consular access. He had attended each and every Consular visit when most Ambassadors would usually leave those duties to their staff. His presence inspired hope and confidence in knowing that he would never leave us to rot in an Asian prison. He was always there.

'Welcome,' he said, smiling as soon as we stepped from the car. I almost fell into his outstretched arms.

'Thank you,' I hugged him even tighter. 'Thank you so much!' I cried.

It suddenly dawned on me that we were about to impose on his personal life. It was different somehow relying on him desperately for all those months and not thinking of him as a husband or father. Our lives had consumed him as much as they had us and suddenly, I felt a little ashamed that we had become such a burden. But Jonathan wouldn't hear of such things and set my mind at ease quickly, telling me that he was more than delighted to have us in his home. Jonathan's wife Eve was away for the night and would not be returning until the morning. He said she was looking forward to meeting us.

I wondered how awkward it was going to be explaining our arrival to his household staff. But it wasn't awkward at all as they made us feel welcome. Of course, they must have heard about our story, but to their credit, they never let on. I began to feel a little more at ease. I kicked off my sneakers and handed them to Kerry.

'You do it,' I said quietly.

'What's going on?' Jonathan looked puzzled as Kerry clutched at my shoes.

'Long story. But basically there's a very important letter in the sole of her shoe,' Kerry explained. 'It needs to go to Thailand with some urgency.'

'Okay. I'll talk to Robin. He can translate it so we can be sure of its integrity,' he responded.

We couldn't argue his logic since neither of us could read Thai that well. The letter was from a prisoner who'd been living a nightmare inside Laos for close to twenty years. When it was eventually translated we learned that he had simply wanted to let his Mother and Father know he was still alive and begged them to go to the temple to make merit for him. The Embassy hand delivered the letter to his parents who lived just on the other side of the Thai-Lao Friendship Bridge. I was so glad that we were able to do that for our dear friend and more glad when the Thai Embassy took a special interest in his case.

***

Our room was on the second floor to the far left. It was beautifully decorated in soft muted tones that drew my gaze to the French doors that opened out onto a small balcony. I was instantly reminded of another time, before Phonthong when we lived with our three children in our French style villa in Saphanthong Village. I closed my eyes momentarily, afraid that I would wake up and suddenly be back in Phonthong prison where the sewage ponds and mosquitoes with their diseases greeted me each morning. But when I opened my eyes again, I didn't see any three-strand razor wire keeping us in, only palm fronds of rich dark green. How I wished Mon and the others could have shared this day with us. Suddenly I felt very sad and pushed my happiness beneath a wave of guilt as I stared out over the lush green lawns, wondering how

I would ever move past the pain of leaving so many dear friends behind.

'Hey Kay check this out,' called Kerry.

Jonathan stood by the door watching me silently. I didn't know that he had caught the deep sadness in my eyes, as I made my way to where Kerry was marvelling at the giant bathroom.

'It's huge,' I said, in true amazement as my eyes widened. 'It's as big as our cell.'

The bathroom glistened. Jonathan laughed when I caught sight of myself in the wall mirror and jumped in alarm. I didn't recognise my own reflection. I hadn't seen it for almost twelve months and for a moment, wondered who the gaunt, dark haired woman was, standing there looking back at me. My head tilted to the side and then straightened as I became preoccupied with my appearance. I thought of all the moments I had gazed into a shallow water trough in our tiny prison washroom and tried to catch my own reflection. But the water was dark from the slime that grew at the bottom of the trough so it hardly revealed anything. My hands slid over my thighs to feel only bones that had once been generously covered with fat. I faintly heard Jonathan excuse himself and said he would see us at dinner. I touched my fingertips to my face and noticed that my skin was considerably darker than when I first went to Phonthong. I looked like those people who spent every day of their lives on a beach. My face was free of make-up and my eyes seemed bigger than usual as they stared back at me. I had changed so much, and loosened my hair from the ponytail I'd become accustomed to wearing. My dark hair fell unevenly to just below my shoulders.

'Ugh, I need a haircut,' I whispered to Kerry who I saw was taking great pleasure in shaving with hot water.

'You look beautiful,' he said as he smiled at me in the mirror.

I smiled over my shoulder and slipped a red pinafore style dress over my head. 'Hurry up, we'll be late.'

CHAPTER EIGHTEEN

House Arrest

'Well, it's nice to have you both here at last, we've been waiting a long time,' Jonathan's wife Eve said gracefully the next evening. 'Let's eat shall we?' We weren't used to eating real food or sitting at a real table, drinking out of crystal clear glasses and eating with a silver knife and fork. The objects looked so alien in my deeply tanned hands. So many little things distracted me all the time, which made doing even basic things difficult. In the prison, we had gotten used to eating with our fingers and a spoon.

Eve had kindly asked the house-cook to prepare simple rice dishes, to wean us back on solids. She was so thoughtful. I cried with the first meal they served because it was green beans and rice, cooked in oyster sauce. My heart wrenched as I thought of my friends left behind in Phonthong. Their lives were so difficult. Sue slaved every day over her prison bean garden that we called `Mama's beans'. I silently wondered if they too were lamenting, as they noticed the empty space where my bedding had been. I spent a lot of my time feeling sad. I cried quietly in the shower and down by the swimming pool, as Kerry ran around it for an hour to keep fit. I often found myself staring at the blue sky above, thinking of my friends in Phonthong. They were only ten minutes down the road and yet they could have been as far away as Mars.

Would there ever be peace in my mind from Phonthong? Flashbacks and nightmares haunted me as I imagined the secret police coming for us again. One night, Kerry found me huddled in the corner whispering 'They're coming!'

But no one was coming. Kerry smoothed my hair, gathered me in his arms and whispered, 'Sshh go to sleep.' Just like my dear sister Mon used to do.

I thought I was reasonably sane for the most part, but on the other side of freedom I felt like I was losing my grip on reality. Prisoner's voices echoed in my head and always, Bounmaly Vilayvong tormented my dreams.

The pains in my chest increased and were like having a constant heart attack. Dr Ben told me that it was only anxiety and was one of the more common symptoms of Post Traumatic Stress Disorder (PTSD). In time, it would pass. But the days at the Ambassador's Residence went by so slowly and I was forever fearful that I would never get back to normal.

Kerry found me one morning filing my fingernail to the bone because I was anxious that I couldn't get it straight. I didn't notice that my nail was bleeding, nor did I notice that Kerry was speaking to me. I was simply lost in my own anxiety. When eventually I came back from wherever I was in my mind, I found myself sitting on the lounge downstairs with Kerry and Eve standing over me. Only I couldn't see them because I had a brown paper bag over my head. Evidently, they had got the doctor's instructions a little mixed up. I was supposed to breathe into it, not wear it.

Mostly I worried that somehow the Lao authorities would find a way to keep us under house arrest for the duration of our sentence. Of course, Jonathan kept reassuring us that everything would work out, but none of us really knew for sure. Our Australian Foreign Minister made a telling public statement about our release, and in it, he again stressed that our imprisonment had never been justified, and that he was now working to allow us to leave Laos altogether.

The Lao authorities took our application for clemency with maximum bureaucratic heel dragging, or so Jonathan said when he updated us the next day. From the Prosecutor General's office, the application was supposed to have gone straight to the Lao President, since he was the only one who could grant a pardon. But the Lao authorities were unsure where the document was at present.

The Embassy Doctor, Ben Burford spent a lot of time talking with me about Post Traumatic Stress Disorder and these conversations helped me gain a better understanding of the emotional changes I was going through.

***

The next evening we were sitting at dinner when Jonathan announced that Foreign Minister Lengsavad was continuing to speak to the media.

'Oh, what's he been saying now?'

'Well, Lengsavad's been hyperactive in giving his version of the case. No longer confining himself to sympathetic Thai outlets, he gave a televised interview with Jason Bleibtreu of *Channel 9*, who is in Vientiane from his base in Bangkok.' Jonathan paused to sip his beer. 'According to Jason, the Lao Ministry of Foreign Affairs has encouraged him to interview you guys,' he concluded.

'Oh?' Kerry asked puzzled. 'Probably banking on us saying something derogatory.'

'Most likely,' said Jonathan.

'Yeah well I think we've made it more than clear to our lawyer that we won't be speaking to any media while we're still in the country,' I conceded.

'He's got a swarm of media at the Novotel Hotel where he's been staying during your detainment,' Jonathan revealed.

'That would have cost Securicor a fair bit,' I replied dryly.

'The police are patrolling outside the main gate,' Jonathan commented.

'It is safe here isn't it Jonathan?' I asked. He saw the concern in my eyes and smiled reassuringly.

'Yeah ... so long as you don't put your big toe outside the gate,' he winked.

'Huh ... well all I can say is ... if they think they're taking me back to that hell ... you'll be coming too!' I pouted.

'Oh, Jason said that during his interview with Lengsavad, he was mostly diplomatic but did claim falsely, that you had confessed to guilt,' he added on a more serious note.

'Typical!' said Kerry. 'Suppose he's trying to get a rise out of me.'

'Probably,' Jonathan responded. 'Don't worry about it though; everyone else knows you are both innocent.'

***

There was more bureaucracy, and more delays, with our Pardon, as the documents were mislaid, sent to the wrong person or department, or were being carefully checked due to the one-off nature of our case. It was the same old delaying tactic, and as the days went by I became more fearful for our safety. I couldn't go back to Phonthong, that much I knew.

On 18 October 2001, the Embassy again asked the reason for the delays. The Prosecutor General's office confirmed that the wording was now acceptable and would be submitted to the National Assembly. Our lawyer advised us to prepare for an afternoon departure. But as usual, the call never came.

'That's why I didn't bother getting dressed!' I said to Eve as we sat down that evening to watch the news.

On 20 October I turned 34 years old and the next day, Kerry turned 43. Jonathan threw a big party for us, which was attended by friends we knew before Phonthong and even the new incoming US Ambassador, Douglas Hartwick. Kerry and I were so surprised when we saw our Boston lawyer Bobby striding towards us.

'We made it Bobby,' I cried into his bear-like embrace.

'That's my girl,' he smiled.

Just hearing his voice brought a flood of memories back to me as I remembered the last time we stood together, embracing, uncertain what the future held. It seemed a lifetime ago. It was such a nice party despite the fact that I didn't remember much of it. There was simply too much happiness in the one tiny space that I felt completely disorientated.

On 22 October, our lawyer told the Embassy that we would be attending a ceremony at which the President himself would personally hand over our Pardon. It never happened. According to media contacts, Bounmaly had become personally involved in opposing our release.

Then on 23 October, Downer wrote to his counterpart, Lengsavad hoping that he could impress upon him the Australian Government's continued desire to hurry along our return to Australia. I was becoming increasingly nervous with every delay and feared our release would be cancelled altogether.

Within hours, we were given more bad news. Rumour had it we were going to be kidnapped.

'Well, that'd be right and there'd be no stopping them either,' I said dryly.

The previous Ambassador had given the Lao authorities the Embassy's arsenal in the interests of good will. With the great bilateral relations the way they were, Kerry and I wondered if our government would even allow us to defend ourselves. Our lawyer was equally worried about my emotional and physical well-being. Some friends wanted me to consider leaving the Residence as soon as possible, even if it meant being smuggled out of the country. We would never both be able to escape like this, so it would mean Kerry being left behind, and I just couldn't do that.

'There's no way I'm leaving my husband. He'd be dead before I ever got back to Australia and for that matter, so might I,' I explained. I realised people were worried about me, but our children needed two parents and there was no way I was leaving Kerry, especially since we'd come so far together. I knew if I left, it would be like signing his death warrant and nothing would make me do that.

Not only that, but before we had left Phonthong, one of the prisoners warned me about secret evacuations. He had lived long in the Communist system and said that if I ever did attempt to escape, I would regret it. Jonathan was relieved that I turned the offer down. It would have undermined the initial agreement that was set between Laos and Australia that enabled us to be released into his care. Besides, his wife Eve was wonderful company.

As each day passed, my mind began to heal but obviously, there was still a long way to go. Dr Ben had prescribed some sedatives to help me fend off the nightmares and I continued on the anti-depressants previously prescribed while I was in prison. Eve was equally as wonderful as Jonathan and I couldn't imagine leaving them, not yet anyway. It was marvellous to talk by telephone to our children each night, although they still harboured thoughts that we'd be scuttled back to prison. We hadn't told them anything about the kidnapping rumours. Instead, I reassured them by saying that I had a firm hold of Jonathan's arm and wouldn't be letting go. It wasn't easy on our families and closest friends and despite us being released from prison, they still worried. My own parents were nearly sixty, and worked full-time to pay off their mortgage. How they'd managed for almost a year was beyond me. My Mum knew something was wrong. For almost a year, I had been living the life of someone else, someone who was willingly submerged into the Communist Lao culture, in order to survive. But how could I even begin to explain that to my Mum?

CHAPTER NINETEEN

Farewell to Friends

On 30 October 2001, having collected the contents of my private bank account, including my Thai payroll, Louise Waugh and our lawyer paid the 'ransom for our freedom' to the Court Verdict Implementation Unit (CVIU) of the Ministry of Justice.

As they were leaving the Implementation Unit, our lawyer advised the Lao official that reservations had been made on a flight leaving Vientiane at 1.40pm that same day. He asked that final formalities for our departure be completed urgently. The Lao official said that he intended to proceed directly back to his office and immediately follow-up on obtaining the official document of Pardon from the President's office. However, once again the authorities dragged their heels. When he next contacted the Australian Consul at 11.45am, he regretted that, because President Khamtay Siphandone was 'up-country' and not expected to return to Vientiane until Friday, 2 November 2001, the document of Pardon would have to wait until then.

The Australian Ambassador spoke with another more senior official and emphasised the high priority the Australian Government continued to attach to our earliest possible release.

Jonathan sought an explanation for the repeated interruptions and delays in the process.

'It is because there have been differing approaches within the Lao Government and that these final problems result from the coordination between the departments,' said the Lao Minister.
The Australian Embassy requested that the document be faxed to the President but this request was denied outright because he was in a remote part of the country and they were not sure when he would return.

At 3.15pm Jonathan made representations to the Ministry of Foreign Affairs about the inordinate length of time—now 23 days—the Lao authorities had taken since our transfer from custody to the Australian Embassy. Consul related the day's events stating that the Australian Government had been extremely disappointed to learn of yet another unanticipated, last minute setback.

'His office tells us he's working at his party Headquarters and that the Pardon for your release is waiting there for his signature,' said Jonathan.

Dinner that evening at the Australian Ambassador's residence was a quiet occasion. I listened intently as Jonathan explained how he and his staff had continued to work around the clock. How frustrating it was for them to be constantly in the dark.

'Well, we're not worried,' Kerry said. He looked across the table to me. 'I think it will give us time to sort our thoughts.'

'Yeah just so long as they can't take us back there Jonathan,' I spoke softly.

Jonathan looked at me with the same sincerity that he'd shown in the last ten months. 'You won't be going back there Kay.'

I didn't really think of Jonathan so much as an Ambassador as I did a trusted friend. He had become someone I could truly depend on for my life. The only other person in all the world that I could say that about was Kerry. My husband kept me going inside Phonthong while Jonathan's continued presence, at each weekly Consular meeting, became my life-line to freedom. Subconsciously

I convinced myself that if anything happened to Jonathan, we would be sent back to Phonthong and lost forever.

***

The hours passed and Jonathan returned several times throughout the day to update us. Kerry and I used the time to call his brother Leslie in Bangkok and for at least half an hour, I stood at the top of the landing listening intently to Kerry telling his brother how important it was that they gather all my company records for an audit. I watched him hang up the phone and run his hand through his short hair in obvious frustration.

'What is it?' I asked, walking to sit at the bottom of the internal staircase. My bare feet concealed my approach.

Kerry was angry because his brother wasn't able to furnish us with the accounts we requested.

'He says he can't because he gave them to the Thai SWAT to manage,' Kerry said.

'He did what?'

'Yeah. He gave your company accounts to the SWAT and he's just been signing everything they put in front of him for ten months.'

'Jeez! Are they running bi-lingual accounts like I instructed?' I asked

'No! It's all in Thai and he can't read a word of it. For all he knows, he could be signing for a shipment of heroin and be none the wiser!'

With my elbows resting on my knees, I slowly allowed my head to fall silently into my hands. The realisation hit me that my Thai Company wasn't as protected as I had been led to believe.

'My God' I cried. 'It's a disaster! What if they haven't accounted properly? What if they weren't paying tax? Bloody hell … it's a conflict of interest for a start!' I whispered.

Thousands of questions raced round my head as I began worrying about a whole new set of possibilities. What mess lay in Thailand? I had no idea. Everything seemed to be going from bad to worse and I had no way of controlling any of it.

'You're gonna have to somehow find out what they've been doing since we've been in jail Kay. You can't risk anything else coming back on your clients,' Kerry warned.

'Well I thought everything was under control,' I replied.

'Yeah well, it's obvious it's not under control and you can't risk the fall out if things aren't kosher down there.' Kerry echoed my own thoughts.

'God I hope this doesn't come back on me too!'

***

The next day, four of our former Securicor staff visited us. They said the Ministry of Interior had taken control of the Lao Securicor operation and if Kerry wanted to, he could return to help them manage it.

'The job is very difficult Mr Kerry,' said Somphone.

The young Laotian man had started in the company as a security officer and later, an instructor at the Securicor training camp. He had quickly worked his way up to become an assistant to the Operations Manager.

'Now they say I am to become the Managing Director!' he said in disbelief.

'That's great Somphone,' I laughed. 'I always told you one day you would be the Director of Lao Securicor and you never believed me!'

Somphone's face was like that of an innocent child. He held out his hands in exasperation. 'Madam, I cannot do the same as Mr Kerry but they tell us that we cannot leave,' he replied.

'What do you mean you cannot leave?' I asked cautiously.

'It's true Madam,' said Noy, who worked in the accounts section. 'The Ministry of Interior said that if we want to leave we can go stay in Phonthong,' she whispered. Noy's dark eyes widened and her face became animated as she described the conditions they were now forced to endure.

'They reduce all the salaries. Now we only get paid US$10 per month,' said Khampang who's salary under Kerry had once been US$250 per month. 'It is not good now because we cannot know how to do everything. The clients do not want us anymore,' he concluded sadly.

As our former staff sat and poured out their problems to us, I began to realise that our detainment had even greater, far-reaching implications than we could know. I felt miserable for our staff and helpless to do anything for them. So many times, I had encouraged them to keep challenging themselves. I had told them that even if they no longer worked at Lao Securicor, they would be valuable to other foreign investors because of the skills and training they had acquired with us. Our staff believed that if they worked hard they could escape poverty, but all that now seemed to be nothing more than a dream. With the change in management, their working opportunities had been severely reduced. Effectively, they were prisoners of a regime that held them captive behind invisible bars.

'The Ministry of Interior want us to ask you to call anybody who left the company to return to Laos,' said Somphone.

'What for?' asked Kerry.

'Because someone ran away to Thailand and took the money from the company,' Somphone claimed.

'What money?' I asked.

'Someone went to the bank and took all the salary for the guards. Then they ran to Thailand in the company car,' added Noy.

'They what?' Kerry exclaimed.

'Now all the guards will not get paid and the authorities want them to come back to Laos and explain why they did this,' Somphone said. His face was serious.

'Look we don't know anything about what Securicor have been doing since our detainment,' Kerry explained quietly. 'I can't bring anybody back, Khampang! Of course I would if I could, but we have no contact with anyone anymore. We don't know where anyone is!'

'I'm so sorry you got so many problems,' I addressed our former staff. Clearly, they were upset at the prospect of working for nothing, and who could blame them?

'Oh Madam, we got a big headache now,' Somphone responded. His youthful face was lined with stress, ageing him.

'I don't know what you can do,' Kerry stated. 'It's no longer my area of responsibility.'

'But the Ministry of Interior said you can come back and help fix the problems. They forgive you about the criminal case.' Somphone's voice was filled with hope now.

'Forget it,' Kerry laughed. 'I'm not going down that road again. Hell, they would probably put me back in jail for something they allege the acting manager did in our absence.'

'No Mr Kerry. They do not believe like that. You can help save the company,' Somphone insisted.

Kerry and I both felt awful that our staff were suffering and needed our help, but there was nothing we could do.

'I'm sorry Somphone. It's too late. Your government did the wrong thing by us and we cannot stay in Laos,' Kerry advised.

'I cannot say anything about your case, except that the Ministry of Interior accepts that you can return to work if you want to,' Somphone argued.

'Well, you can thank them for me but tell them that I am going home!' Kerry concluded.

As we said goodbye to our former staff, I felt sorry that they were left to face all those problems alone. I knew they would face even further hardships down the track and most likely, it would be impossible for them to rebuild the company to its former success. They were just another group of victims of this regime, another set of prisoners, trapped in the Lao system. Part of me wanted to go with them, to guide them as we had once done. But I knew that was a fanciful notion. I hugged each one of them goodbye, probably for the last time. As I did, I pressed a one hundred dollar bill into Noy's hand.

'It's not much, but I hope it will help a little,' I whispered and kissed her goodbye. Considering the average monthly salary for the nation was US$10 per month, it was actually a significant amount. Tears welled in Noy's eyes as she looked deep into mine.

'I'm so sorry Madam that you go through so much,' she said softly. 'Take care Madam and thank you.'

'Goodbye,' Kerry and I said in unison as we walked them to the door.

We couldn't stand in the doorway and wave goodbye because the press were waiting outside with their cameras. So we said our goodbyes and closed the door quietly behind them. A few hours later, Mr Wan came to see us. He had been the Lao Securicor handyman and was most fond of Kerry. When he saw us, he cried and fell to his knees. The tears streamed down his face as he broke down with anguish and relief. Kerry walked over to Mr Wan and drew him up from the ground. They stood for what seemed like ages, as Wan held Kerry in a fierce embrace.

'Oh Boss, I wait to see you again and worry. I try many times to come to the prison but the police say cannot,' he cried.

'Oh Wan we got your fried bananas in the prison, thank you!' I said to comfort him and gently patted him on the back.

'You get them? I think they don't give to you,' Mr Wan exclaimed and wiped the tears from his thick black eyelashes that clumped together. Wan always brought crunchy, fried bananas to us at the office—before we got arrested.

'I remember you and Madam like the fried bananas. I just wait all this time to see you,' he said.

'We're both fine, Wan. You don't worry anymore. We're fine,' Kerry said.

For an hour, we sat and talked about the three years we had lived in Laos. We had known Mr Wan for all that time. He was a good man with a good heart and funny too, like a Lao version of UK funny man Mr Bean. We laughed so many times because of the silly things Mr Wan did. I remembered a time when Kerry was forced to design a lock box for the telephones deployed at posts because our guards kept ringing their girlfriends and the client would get the bill.

Mr Wan made the lock boxes and followed his own blueprint much like the time he had installed ceiling fans at our training camp at the incorrect height, which resulted in a series of head injuries to our staff. His lockboxes were useless because none of the guards could activate the telephones for teleprotection. Wan forgot to cut a hole in the box for the auto dial button. Then there was the time that he had wired all the Embassy telephone lines together and we got a complaint from the Indian Ambassador. He couldn't ring out because our guard kept telling him, 'Please Sir, don't use telephone, emergency may be coming.'

Leaving friends like Wan made leaving Laos harder still because we never knew if we would ever see them again.

CHAPTER TWENTY

Homecoming

'I think we should travel via Cambodia or Vietnam.'

'Vietnam! You're kidding right?' I was shocked that Tzovaras would even suggest such a thing.

'There's no need to worry about travelling through Vietnam. We can go through Ho Chi Minh City,' he explained. 'It's safe, I assure you.'

'Yeah well the only flights going in that direction are on Lao Aviation. Surely you don't expect us to risk our lives flying with them?' I questioned our lawyer's plan, which seemed hazardous.

'We'll be fine Kay,' he insisted.

'But I need to go to Thailand. I have to make sure everything is okay with my company,' I declared hotly.

'Look Kay, forget Thailand. You can't go there!' he responded abruptly. 'People are looking for ways to create problems for you.'

'I'm not concerned about them,' I responded anxiously.

As much as I hated to admit it, he was right. My reputation was in tatters. By our third week under house arrest, the Australian Foreign Minister telephoned the residence to speak to Kerry. I sat with Jonathan in the adjoining sitting room and listened as Kerry tried to get the Foreign Minister to send him to Afghanistan to rescue two West Australians held hostage by the Taliban.

'I believe there are 100 SAS going,' Kerry said. 'Care to make it 101?' he laughed.

'Gosh you'd think he'd had enough adventure for one year!' I said.

***

Newspapers all over the world announced our imminent release and provided a recap of our detainment, saying that we were 'gem smugglers'.

'They're making us look like crooks,' I responded with a shake of my head.

'Here's another one,' said Kerry. 'Downer says … it is especially a relief for the couple's three children. There have been many false dawns in this effort to try and get them released and there have been occasions where the children have been told that their parents are on the verge of being reunited with them back in Brisbane and it hasn't happened. I'm very sorry that those kinds of false hopes sometimes have been raised because my view has always been that this would take a bit of time and patience.'

'Yeah well whose fault is that?' I complained. 'I told them so many times to stop raising their hopes!'

***

It was a quiet afternoon when the Embassy staff rang with the news that we were being summoned to the Ministry of Foreign Affairs to receive a Presidential Pardon.

'It's wonderful!' the Ambassador's wife said hugging us.

'What am I gonna wear?' I turned to Kerry, who wasn't at all as flustered as I was.

'You should wear a *Pha sin* Kay,' Eve advised. This was a traditional Laos skirt.

'But I don't want to dress as a Laotian. I want to go as a foreigner!' I pleaded with her even though I knew that what she said made a great deal of sense. In the end, I gave in. The gesture would ease the tension, and I was willing to do a lot to help things along.

The soft silk folds of the skirt with matching shirt shimmered in the sunlight and reminded me of my former cell mate Pang who once described Lao silk as too beautiful to resist. The material clung lovingly to my skin as each tiny thread lay delicately in place. As a birthday present to me, Louise sent a French hair dresser to the Embassy. He cut my dark hair into a short bob style and Eve and I laughed as he made us look like twins.

Having dressed, I gently pushed my sapphire engagement and wedding ring onto my left hand. Looking at them sparkling back at me I wondered if it was such a wise choice to wear them at all.

'If they thought you stole them they wouldn't have given them back,' Kerry reminded me.

'I know. But I feel kinda odd wearing sapphires now,' I said fidgeting with my rings.

Kerry hugged me gently and told me never to worry about what other people thought. We knew the truth and that was all that mattered. He was right, of course, but it still felt a little strange.

***

Half an hour later, I sat between Jonathan and Kerry as we travelled by Embassy car to the Ministry of Foreign Affairs for a low-key ceremony signifying the final stage of our release. A large number of middle-ranking officials attended the meeting.

The Director-General of the Lao Consular Department greeted Jonathan upon arrival and motioned us towards a small room at the end of a narrow hallway. One of the Lao officials apologised for the cramped conditions as we all squeezed inside. I thought briefly of my prison cell. It was considerably smaller but I said nothing. The Presidential Pardon was read aloud in the Lao language and then roughly translated afterwards.

I bit my tongue when I heard them call me a criminal and smiled falsely when the official congratulated us and said we were now free to engage fully in normal activities. He said that the Lao PDR would welcome us back at any time. The Ambassador made a short statement to acknowledge the Australian Government's gratitude, that the matter which had preoccupied both governments for almost a year was now resolved. He was very pleased that they had reached the point at which we could now return to our children. He expressed respect to the President and National Assembly of the Lao PDR for having granted the Pardon so quickly.

Tzovaras warned us not to engage the Lao officials at the ceremony but upon departure from the small room several of them commented on my choice of attire.

'Madam is very beautiful,' said the official as his beady brown eyes raked over my body. I replied politely, and said I wished to go to the morning market, but I kept it at that.

Back at the Embassy residence, we waited for our passports to be returned and celebrated our pardon by toasting a few glasses of fine Australian red wine from the Embassy cellar. It mixed surprisingly well with the medication I was on and for a few fleeting moments, I felt at peace. Kerry rang our children and told them the good news.

On 8 November 2001, we would leave Laos on the Lao Aviation flight to Ho Chi Minh City. But before we left, the Australian Embassy staff, who had all worked tirelessly for our release, joined us for a lovely morning tea. An hour later, I felt like a queen as I sat beside the Ambassador in the official Embassy car. The media were waiting for us at the Wattay airport when we arrived.

'So how does it feel to be a convicted criminal?' one reporter hammered out, as I climbed from the Embassy car. I said nothing but smiled.

'She's aggressive,' I whispered to Jonathan. 'Must be en route to interview Bin Laden!'

Jonathan smiled. Secret police stood within earshot of everywhere we went but quite obviously the reporter was oblivious to them. Our former security staff greeted us warmly as we entered the security screening area and for a split second, I remembered when I first arrived in Laos.

It was a relief when the reporter didn't follow us through customs, but much to our surprise, Mr Wan came walking towards us.

'Wan, how'd you get back here?' Kerry asked in amazement.

'Oh, I can do anything, Boss,' he said, smiling.

'Of course, I forgot,' Kerry replied.

Mr Wan had walked right through the customs officials to give his 'Kangaroo brother' a fierce, farewell embrace.

'We'll meet again, Wan. We won't forget you,' Kerry reassured him.

'I never forget you boss!' cried Mr Wan.

***

The secret police and Lao officials waited in the departure lounge for the boarding call. They were ever watchful as I walked to the far corner of the waiting area to escape their prying eyes. A bearded man, who had stood next to us at check-in, lingered nearby. Was it just my imagination or was he a spy? Had my life now become one of constantly looking over my shoulder as I was now, wondering who was or was not working for the communist regime?

The moment finally arrived when the airport staff called all passengers for boarding. It was time to leave Laos and all the pain it represented. I walked to stand near Kerry and listened to him thanking Jonathan for saving our lives. Quietly, the other passengers filed through the gates until we were the last ones remaining. Part of me did not want to leave, but only because I felt enormously safe when I was with Jonathan.

'Thank you so much,' I said in a whisper as I hugged him goodbye.

Letting go was harder than I ever imagined but as Jonathan smiled down at me I felt instantly reassured by his words, 'See you again soon!' he smiled.

My body trembled as I finally found the courage to turn and walk away. Kerry and I walked through the gates and only turned back about five or so times to wave to Jonathan and Eve and our friends who smiled from behind the glass petition.

'Goodbye!' I mouthed the words and made myself look happy.

Absently I turned my gaze to the tarmac below, hoping to catch a final glimpse of the guards maintaining the security of the airside. But instead of the pale blue uniform catching my eye, something else did and immediately I became fearful.

'Kerry! The black cars,' I spoke quietly in alarm. An entourage of black limousines waited for the return of Foreign Affairs Minister Lengsavad. It was a daunting sight and it reminded me of the last time I saw the secret police standing around the black cars. That was the day they kidnapped my husband.

'It's okay. Let's get the hell out of here,' Kerry said.

I turned to wave just one more time to Jonathan and then boarded the plane with great trepidation. It was finally over. Or was it?

★★★

We left Laos at 1pm on Wednesday, 7 November 2001. I sat by the window and as the aircraft banked over Vientiane, I tried to find Phonthong but was confused by the landscape below. I waved regardless, to keep my promise. We often saw planes leaving Laos and whenever a prisoner left Phonthong, we'd wave to the planes thinking that our friends were on that flight. With my fingertips touching the windowpane, I said goodbye to friends that I would probably never see again, but they would remain forever in my heart.

I wanted to cry but didn't because a cameraman was filming from across a row of seats. So instead, my face remained a mask and I cried on the inside; for my friends who I would never forget. Nor would I forget their struggle to endure. I would never again let time slip away without making each moment count. Nor would I forget my promise to tell the world that they exist, lest they become like water in a glass, evaporating into the air as each day passes. The horizon slowly faded away as the plane climbed higher and higher, until white clouds took me far from the land that had once been my home.

We landed unceremoniously in Ho Chi Minh and when an entourage of Vietnamese military and police surrounded the plane, I felt dread wash over me. I felt frightened without the protecting arm of my Ambassador wrapped around my shoulders, so I clung to Kerry's hand instead. We walked across the tarmac under the watchful eye of the military and Viet police presence and for a moment, I wondered if we'd ever left Laos. Their faces reminded me of those dark evil expressions I'd seen on the 'Lumpini Torture Police' in Phonthong.

'I'm frightened,' I whispered to Kerry, who put his arm instinctively around my shoulders.

The steps to the mini-bus were a few paces in front of me. It would transport us to the terminal where we knew the Australian Government officials waited.

'Just keep moving Kay. Don't look at them!' Kerry ordered softly. 'Don't get off that bus whatever happens!'

My world moved in slow motion as the blood pounded in my ears and blocked out the usual airport noises.

One. Two. Three. I held my breath as I sat down on the small vinyl seat three rows back from the driver of a mini-bus. The rest of the passengers boarded without fuss but I shut my eyes, willing them to hurry. I just wanted the engine to start so that we could get the hell out of there. I felt Kerry tense beside me and opened my eyes to see why. Then I saw a soldier standing in the doorway of the mini-bus, speaking to the driver. His rifle was slung over his shoulder as his hand gripped its leather strap. The minutes ticked slowly by. Slowly he stepped away, ordering the driver to depart. Gradually the mini bus pulled away from the plane as I expelled my breath and wiped my sweaty hands down both sides of my trousers.

'It's okay babe,' Kerry comforted me.

We were greeted at the terminal by Mr Hugh Le, the Consul for the Australian Embassy and other members of the Australian Department of Foreign Affairs.

'Glad to see you!' he smiled warmly and extended his hand in greeting.

I felt slightly more at ease when we entered the airport lounge to wait for our next flight to Singapore. We didn't have long to wait and within hours were saying our goodbyes to the Australian Embassy staff.

Upon arrival at the Singapore International Airport, Phillip Brown, Attaché, and Vice-General of the Australian High Commission, and Mark Porter, First Secretary to the Australian High Commission met us. 'Changi' Airport was like stepping forward in time from our experience in Vietnam. Had we been there under different circumstances, it would have been nice to explore the excellent shops and carpeted walkways of the world's best airport. I quietly sipped my coffee and listened to our lawyer, who had met us here, explain to Kerry that our employers wanted to speak with him before we returned home. Reluctantly, we boarded a plane from Changi to Hong Kong. It was 1am when we finally arrived, exhausted. A *Channel Nine* reporter had waited so long to see us and all I could say to him was that I felt both happy and sad to leave Laos. As we departed from Hong Kong International Airport, in a black Mercedes Benz that was waiting outside the terminal, my mind came to a complete stop. Vaguely I heard Kerry's employer asking if I'd ever been to Hong Kong before.

'No,' I replied.

All I wanted to do was sleep. We would be staying the night at the famous, five star, Mandarin Oriental Hotel overlooking Victoria Harbour on Hong Kong Island. The rooms had balconies and panoramic views of the harbour. Before retiring, we joined Kerry's boss for a tall glass of champagne.

'To your freedom!' he said in a salute.

Our conversations were kept light and nothing was ever mentioned about the ins and outs of our detainment. Quite simply, we were both exhausted and just wanted a good night's sleep. After bidding them goodnight, Kerry and I took a shower and slipped in between the expensive sheets that adorned the biggest bed I had ever seen in my life. Within seconds, we were fast asleep, wrapped in each other's arms.

The next morning we awoke early and while Kerry met with Jardine Securicor, I went to the hairdressers for a relaxing few hours. I felt almost human again. In the evening, our employers arranged our transportation to the airport.

***

We boarded a Qantas flight for our journey home and were seated in business class. At first I couldn't figure out why we weren't given a newspaper as they normally do on flights. Kerry and I were both anxious to catch up on the world news and all that we had missed. It wasn't until our plane took off that a crew member passed us a paper which explained everything. We were front-page news!

We arrived at Brisbane Airport on 9 November 2001 and were greeted by an Australian Foreign Affairs representative, Roman Anorov, State Director Attorney General. He walked with us, and a friendly Group 4 security guard with a Scottish accent, to where the government car stood parked in the underground Government parking bay. We departed the airport and made our way to the Conrad International Hotel, in the heart of Brisbane City, where I knew our children were waiting. Within 45 minutes, we arrived and were greeted by a group of highly impressive security guards engaged to keep the swarming media at bay. This gave us a clear run from the basement to our room. Our kids were behind a heavy oak door and as I turned the handle, I thanked God we had finally arrived. This was the moment we'd waited almost a whole year for, and soon our waiting would be over.

The door opened, slowly. Stepping inside was like stepping into a whole new world. My Mum was the first person I saw and she looked older than I remembered. My sister Karen stood nearby smiling. But it was the sudden movement coming from the right of us that caught and held my attention. Half-a-dozen arms and legs threw themselves around us as we embraced our children for what seemed an eternity. Our eldest daughter, Jess, smiled and hugged me as she said I looked like a skeleton.

Young Nathan held me so tight that I almost couldn't breathe and Sahra wrapped herself in Kerry's embrace. He said quietly how proud he was of the way she'd handled the entire ordeal and for the next two hours, we all stood laughing, hugging and staring at each other wondering if we weren't dreaming.

By 2pm, our lawyer had arranged a press conference to dispel the media presence that surrounded the Conrad International Hotel. It went on longer than any of us imagined it would. There were two hundred reporters in the main hall and a couple of television cameras but they were all very considerate to what we'd endured. I think some of them were a little confused that we were so jovial but really, we were just thrilled to be home. Cameras clicked constantly as Kerry spoke.

'First of all, I would like to thank everyone for coming and showing an interest in our case. It has been through the efforts of the press, jointly with the Australian Government and obviously our lawyers that we're here today. And we would like to thank the press in particular for the sensitivity they showed throughout the whole ordeal which allowed the procedures with the Government and our lawyers to go ahead unobstructed so that we could be here today, free.'

Kerry talked for ten minutes about the support we received from the Government and how the Australian Embassy provided Consular support. He also took the opportunity to hold up the Australian Flag that he had carried for many years and had taken to Laos to fly proudly outside our office. Kerry is hugely patriotic and doesn't mind sharing that fact. When it was my turn to speak, I felt a little overwhelmed and just wanted to get it over with and return to our kids in the next room.

'Kay, obviously this has been quite a drama for you, but what were your thoughts when you stepped off the plane today in Brisbane airport?' a reporter asked.

'I thought the Qantas stewards were very handsome and then I thought I'd like to fly with that airline again,' I said laughing. Everyone in the room burst out laughing.

'I thought they were handsome as well,' said Kerry.

The journalists laughed even more and I suppose it worked well as a good icebreaker to an otherwise serious occasion. For an hour, we discussed a number of issues relating to our detainment. Listening to our lawyer and Kerry talk so positively about the Lao Government, and how grateful we were for the Presidential Pardon, actually made my skin crawl. I suddenly found myself thinking of all those we'd left behind in Phonthong, and the promises I'd made to tell the world all that I'd seen. This was the perfect opportunity to do that, but somehow the words were caught in my throat.

'The truth is that we are innocent,' said Kerry. 'We were caught up in a situation which meant we were the ones they decided to arrest. I believe that once the truth is told everyone will have a full understanding of our position.'

The opportunity for me to tell the world that truth was apparently not going to be there and then. In years to come, I would often wonder if I should not have asserted more control. My intuition told me that it was an ideal moment to tell them about the torture and horrors of Phonthong but the pain in remembering was almost too difficult to bear so I pushed it all away.

Following the press conference, several journalists accused Downer of brokering an unjust agreement with his Lao counterpart, Lengsavad, in order to secure our release. It was confirmed by Lengsavad that Mr Downer 'guaranteed' on behalf of the Australian Government, that we would pay over one million dollars in compensation. The key question asked by a *Melbourne Age* reporter was: 'How did a small and struggling state, which receives AU$20 million a year in aid from Australia, apparently dictate terms to such an extent? For a year, Laos treated direct appeals from the Governor-General and the Australian Prime Minister, as well as the best efforts of a special envoy and Australia's Ambassador, with contempt!'

'One could be forgiven for thinking that the payment of ransoms for the release of innocent people held by corrupt regimes is now an acceptable practice,' said another reporter.

Questions about Australia's relationship with Laos remained unanswered and many people felt that the Lao leadership should not have been allowed to get away with taking us hostage. But not much else was said to that effect. Downer clarified to *ABC* television that the Lao authorities did not expect us to pay compensation. 'They have no expectation of ever receiving the money, but it's a case of face being saved all round,' he said.

I worried less about the Laos regime and more about how our family would put the past year behind us, particularly when our son Nathan constantly waited outside the bathroom door thinking I'd disappear. How could I explain that what happened wasn't likely to happen again? How could any of us be sure of anything anymore? We began arranging the shattered pieces of our lives but having a conviction in any court, let alone a communist one, has the capacity to throw your life into disarray.

Ultimately, the Presidential Pardon we received and invitation to return to Laos any time did not mean much in reality. It hindered us from getting insurance and renewing our security and firearms licences. We asked the Department of Foreign Affairs and Trade to write a letter explaining our situation to various Australian Government departments. They wrote a standard letter that they said could suffice for any other situations where we needed to clarify our position, and their support.

I wasn't sure that this was enough to reverse the fact that our names had been tarnished through no fault of our own, but at least we were now home and safe. But the memories of our ordeal in that gulag in Laos would never leave me, as the thoughts of the many friends and truly courageous people I had met there would stay with me forever. It was important for me that their stories would be told.

CHAPTER TWENTY ONE

The Journey Continues

Although I returned to a normal life in Australia, I didn't forget my promises to my friends in Phonthong. In October 2002, I received an invitation from Dr Sin Vilay, who represented the General Assembly of Laotians Abroad. He asked me to testify at a US Congressional Forum in Washington D.C. on the atrocities I witnessed in Laos. Dr Sin Vilay was excited about my trip, as was a man who I can only refer to as 'Don.' Don had fought for our release from day one and I spoke to him several times on the telephone when we came home. Secretly, he had organised ex-CIA operatives to conduct covert surveillance to rescue us in the event that the Australian diplomatic relations failed. Sadly, however, Don and I never met because he died of a heart attack only a week before I was due to depart for Washington D.C. I did however, meet one of his associates who said Don's rescue team was never deployed because ex-members of an elite Australian Special forces group were thinking of doing something similar. That explained why the Headquarters of the Special Forces Operations in Canberra issued the message during a Consular visit: 'Do nothing. I repeat. Do nothing! Allow the diplomatic negotiations to fully exhaust themselves!'

As I stood before the US Congressional forum, I read aloud a letter written by Mensuh, one of the young Africans I knew in Phonthong:

'I came to Laos to renew my visa then was arrested by the Lao police, for what, I do not know. I was beaten badly. Even up to now, they are still beating me. They laid a stick on my feet and two policemen stood on it, for more then five hours and since then I am unable to walk anymore. They beat me in the chest that I am now coughing with blood.
They beat my stomach with iron that whenever I go to the rest room I put out blood and suffer tender pains. They burn my penis with fire and tell me I am not going to have any child in my life. They even beat my head so badly that my remembrance is no longer like before. Sometimes the blood comes from my nose. I am asking you to please help or else I will be dead. The police told me they can kill me and nobody will ask them why. They said they don't care about my country. I have no Embassy in Laos therefore; they are even brave to kill me if you do not come to my rescue quickly. I am dying slowly! Please!'

He was actually one of the lucky ones. Abrahim, I learned, had been beaten to death in his cell, under the supervision of Tan Sombut, but within two years, Mensuh had left Laos. Of course, the Lao Government was informed that I had raised his case to US Congress, and that I had made several television appearances campaigning for human rights. I wasn't afraid to speak out with so many Laotians living in exile standing beside me. They had lost their country when the United States Government of that time had tried to walk a fine line between its real interests in Laos and its diplomatic façade, before abandoning the Hmong to their fate. I felt honoured to be standing amongst former war veterans, like Colonel Khambang Sibounheuang, Brigadier General Ed. Y. Hall and Colonel Khamphan Thammakhanti, a POW and former military advisor to the Royal Lao Army. They and the hundreds of others who attended gave me the courage to call Laos a country of corruption and to share the horrific experiences of those detained in places like Phonthong Prison.

Attending the Congressional Forum were Congressmen Kind, Rohrabacher, Green and Kennedy. They each submitted their strong support to pass a resolution to ensure all adult citizens of Laos are able to vote and run for public office regardless of their gender, race, ethnicity, religion, economic standing, or political affiliation, that the citizens of Laos would be allowed to assemble and peacefully protest against the Lao Government and public officials and to organise themselves into political parties; and to allow unrestricted access by international human rights and election monitors.

I hope that one day the people of Laos will be in a position to enjoy those simple freedoms that we so often take for granted. The Lao Government did request my extradition to Laos for speaking out against the regime, but since there is no treaty between our two countries allowing for this, I am safe for now.

***

Kerry returned to the military as a Senior Instructor, training Special Forces soldiers in hostage rescue, among other things. Life had come full circle. He went overseas on various military deployments and the Army promoted him to Regimental Sergeant Major of the Special Forces Training Centre. It wasn't all smooth sailing because there were some in the Military who still didn't understand what we'd been through or why Kerry was still serving despite having been convicted of criminal offences in Laos. We just told them to take the matter up with our Foreign Minister Alexander Downer.

My bodyguard company collapsed while I was in prison. In my absence, company money was borrowed and never repaid, and I found that my sub-contractors set up their own security company. I was bitterly disappointed to learn the truth. After a bitter battle to salvage my reputation, I was forced to admit defeat. I lost everything.

For a long time I wondered if it was possible to start again. I felt plagued with resentment for those who betrayed me, and bitter with the Lao authorities for destroying my reputation and traumatising my family in the process. Then a friend rang and told me he'd seen a book for sale at the Brisbane airport that was supposedly all about us. I immediately drove to the bookstore and read an account of our ordeal. We hadn't co-operated with the book, and so it was missing important parts of the story. Inevitably, I suffered a nervous breakdown because I couldn't cope with the reality of all that had happened to us.

It has been a long struggle for Kerry and I to rebuild our lives. When you are denied justice, you feel like you are drowning in despair. There are currently no legal avenues in Australia, under international or Australian law, enabling us to have our case re-heard in Australia. Despite having overwhelming evidence that we were wrongly convicted, and even with a Presidential Pardon, it does not change the fact that a terrible wrong was done to us. It also doesn't change the fact that while this terrible ordeal was going on, we lost control of my own company and faced huge costs in trying to clear our names. I would settle for a finding under Australian Law that said 'under Australian law this person would not have been found guilty.' At least it would be a form of justice. As a consolation, our case impacted and brought change and hope to others as stated by the Australian Ambassador, Jonathan Thwaites:

'They took a lot more notice of what was happening to other prisoners than, in many cases, they did to what was happening to themselves. It was quite evident, as time went on, that the detention centre was becoming a better place, largely through the efforts of Kay and Kerry.'

Though our story remains a painful reminder to our family, it is important to share with others because it represents too the plight of many families, when in 1975, they lost their country to an invading communist force. Thousands of Lao people still struggle today to find peace as they remember loved ones either dead or imprisoned in the death camps scattered all over Laos. The time is well overdue for the US Government and the United Nations to investigate and stop the atrocities committed against the Hmong ethnic minorities, the people of Laos and the political prisoners who survive on the hopes that we will never forget them.

**

Then, exactly one year after I left Laos, I received a letter from my former cell mate, Pang:

'Mai Kue, things get better here now since you go home. Still have torture but not like before. Prisoners can now play badminton everyday. It is not good here but is better. Thank you. Everybody in Phonthong knows that you and Kerry keep your promise to make life better for the prisoners here!'

In March 2004, Pang and her sister Sue were released from Phonthong. I immediately made plans to meet them and flew with my sister Karen, to San Francisco. We spent a few days sightseeing to recover from the jet lag of our transpacific flight. When we toured the famous prison 'Alcatraz', I laughed when Karen asked me what the conditions were like by comparison to an Asian jail. 'Luxurious!' I responded.

Three days later, I sat beside Karen on the United Airlines flight destined for Atlanta, Georgia. I felt nervous about how I would react to seeing my former cell mates again. Staring out over an ocean of green fields, I remembered leaving Laos and how I'd searched the vast landscape below me for Phonthong prison and a glimpse of those I was leaving behind.

Half an hour later, Pang and I stood hugging each other inside the busy Hartsfield airport terminal. The hell of the grimy prison cell we had once shared seemed an entire world away. I wept, thinking of those days when I would ask Pang if we would ever get home to our families.

Over the next few days Pang, Sue and I sat for hours talking about life then and now. Dressed in our pyjamas we whispered through the night as we had done so many times in Phonthong. During the week, Pang's father took us to Stone Mountain, the largest high relief sculpture in the world. Pang insisted we climb it, which took two hours. I was exhausted by the time we got to the top, but in awe as we looked across Georgia, to the city of Atlanta that lay distant on the horizon. The view was breathtaking as we felt the cool wind caress our faces.

'It's a long way to Phonthong, Pang!' I whispered, standing beside my best friend.

'Sure is Mai Kue,' she laughed squeezing my hand. We were finally free!

Hours later, with Stone Mountain behind us, we returned to Lawrenceville. Word had spread throughout the Hmong community that I was visiting Pang and Sue. When we arrived back at Zang's house, the most bizarre thing happened.

Pang stood on her brother's driveway waving for me to hurry up. I walked to Pang as her relatives came outside to greet me. My sister followed behind with Pang's father, Nhia. As I turned to tell Karen to hurry up, I shivered, despite the southern-Atlanta heat. 'I think someone just walked over my grave,' I said.

My friend Joe from Chicago, who resembled a giant lumberjack, stepped from the car with his bag slung casually over his broad shoulders. His six-foot tall towering frame walked towards me smiling. Joe was a vigilant human rights activist who had felt a great empathy for the Hmong people in particular.

'You okay?' he asked.

I was rooted to the spot and stood staring at the dark blue sedan that pulled up to the curb. A young Asian man opened the driver's side door and got out. The rear passenger door opened seconds later but the occupant remained in the car. An older man seated in the front of the car walked to open the rear door. Pang's relatives told me to come inside but I was unable to move. Just then, Pang moved towards me and put her arm around my shoulder.

'Who is she?' I whispered to Pang. An old woman walked slowly towards me.

'Mai Kue,' said Pang quietly. 'It's the mother of Mr Joy.'

The old woman's eyes crinkled with unshed tears as she continued to walk towards me.

'My God!' I cried and embraced her.

It took a while to regain my composure but when I did, we went inside and talked for hours about her son, detained in Phonthong as a political prisoner.

'I wish you could see his face. He's always smiling,' I told the old woman. Joe translated everything I said into the Hmong language.

'He loved to sing John Denver songs.' I started to sing 'Annie's Song' to her. The room was quiet as everyone absorbed my pain and my memories.

'Joy would be so happy to know I have met you,' I spoke softly.

'He hopes one-day there will be change in Laos. He is inspirational and is partly the reason why I survived.'

I stood with Mr Joy's mother as my sister took our picture. Somehow, I would find a way to send it to Mr Joy.

***

I returned to Washington DC following my visit with Pang's family and again testified to US Congress on behalf of the political prisoners of Laos. I was encouraged that twenty-three Congressmen were now supporting those same resolutions that we had raised in October 2002. Furthermore, they called on President George W. Bush to block a drive by Laos for normal trade relations. They cited alleged human rights violations and stated that: 'Laos continues to be one of the world's most reprehensible abusers of human rights—with a repertoire that includes torture, harsh restrictions on the press and free speech, and imprisonment of people for their religious beliefs.'

I began to understand the true value of my journey through Phonthong Prison. One voice whispering in the vastness of this world can make a huge difference in the quest for freedom and democracy. However, it was just the beginning.

When I returned home weeks later, I received a letter from a young man in the United States. He was the brother of Mr Joy. Vang wrote thanking me for helping him get to know the older brother he never knew. Joy's family is now in contact with the US Embassy, trying to reopen the case. Another letter arrived from Phonthong Prison, and in it, I learned that everyone still missed me and said that at times they could hear my laughter, as if caught on the wind. I am glad my spirit remains in that place to comfort those I left behind.

My dear friend Chao was sentenced to fifteen years by the court for political reasons and was now able to go to the Thai Embassy every month for Consular access. This lifted my spirits knowing that my constant campaigning had finally achieved a positive result for him.

Another of my former prison companions, Joe Hay, had been detained for almost a decade without charge. No one knew why, not even the Lao authorities. In my last goodbye to him, I remember telling Joe to be patient. I wrote every week to the French Embassy begging for their support. Joe was so childlike that I feared they wouldn't understand his strange behaviour. After two years of pleading his case through a constant stream of letters,

I began to see results. Joe's name wasn't really Joe. It was Dieter Roux, from Dijon Ville in France and for eight years his family had been searching for him. My journalist friend Nikki was so moved by Joe's plight that she joined my campaign for his release. With her support, the French Embassy began diplomatic negotiations with the Laos Government and finally in 2004, Dieter Roux, aka Joe Hay, was released on medical grounds.

The Laos Government said 'he suffers from schizophrenia', and asked who would pay his travel costs to France and for the nurses to fly from France to collect him? The question was argued for almost a year without resolution. I offered to pay but for some reason, I wasn't allowed because I was too political. Finally, two French doctors offered to go free of charge. But no one can ever give Joe back those ten years that were stolen through a decade of arbitrary arrest. The only good news is that Joe is now home.

My Thai friend Pooperk was released from Phonthong, on 18 October 2001, just two days before my 34th birthday. Pooperk returned to Bangkok and works at a travel agency. He dedicates his spare time to helping Thai prisoners still in Phonthong. We remain great friends.

The Canadian I first met when I arrived at Phonthong Prison, Anouhack, was released from prison in 2001. He and his wife Phaiwan returned to the United States where his brother lives in California. I usually get a Christmas card each year but never a letter. I guess life is hard enough for some to move forward again without constantly looking back.

In 2003, I received information that Madam Gin-Gin and the other Chinese prisoners I met were released from Phonthong. I have no way of confirming with the Chinese government if this information is correct. But I hope it is.

Twenty-two political prisoners were transferred from Phonthong in November 2001 to the domestic jail called Somkhe. Noi from my cell was amongst them. She had lost her husband to the dark room of Phontan Domestic jail. A decade and a half has passed since Noi saw her two young children. I remember the many times we sat and sang sad songs of home. We longed to see our loved ones again. We longed to be free. I was lucky. I got to feel the warm embrace of my children. Chances are Noi may never see her children again.

My Hmong friends Mr Joy, Bounmy and Nor Neng, were all taken to the Lao court and sentenced to twenty years each for allegedly calling for democratic reforms—those same reforms that Laos says it has adopted in order to receive foreign aid and enter into free trade agreements with the western world.

In March 2005, our Thai friend Tanaphan, who helped Kerry administer first aid to the tortured Africans, was released from Phonthong after twenty years as a Prisoner of War.

Finally, I received a letter from my dear sister Mon who had been trying just as I was to say sorry for not saying goodbye. I smiled when she asked me in the letter if I wanted to drink coffee. 'Café me Kha?' Mon wrote. It brought back so many happy memories but inevitably caused my heart to ache as I remembered all the times we shared in that hell called Phonthong Prison.

***

One day things will be different and I will be able to return to Laos with the thousands of Laotians now living in exile. But until then, I'll just keep chipping away at the wall of secrecy the regime has built to hide the suffering and atrocities of the Lao people's daily existence. My experiences haven't changed the person I've always been, or Kerry, but they've made me more aware. I doubt I'll be free of those images I'd rather forget, or forget the feeling of overwhelming frailty during those months of torment. They made me believe tomorrow would never come, but it did.

My husband and I survived behind the razor wire of a communist prison because we dared to believe that nothing is impossible, that we can overcome our struggles and that every day is precious. More than anything, we never gave up on each other. I still think my husband is the most honourable and remarkable man in the world. The emotional scars cut deeply into my children's hearts. I doubt they will ever fully recover from our ordeal, but I am glad that they choose to remember the good things about Laos, and the happier times we once had when it was our home.

Nowadays, I actively campaign for prisoners and human rights all over the world with Tony Fox who founded the online advocacy service; Foreign Prisoner Support Service (FPSS). Too few people in this world care for others and never expect anything in return. Tony is one of those people. We support thousands of prisoners interned in foreign prisons, and assist their families in dealing with that internment. Some of the cases are heartbreaking, while others are inspiring.

It has been a huge commitment. We get thousands of emails and letters from all over the world. Many are from ordinary Mums and Dads desperate for answers and grateful for our support.

My journey continues but now in so many directions. I still lobby for the restoration of human rights for the people of Laos but I also find myself in places I would never expect to be.

In May 2005, I found myself dodging a frenzy of media cameras that blocked the wooden doorway to Kerobokan Prison, Indonesia. I was there to see fellow Australian, Schapelle Leigh Corby, a 27-year-old trainee beauty therapist from the Gold Coast who'd been arrested on drug charges in October 2004.

It was the first time since my own incarceration that I had set foot inside Asia. Each time a police officer passed by I almost went to my knees, as I was once conditioned to do in the Laos prison. Then I remembered that I was merely an observer to Schapelle's nightmare. I hoped that through my experiences, I would be able to give her some comfort and to her sister Mercedes, whom I had become good friends with. It was obvious to all who knew Schapelle that she had simply fallen victim to foul play. But here she was, an innocent young girl doing time for something she absolutely didn't do.

I later sat in the front row of the Denpasar District Court alongside Schapelle's family and friends. I was one of the few people there who truly understood the anxiety she was feeling as she sat quietly before three Indonesian judges. I thought of the time I'd stood before three Laotian judges, then watched Schapelle's shocked reaction to the 20-year sentence they handed down. I felt a weird sense of detached understanding because I knew her ordeal was far from over. I returned to Kerobokan Prison the next week and took her some basic supplies – soap, noodles, toothpaste, cigarettes and food for some of the other prisoners detained. It was difficult to say goodbye and leave her in that God-forsaken place but I knew Schapelle would never give up and neither would those of us who believed in her and continue to lobby for her release.

***

I used to be that person who said 'hang the drug traffickers!' But now I understand that people make mistakes. Sometimes they do things out of desperation. Sometimes they risk their lives in order to make their life better and think that a one-time deal will erase all their problems. Those who are guilty already know they have done wrong. Their perception is that they are worthless and when a person feels like that, it is difficult for them to turn their life around. On the other end of the spectrum, there are prisoners detained for no reasonable explanation, like the many I met in the Laos prison. They live every day wondering if they will see their loved ones again and sadly, many of them won't. Imagine if you or your loved one was taken to an undisclosed location, tortured and detained for an indefinite period. How would you cope?

I know exactly how it feels to have your innocence cast aside for political reasons. I was forced to listen to the agony of other humans being tortured and ill treated for no particular reason, other than that they were Hmong, or were an inconvenience to the government's aims. I came to realise that guilty or not, for every person detained in these appalling places, there is always a family or loved one quietly agonising for their return. Some of course deserve to be there but in my humble opinion, everyone deserves at least one-second chance.

I can never return to that life of carefree ignorance that I once enjoyed and nor will my family ever forget the agony we all endured. But in the words of a former American President Theodore Roosevelt:

'It is not the critic who counts, nor the man who points out how the strong man stumbled, or where the doer of deeds could have done them better. The credit belongs to the man who is actually in the arena, whose face is marred by dust and sweat and blood; who strives valiantly; who errs and comes short again and again; who knows great enthusiasms, great devotions; who spends himself in a worthy cause; who, at the best, knows in the end the triumph of high achievement, and who, at the worst, if he fails, at least fails while daring greatly, so that his place shall never be with those timid souls who know neither victory nor defeat.'

I am inspired every day by these words, and reminded that we each have a part to play in preserving humanity, in reaching out and showing kindness, and in fighting injustice and cruelty. If we don't, there will be nobody safe in this world. What happened to my family could easily happen to yours.

In Memoriam

Bounmy Phong Xiong

Laos, 7 November 2005

On 20 October 2005, coincidentally my birthday, after having lived in Lao prisons for over 11 years without trial, my dear friend Bounmy Phong Xiong was released from Somkhe prison, Vientiane. A couple of weeks later, he was hospitalized with heart complications. On 7 November 2005, again coincidentally the same day I left Laos four years earlier, Bounmy passed away. He died a free man!

A Short History of Laos

Laos covers a large area of over 200,000 square kilometres, and is bordered in the North by China, the Northeast by Vietnam, the South by Cambodia, the Southwest by Thailand and in the West by Burma. It is sparsely populated, with the second lowest population density in Asia, after Mongolia.

It is not strategically important in its own right, but has appeared throughout history as a buffer state dividing powerful neighbours and colonial interests.

As with much of South East Asia, the history of Laos has seen proud kingdoms crumble and colonisation come and go, with the declaration of an independent state coming as late as 1953. The young state couldn't help but become embroiled in conflict as world powers played with its borders and strategic position on the world stage, especially during the Vietnam War. Laos remains the most bombed country in the history of the world.

The US-backed Hmong people, who fought the communist North Vietnamese and who made up 5-10% of the population, were eventually abandoned to their fate as America withdrew its troops and financial support. In 1975, the North Vietnamese Army swept in, and the Laos king and queen, along with hundreds of thousands of ordinary Lao people were sent to gulags to be 'indoctrinated', where many died of illness, starvation or torture. Many still do.

The Hmong are still the largest and most vocal minority in Laos. Their struggle with the Communist government goes on in remote regions to this day. However, not only the rights of the Hmong minority, but all human rights are at risk in this country.

The Laos government in exile continues to lobby for reconciliation, peace and democracy for Laos, but the regime is unrelenting. The rest of the world needs to listen to the cry of the people, and to make the current Laos government accountable for its gross human rights transgressions. The regime, however, rejects all allegations of corruption and massacres, and even today denies the existence of re-education camps. The evidence to the contrary speaks for itself.

Foreign Prisoner Support Service is a volunteer prisoner advocacy service founded in 1995 by Mr Tony Fox, to support families with loved ones interned in foreign prisons worldwide.

Foreign Prisoner Support Service
http://www.foreignprisoners.com

FOREIGN PRISONER SUPPORT SERVICE
Save-A-Life

The International Relief Centre offers humanitarian support to assist the impoverished people of South East Asia, and is proudly supported by the Cambodian government.

International Relief Centre, Inc.
3306 Olsen Lane,
Nashville, TN 37218
Web site: http://ircsea.org